Heirloom Projects *for* Woodworkers

Heirloom Projects *for* Woodworkers

**Plans and time-honored techniques
for building 20 masterpiece designs**

by the Editors of
The Woodworker's Journal

We at Madrigal Publishing have tried to make this book as accurate and correct as possible. Plans, illustrations, photographs, and text have been carefully researched by our in-house staff. However, due to the variability of all local conditions, construction materials, personal skills, etc., Madrigal Publishing assumes no responsibility for any injuries suffered or damages or other losses incurred that result from material presented herein. All instructions and plans should be carefully studied and clearly understood before beginning any construction.

For the sake of clarity, it is sometimes necessary for a photo or illustration to show a power tool without the blade guard in place. However, in actual operation, always use blade guards (or other safety devices) on power tools that are equipped with them.

Printed in the United States of America.

Library of Congress Cataloging-in-Publication Data
    Heirloom projects for woodworkers : plans and time-honored techniques
        for building 20 masterpiece designs / by the editors of the
        Woodworker's journal.
            p.   cm.
        ISBN 1-880618-03-6 (pbk.) : $18.95
        1. Furniture making—Amateurs' manuals.   2. Woodwork.
    I. Woodworker's journal.
    TT185.H394   1993
    684.1'04—dc20
                                                    93-29871
                                                        CIP

Madrigal Publishing Company
517 Litchfield Road
P.O. Box 1629
New Milford, CT 06776

CONTENTS

Projects

Techniques

Sources

Introduction

We are, indeed, fortunate to enjoy the craft of woodworking, where our unique and wonderful skills enable us to create things of lasting value and beauty—things that can be passed along to future generations long after we are gone. As we carefully cut and shape wood, creating a project, we often unknowingly impart to it a little bit of ourselves, perhaps in the way we move a smooth plane over a tapered leg, or maybe in the manner we delicately round the underside of a table top. Some small part of our personality then becomes a permanent part of the piece, there to be long enjoyed and appreciated, perhaps even a hundred years from now by a grateful descendant. What had started many years earlier simply as a woodworking project has now become something very special—a family heirloom.

There are 20 heirloom projects in this book, all classic designs, and chosen because we felt their beauty and function would enable them to stand the test of time. There is no fad furniture here, nothing that will be the rage today but quickly out of style tomorrow. Many of these project designs have been around for more than 200 years, and it's likely they will continue to be treasured, even as we approach the end of the next century. We hope you enjoy building each one of them.

We want to extend our thanks to the following individuals who provided valuable project contributions to this book: ***Roy B. Cook***, Houston, Texas, for the Grandfather Clock; ***Paula Garbarino***, Somerville, Massachusetts, for the Tilt-Top Table and the Pennsylvania Small Chest; ***Dennis Preston***, Brookfield, Connecticut, for the Highboy and the Jewelry Chest.

In addition, our thanks to ***Berea College***, Berea, Kentucky, for the Slant-Front Desk, the ***Washington Historical Museum***, Washington, Connecticut, for the Gate-Leg Table and the Federal Period Washstand, ***Woodcraft Supply Company (Mason and Sullivan)***, Parkersburg, West Virginia, for the Vienna Regulator Clock; and ***Weston Thorn Antiques***, Bantam, Connecticut, for the Cutlery Tray.

Also, many thanks to ***John Kane*** of ***Silver Sun Studios***, New Milford, Connecticut, for the cover photo and many of the project photos.

The Editors

Projects

Grandfather *Clock*

Clocks of this style, called long case clocks, originated in England sometime before 1660. In 1876, the American Henry Clay Work wrote a song about a long case clock which began *"My grandfather's clock was too big for the shelf so it stood ninety years on the floor . . . ."* The song was quite popular in the 1880's, and ever since the name grandfather has become synonymous with the long case clock.

As a general rule, grandfather clocks stand between seven and eight feet tall. A somewhat smaller version, appropriately called the grandmother clock, usually measures around six feet high.

Grandfather clocks come in a variety of shapes and styles, but we think this one is especially handsome. It has a number of interesting features, including ogee feet, a raised arch base panel, arched panels for the waist and hood doors, a broken arch pediment and a calendar moon dial. We used walnut for ours, but oak, cherry, or mahogany are also quite appropriate.

Before starting, it would be prudent to have all the hardware on hand, including the moon dial and movement. You don't want to build the entire clock and then find out that some important parts are no longer available.

Making a grandfather clock often involves using a shaper—a tool few woodworkers own. We feel that one of the important features of this design is the fact that a shaper is not needed. The operations normally done with the shaper have been worked out so that a table saw molding-head cutter or a router table will do the job.

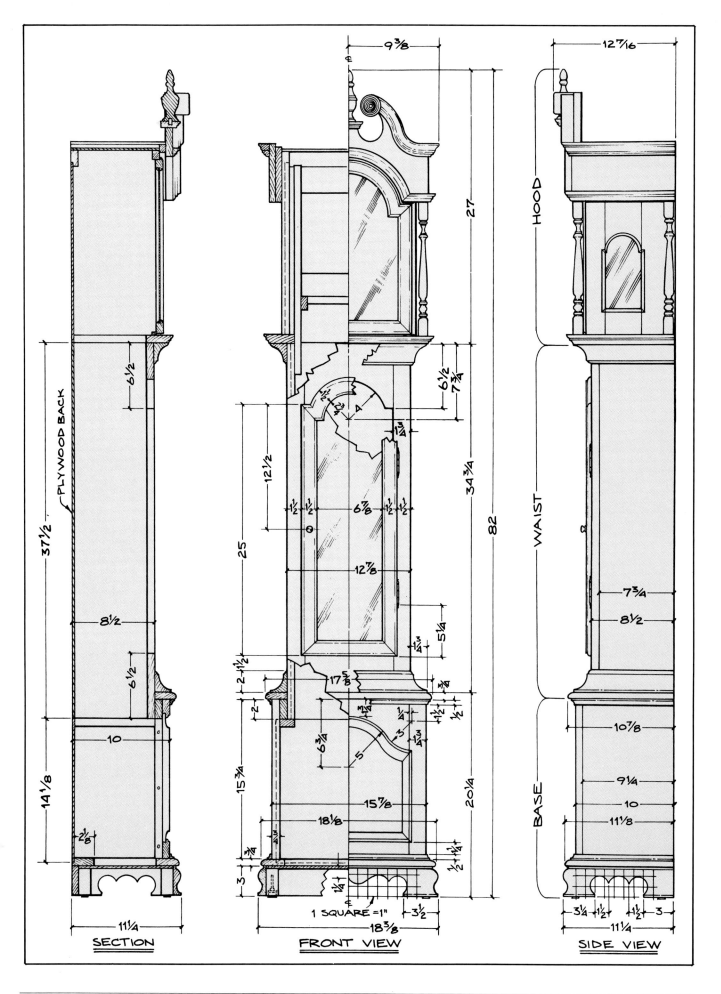

SECTION

FRONT VIEW

SIDE VIEW

1 SQUARE =1"

HOOD

WAIST

BASE

PLYWOOD BACK

Bill of Materials
(all dimensions actual)

Part	Description	Size	No. Req'd.	Part	Description	Size	No. Req'd.
A	Side Ogee Foot	3/4 x 3 x 11 1/4	2	VV	Hood Base Front	3/4 x 3 1/8 x 17 5/8	1
B	Front Ogee Foot	3/4 x 3 x 18 3/8	1	WW	Side Spacer	5/8 x 5 1/2 x 9	2
C	Foot Support	3/4 x 3 x 16 7/8	1	XX	Front Spacer	5/8 x 5 1/2 x 15 1/8	1
D	Base Side Molding	3/4 x 2 3/8 x 11 1/8	2	YY	Scrollboard Side	5/8 x 5 3/4 x 10 1/4	2
E	Base Front Molding	3/4 x 2 3/8 x 18 1/8	1	ZZ	Scrollboard	5/8 x 11 1/2 x 17 *	1
F	Base Molding Support	3/4 x 2 3/8 x 13 3/8	1	AAA	Hood Top End Molding	See Fig. 30	2
G	Base Side	3/4 x 9 1/4 x 15 3/4	2	BBB	Swan's Neck Molding	See Fig. 30	2
H	Base Frame Stile	3/4 x 1 3/4 x 15 3/4	2	CCC	Finial Base	5/8 x 2 1/8 x 2 7/8	1
I	Base Frame Top Rail	3/4 x 5 3/8 x 12 3/8	1	DDD	Finial Pin	1/2 dia. x 3/4 long	1
J	Base Frame Bottom Rail	3/4 x 2 x 12 3/8	1	EEE	Finial	1 7/8 dia. x 5 3/16 long	1
K	Base Panel	3/4 x 12 7/8 x 12 1/4	1	FFF	Rosette	See Fig. 40	2
L	Panel Block	3/4 x 1 x 15 3/4	2	GGG	Spindle	1 1/8 dia. x 13 1/8 long	4
M	Support	3/4 x 1 1/2 x 8 1/4	2	HHH	Spindle Pin	1/2 dia. x 3/4 long	8
N	Spacer	3/4 x 2 x 8 1/2	2	III	Scrollboard Side Molding	See Fig. 33	2
O	Cleat	3/4 x 2 x 12 3/8	1	JJJ	Scrollboard End Molding	See Fig. 33	2
P	Base Back	1/4 x 15 1/8 x 14 1/8	1	KKK	Scrollboard Arch Molding	See Fig. 33	1
Q	Base Side Molding	1/2 x 1/2 x 10 1/2	4	LLL	Cleat	1/2 x 1/2 x 12 3/8	1
R	Base Front Molding	1/2 x 1/2 x 16 7/8	2	MMM	Frame Pin	3/8 dia. x 1 long	4
S	Bottom	1/4 x 9 3/4 x 16 7/8	1	NNN	Hood Back	1/4 x 13 1/8 x 17 3/4	1
T	Leveler Block	See Fig. 9	4	OOO	Back Lock	3/16 x 5/8	3
U	Leveler	See Fig. 9	4	PPP	Hood Top	1/4 x 13 7/8 x 9	1
V	Waist Side Molding	3/4 x 2 3/8 x 10 7/8	2	QQQ	Hood Door Stile	3/4 x 1 3/8 x 12 7/8	2
W	Waist Front Molding	3/4 x 2 3/8 x 17 5/8	1	RRR	Hood Door Right Arch	See Fig. 35	1
X	Waist Side	3/4 x 7 3/4 x 37 1/2	2	SSS	Hood Door Left Arch	See Fig. 35	1
Y	Waist Frame Stile	3/4 x 1 3/4 x 37 1/2	2	TTT	Hood Door Bottom Rail	3/4 x 1 3/8 x 13	1
Z	Waist Frame Top Rail	3/4 x 6 1/2 x 9 3/8	1	UUU	Hood Door Glass	1/8 thick	1
AA	Waist Frame Bottom Rail	3/4 x 6 1/2 x 9 3/8	1	VVV	Rubber Glass Retainer	3/16 quarter round	as req'd
BB	Waist Back	1/4 x 12 1/4 x 37 1/2	1	WWW	Brass Latch	1/2 dia.	1
CC	Waist Door Hinge	Am. Clock p/n 40406	2	XXX	Hood Door Top Hinge	See Fig. 38	1
DD	Back Lock	3/16 x 5/8	10	YYY	Hood Door Bottom Hinge	See Fig. 38	1
EE	Waist Side Molding	See Detail	4	ZZZ	Front Mounting Post	3/4 x 1 1/4 x 21	2
FF	Waist Front Molding	See Detail	2	AAAA	Back Mounting Post	3/4 x 1 1/2 x 18 1/4	2
GG	Waist Door Stile	3/4 x 1 1/2 x 25	2	BBBB	Seatboard Cleat	3/4 x 1 3/8 x 7	2
HH	Waist Door Top Rail	3/4 x 4 1/4 x 9 7/8	1	CCCC	Front Seatboard	3/4 x 1 1/4 x 9 3/8	1
II	Waist Door Bottom Rail	3/4 x 1 1/2 x 9 7/8	1	DDDD	Back Seatboard	3/4 x 1 x 9 3/8	1
JJ	Waist Door Glass	1/8 thick	1	EEEE	Chime Board	1/2 x 8 x 11 3/8	1
KK	Rubber Glass Retainer	3/16 quarter round	as req'd	FFFF	Chime Block		1
LL	Brass Latch	1/2 dia.	1	GGGG	Dial Board	See Fig. 39	1
MM	End Frame Back Stile	3/4 x 3 3/8 x 18 1/8	2	HHHH	Moon Dial		1
NN	End Frame Front Stile	3/4 x 2 x 18 1/8	2	IIII	Movement		1
OO	End Frame Top Rail	3/4 x 3 5/8 x 9 3/4	2	JJJJ	Hands		1 set
PP	End Frame Bottom Rail	3/4 x 3 5/8 x 2 5/8	2	KKKK	Cable Hanging Plate		1
QQ	Front Stretcher	3/4 x 5 3/8 x 12 3/8	1	LLLL	Pulley		3
RR	Back Stretcher	3/4 x 1 1/2 x 12 3/8	1	MMMM	Weight Shell		3
SS	Glass Panel	1/8 x 4 1/4 x 8 3/16	2	NNNN	Weight Filling		3
TT	Rubber Glass Retainer	3/16 quarter round	as req'd	OOOO	Pendulum		1
UU	Hood Base End	3/4 x 3 1/8 x 10 7/8	2		* Length and width dimensions allow extra stock.		

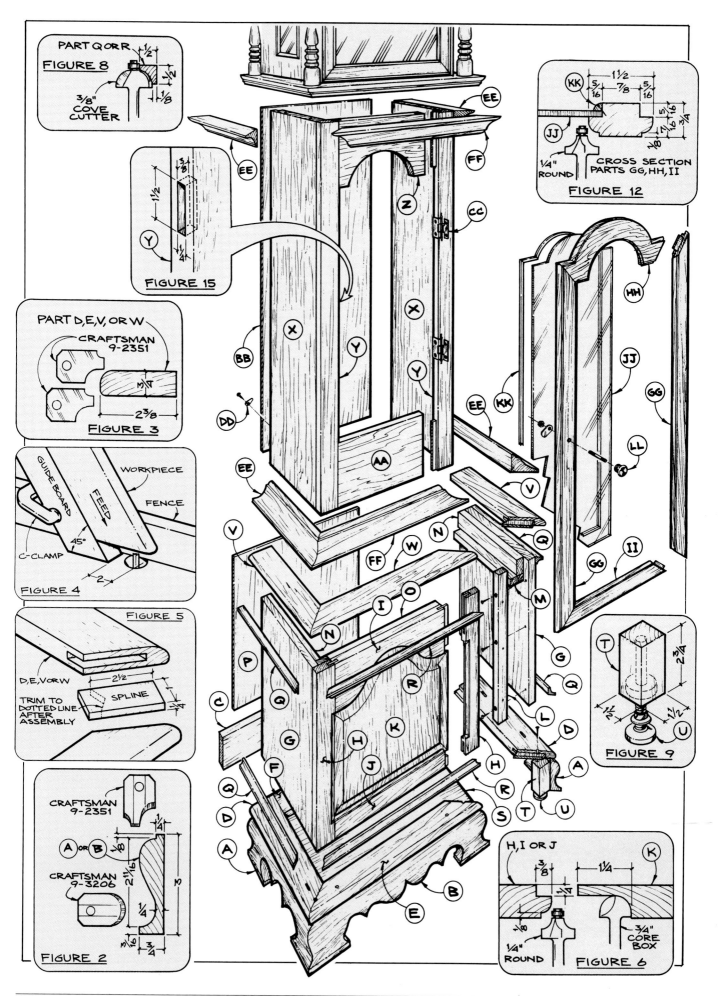

PART Q OR R

FIGURE 8

3/8"
COVE
CUTTER

1/2
1/2
1/8

FIGURE 15

3/8
1 1/2
1/4

Y

PART D,E,V, OR W

CRAFTSMAN
9-2351

M

2 3/8

FIGURE 3

GUIDE BOARD
WORKPIECE
FEED
FENCE
45°
C-CLAMP
2

FIGURE 4

FIGURE 5

D,E,V OR W
2 1/2
SPLINE
1/4
TRIM TO
DOTTED LINE
AFTER
ASSEMBLY

CRAFTSMAN
9-2351
1/4
1/8
A or B
2 11/16
CRAFTSMAN
9-3206
1/4
3
3/16
3/4

FIGURE 2

KK
1 1/2
5/16
7/8
5/16
5/16
5
1/16
3/4
JJ
1/8
7/16
1/4"
ROUND
CROSS SECTION
PARTS GG,HH,II

FIGURE 12

EE
EE
FF
Z
CC
N
X
Y
Y
BB
X
DD
AA
EE
HH
JJ
GG
EE
KK
LL
V
Q
GG
II
N
W
N
O
FF
I
M
G
Q
P
Q
R
L
D
C
K
G
H
H
J
R
T
U
F
Q
S
A
D
B
A
E

T
2 3/4
1 1/2
1 1/2
U

FIGURE 9

H,I OR J
3/8
1 1/4
1/4
K
1/100
1/4"
ROUND
3/4"
CORE
BOX

FIGURE 6

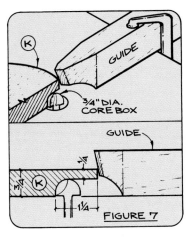

K

GUIDE

3/4" DIA.
CORE BOX

GUIDE

1/4

3/4

K

1 1/4

FIGURE 7

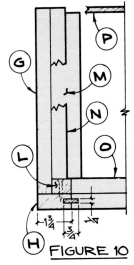

P

G

M

N

O

L

H

1 3/4   3/4   1/4

FIGURE 10

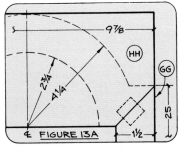

9 7/8

2 3/4

4 1/4

HH

GG

25

1 1/2

FIGURE 13A

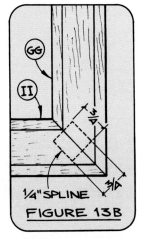

GG

II

1/4

1/4" SPLINE

3/4

FIGURE 13B

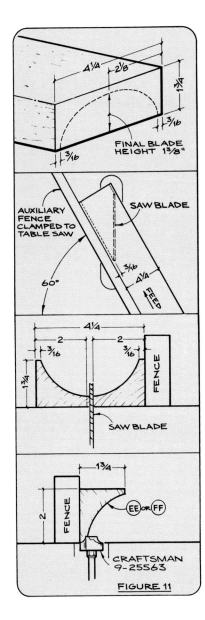

4 1/4   2 1/8

1 3/4

3/16

FINAL BLADE
HEIGHT 1 3/8"

3/16

AUXILIARY
FENCE
CLAMPED TO
TABLE SAW

SAW BLADE

60°

3/16

4 1/4

FEED

4 1/4

2   2

3/16   3/16

1 3/4

FENCE

SAW BLADE

1 3/4

FENCE

2

EE or FF

CRAFTSMAN
9-25563

FIGURE 11

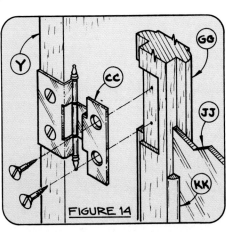

Y

CC

GG

JJ

KK

FIGURE 14

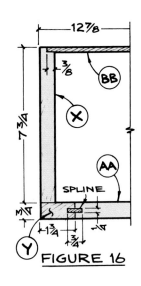

12 7/8

3/8

BB

7 3/4

X

AA

SPLINE

1/4

Y

1 3/4

3/4

1/4

FIGURE 16

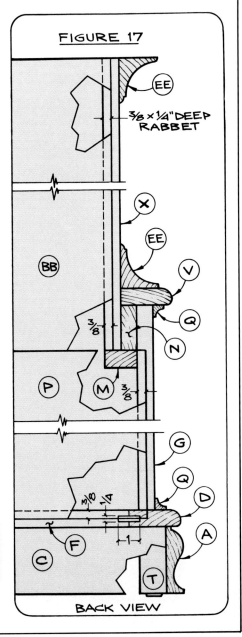

FIGURE 17

EE

3/8 x 1/4" DEEP
RABBET

X

EE

V

Q

N

BB

3/8

P

M   3/8

G

Q

D

3/8   1/4

A

C

F

1

T

BACK VIEW

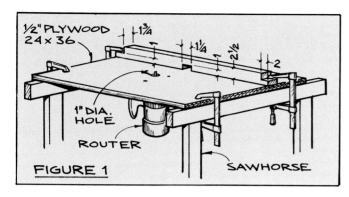

FIGURE 1

A router table is easy enough to make (See Fig. 1). Cut a sheet of $1/2$ in. thick birch plywood to a width of 24 in. and a length of 36 in. Bore a 1 in. diameter hole at the center, then make the fence from $1^3/4$ in. thick solid stock as shown. The 1 in. by $1^1/4$ in. notch is cut across the underside of the fence to allow clearance for the cutter. It also allows clearance for wood chips. Remove the router's plastic sub base, then secure the router to the underside of the table with three screws, each one driven through the top and countersunk $1/4$ in. Two pairs of C-clamps will secure the router table and the fence to sawhorses as shown. Make sure the sawhorses are sturdy as it's important that the router table be stable as the cuts are made.

Part 1: The Base and Waist Sections

To simplify the clock's construction, we've divided the assembly into two parts. Part 1 details the base and waist sections and Part 2 covers the hood and movement.

The ogee feet (parts A and B) can be made first. Cut $3/4$ in. thick stock to a width of 3 in. and a length of 42 in. (length dimension includes extra stock). The molding-head is used to cut most of the curved profile (see Fig. 2), but before starting you'll need a plywood inset for the table saw. The metal one that comes with the saw cannot be used with the molding-head and must be removed. Trace the outline of your present insert on a piece of scrap plywood—$1/4$ in. thick for a Sears 10 in. saw, $1/2$ in. thick for a 10 in. Rockwell Unisaw. Cut the pattern and fit it to the saw, then mount the three 1 in. flute cutters (Sears Craftsman 9-3206) to the molding-head. Lower the cutters below the table, then add the new plywood insert. With the

power off, and the cord disconnected, rotate the cutters by hand to make sure they are below the plywood.

Using a pushstick to hold down the insert, start the saw and raise the cutter very slowly. Continue raising the cutter, allowing it to cut through the plywood, until it is slightly above the desired height (about $1/2$ in.).

Lower the cutter to a height of about $1/8$ in. above the insert, and locate the rip-fence $3/16$ in. from the cutter. Using a pushstick, run the stock through the cutter to make the first pass. Do this three more times, raising the cutter $1/8$ in. after each pass. Making the cut in four passes produces a smooth surface with minimal strain on the saw.

Next, install the $1/2$ in. quarter-round cutters (Sears Craftsman 9-2351) in the molding-head. As before, raise the cutter to its desired height, then rotate the molding-head to make sure they don't hit any part of the plywood insert. Cut the radius as shown, again making the cut in several passes.

The remaining material can now be removed using a hand plane. Plane the stock to the profile shown in Fig. 2, then sand smooth. When planing and sanding, be careful not to reduce the thickness to less than $3/4$ in. at the point where

the $1/2$ in. radius is applied. It's important that this curved face of the stock have two points that are $3/4$ in. thick so that it will rest flat on the table saw when the miters are cut.

Next, cut the 45-degree miters on the front end of parts A and each end of part B. Note that the back ends of parts A are cut square. To look good, it's important for the miters to be cut at exactly 45 degrees, so it's best to make a trial cut with scrap stock. If the joints are square and the miter is tight, you can then proceed to cut the stock.

Now, transfer the curved profiles (shown on the front and side views) to the back side of parts A and B, then cut out with a band or saber saw. It's best to cut slightly on the waste side of the stock, then sand exactly to the line. If you have one, a drum sanding set will prove handy here.

After cutting the foot support (part C) to size (see Bill of Materials), the foot frame (parts A, B, and C) can now be assembled. Apply glue to the mating surfaces of the four joints, then apply pressure with a pair of web clamps.

The base side and front molding (parts D and E), and the waist side and front molding (parts V and W) are made next. Note that all these parts measure $3/4$ in. thick by $2^3/8$ in. wide (see Fig. 3). You'll need a piece of stock that's 41 in. long for parts D and E, and 40 in. long for parts V and W. Keep in mind that both these lengths provide a little extra for

later trimming. Again use the molding-head cutter to cut the $^1/_2$ in. and $^1/_4$ in. radii as shown.

To make the cut with the $^1/_4$ in. quarter-round edge of the cutter, part of the cutter will be into the rip fence. This necessitates an auxiliary wood fence. Straight square stock should be chosen, as long and high as the metal fence and at least $^7/_8$ in. thick. Secure it to the metal fence with a pair of clamps. Move the wooden fence to its proper position with the cutter below the table. Lock the fence in place, then start the motor and raise the cutter to slightly more than its desired height before backing it off a bit. The $^1/_4$ in. radius can now be cut but, as before, do it in several passes.

Cut the 45-degree miter on the front ends of parts D and V, and on both ends of E and W. To cut the spline mortises, a jig is used in conjunction with the router table (see Fig. 4). Use a $^1/_4$ in. diameter straight bit set to a depth of $^1/_8$ in. Start the router, then lower the stock into the cutter. When the workpiece comes in contact with the table, push the workpiece forward so that the bit cuts a mortise as shown in Fig. 5. Continue making $^1/_8$ in. deep cuts until the full $^1/_2$ in. mortise depth is achieved.

The base molding support, part F, can now be made. As shown in Fig. 17, a $^1/_4$ in. wide by $^1/_2$ in. deep spline mortise is cut on each end of part F. A mating spline mortise is cut on the back ends of parts D.

Parts D, E, and F can now be assembled. Cut $^1/_4$ in. splines to fit the mortises, then dry-assemble to make sure all parts fit well. Remember to cut the splines so that the grain direction is at a right angle to the joint line. If the dry assembly is satisfactory, apply glue to the splines and the mortises, then clamp securely with a web clamp. Check for squareness before setting aside to dry.

After cutting the base sides (parts G) to size, work can begin on the base frame (parts H, I and J). Cut each part to the dimensions shown in the Bill of Materials, then use the router table to cut the $^1/_4$ in. wide by $^1/_2$ in. deep spline mortises. Note that on the ends of part I, the spline does not go entirely across the $5^3/_8$ in. width of stock. Instead, the mortise is cut $4^1/_2$ in. long, stopping short of the bottom edge. The mating mortise on parts H are cut to the same length. The

spline mortise is also cut short on the ends of parts J, resulting in a length of $1^1/_4$ in. The mating mortise on the bottom of part H is also cut to a length of $1^1/_4$ in.

Next, on part I, use a compass to scribe the curved profile (see front view). Use a band or saber saw to cut just outside the scribed line, then use a drum sander to sand exactly to the line.

Cut the splines to size and dry fit parts H, I, and J. If all looks satisfactory, add glue and clamp with bar or pipe clamps. Check for squareness before setting aside to dry.

When dry, remove the clamps and equip the router with a ball-bearing piloted $^1/_4$ in. roundover bit (see Fig. 6). Cut the $^1/_4$ in. bead all around the inside edge of parts H, I, and J.

Next, equip the router with a $^3/_8$ in. ball-bearing piloted rabbet bit to cut the $^1/_4$ in. by $^3/_8$ in. rabbet all around the inside back edge (Fig. 6). Once cut, use a chisel to square the corners.

The base panel (part K) can now be made. You'll probably need to edge-join two narrower boards in order to get enough width. Since this panel is a visual highlight of the clock, try to select stock that has a pleasing grain. Edge-join the stock so that you have extra length and width. When dry, rip to final width, then lay the base frame assembly (parts H, I, and J) on the panel and scribe the profile of part I. The panel must actually be $^1/_4$ in. larger than this curved line, so use a pencil to scribe a matching, but larger, profile. Cut out with a band or saber saw, staying slightly on the waste side of the line, then sand to the line with a drum sander. The bottom edge of part K can then be cut to final length.

The radius that's cut all around the

edge of the panel is made using the router table equipped with a $^3/_4$ in. core box bit (see Fig. 6) and a guide clamped to the router table (see Fig. 7). Set the bit to make a $^1/_2$ in. deep cut, then locate the guide so that the first cut removes about $^1/_4$ in. of material all around. After the first cut, relocate the guide and remove an additional $^1/_4$ in. of stock. Repeat this process until the $1^1/_4$ in. width is achieved. It's a good idea to make some test cuts on scrap material before starting on the panel stock. After completing the radius, check part K for a good fit in the frame (there should be $^1/_8$ in. on the top and sides for expansion), then set aside.

After cutting the waist sides (parts X) to size, the waist frame (parts Y, Z, and AA) can be made. Both parts Z and AA are $6^1/_2$ in. wide and have $^1/_4$ in. wide by $5^1/_4$ in. long spline mortises cut in each end. A mating mortise is cut in parts Y. Use a compass to scribe the 4 in. radius curve in part Z (see front view) before cutting out and sanding smooth. Cut the four splines and dry fit the frame. If satisfied, add glue and clamp with bar or pipe clamps. Check for squareness and set aside to dry.

The waist side and front moldings (parts EE and FF) are made as shown in Fig. 11. Cut $1^3/_4$ in. thick stock to a width of $4^1/_4$ in. Clamp an auxiliary fence (at 60 degrees) to the saw table. With the saw blade set to a height of $1^3/_8$ in., note that the fence is located $^3/_{16}$ in. from the blade. Lower the saw blade to a height of $^1/_{16}$ in., then pass the stock through the blade. Flip the stock, end for end, and make the same cut. Raising the blade in $^1/_{16}$ in. increments, continue this process until the final blade height of $1^3/_8$ in. is reached. To be sure your set up is accurate, it's a good idea to make a practice run on a short piece of scrap pine.

Once the cove is cut, rip the piece to a width of 2 in., then final sand. Next, use the router table and a $^1/_4$ in. beading bit (Sears Craftsman 9-25563) to cut the bead along one edge. Note that the cutter is used without the arbor (pilot).

The waist door (parts GG, HH, and II) can now be made. Cut each part to size, then add the 45-degree miters as shown in Figs. 13A and 13B. The mortises for the $^1/_4$ in. thick splines are cut using the same jig that was used to cut parts D, E, V, and W (Fig. 4). However, the final cutter height setting will be $3/8$ in., and the dimension from the guide board to the outside cutter edge will be $1^1/4$ in. You'll need to clamp a stopblock to the table to limit the mortise length to $3/4$ in.

Apply glue to the splines and the mortises before assembling with bar or pipe clamps. Check for squareness before setting aside to dry.

Once dry, remove the clamps, then use a compass to scribe the inner and outer radii on part HH. Cut out on the waste side of the line, then sand smooth with a drum sander.

To cut the front bead on the inside and outside edges of the waist door parts, equip the router table with a $1/4$ in. bead bit that has a ball-bearing pilot (see Fig. 12). The back rabbets are cut with a ball-bearing piloted $5/16$ in. rabbet bit.

Assemble parts G to parts H using glue and clamps. To keep the parts from sliding as the clamp pressure is applied, it's a good idea to first drive two or three small brads in part G, then clip the heads off so $1/16$ in. is exposed.

Apply three or four coats of a good penetrating oil to the base panel (part K) before installing it to the base frame (parts H, I, and J). Parts L, which serve to hold the panel sides in place, can now be glued and screwed as shown. Part O, which secures the panel at the top, is also added now.

Glue and clamp parts N to parts G so that the top edges are flush. When dry, parts M are glued and clamped to parts N and G.

Cut part T to the dimensions shown in Fig. 9, then bore holes to accept the leveler (part U). Glue and clamp part T in place, locating it $1/4$ in. from the top edge of A and B. The bottom (part S) can now be cut to size, given several coats of penetrating oil, and dropped in place.

Apply glue to the top edge of parts A and B, then attach the base molding frame (parts D, E, and F) with $1^1/4$ in. long no. 8 flathead wood screws (FHWS) driven through the frame and into the tops of the leveler blocks. Be sure to locate the screws at a point that will not show after the addition of the part Q molding.

Place the partially assembled waist on top of parts D and E and scribe a pencil line to indicate the proper position of parts G and J. Remove the waist and, with the lines as a guide, bore screw

holes down through parts D and E. Note that the screw holes in parts D are slotted. Add glue to the bottom edge of parts G and J, then join to parts D and E with $1^1/2$ in. by no. 10 FHWS driven up through the bottom.

After joining X to Y, the waist can be joined to the base. Apply glue to the mating surfaces and clamp firmly.

When dry, add glue to the inside edges of parts V and W and slide in from the front. Clamp firmly.

Moldings Q and R (see Fig. 8) can

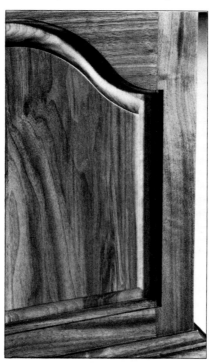

now be cut and applied with glue and several small brads, countersunk and filled. The lower parts EE and FF are added in the same manner, however the upper ones won't be applied until after the hood is added—as detailed in Part 2.

All of the hardware for the base and waist sections can be ordered from The American Clockmaker, P.O. Box 326, Clintonville, WI 54929; tel. 1-800-236-7300. The leveler (U) is p/n 43100, the waist door hinge (CC) is p/n 40406, the back lock (DD) is p/n 42800, the rubber glass retainer (KK) is p/n 43654, and the brass latch (LL) is p/n 40706.

The waist door hinge (part CC) is mortised to part GG, but not to part Y (see Fig. 14). As shown in Fig. 15, a mortise is cut to accept the brass latch (part LL). The glass (part JJ) is cut to fit the door frame and held in place with glass retainer (part KK).

Part 2: The Hood and Movement Installation

The two end frames (parts MM, NN, OO, and PP) can be made first (Fig. 22). Cut each part to the dimensions shown on the Bill of Materials, but allow a little extra on length. Lay out the $1^9/16$ in. radius on one end of each part OO before cutting to shape with a band or saber saw. Make the cut slightly on the waste side of the marked line, then sand exactly to the line.

Edge-glue parts MM, NN, OO, and PP. Note that $1/4$ in. diameter by 1 in. long dowel pins are used (Figs. 22 and 34) to make alignment easier when the parts are clamped. Be sure that parts OO and PP are spaced $5^3/4$ in. apart (Fig. 22). Clamp with bar or pipe clamps and allow to dry overnight.

Once dry, use the table saw to trim the end frames to final length. The cuts must be square, so check your miter gauge before starting.

To apply the $1/4$ in. radius to the outside of the panel opening (Fig. 23), use a router equipped with a ball-bearing piloted $1/4$ in. roundover bit. You'll note the router does not produce sharp corners, so you'll need a chisel to square them up (see photo).

On the inside of the panel opening, a $5/16$ in. by $3/8$ in. rabbet is cut using a ball bearing piloted $3/8$ in. rabbet bit. In order to accept the glass panel (SS), the corners on the inside of the panel opening must be cut square (Fig. 22). This is best cut with a sharp chisel, using the $5/16$ in. deep rabbet as a guide for the proper depth.

Next, cut the front stretcher (QQ) to size, then use a compass to scribe the $5^1/4$ in. radius as shown. Cut out on the waste side of the stock, then shape and sand to the line. The $1/4$ in. wide by $3/8$ in. deep spline mortises are best cut on the router table equipped with a $1/4$ in. diameter straight bit. However, don't make the $3/8$ in. deep cut in one pass. You'll get a smoother cut, with less strain on the motor, if it's done in two passes, each pass removing $3/16$ in. of material. Also, note that the spline mortise does not go all the way across the end of the stock. Instead, it is cut 5 in. long, stopping $3/8$ in. short of the

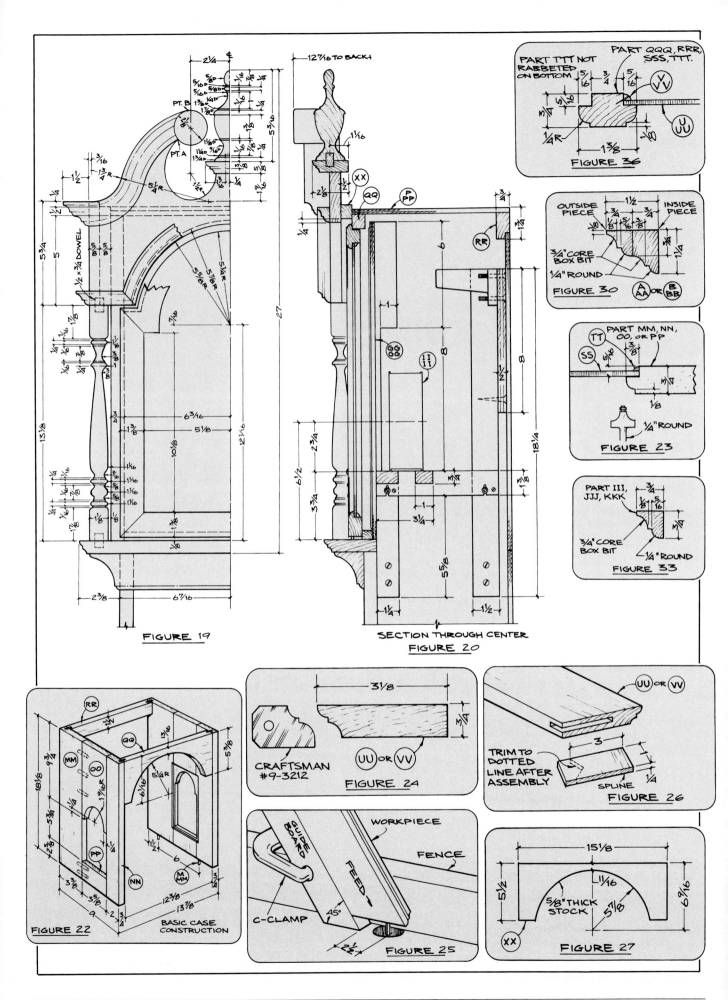

PART TTT NOT RABBETED ON BOTTOM

PART QQQ, RRR, SSS, TTT.

VV
UU

FIGURE 36

12⁷/₁₆ TO BACK)

1¹/₁₆

XX
QQ

PP

OUTSIDE PIECE

INSIDE PIECE

3/4" CORE BOX BIT

1/4" ROUND

FIGURE 30   A AA OR B BB

PART MM, NN, OO, OR PP

TT
SS

1/4" ROUND

FIGURE 23

PART III, JJJ, KKK

3/4" CORE BOX BIT

1/4" ROUND

FIGURE 33

PT. B

PT. A

1/2 × 3/4 DOWEL

RR
QQ

GG
QQ

III

FIGURE 19

SECTION THROUGH CENTER
FIGURE 20

RR
QQ
MM
OO

PP
NN
M MM

BASIC CASE CONSTRUCTION

FIGURE 22

3¹/₈
3/4

CRAFTSMAN #9-3212

UU OR VV

FIGURE 24

GUIDE BOARD

WORKPIECE

FENCE

FEED

C-CLAMP

45°

FIGURE 25

UU OR VV

TRIM TO DOTTED LINE AFTER ASSEMBLY

SPLINE

FIGURE 26

15¹/₈

5¹/₂

11/16

5/8" THICK STOCK

5⁷/₈

6⁷/₁₆

XX

FIGURE 27

bottom edge.

The back stretcher (RR) can now be cut to size. Once again, use the router table to cut the $1/4$ in. wide by $3/8$ in. deep mortises on each end. These mortises are not stopped, but rather cut along the entire length of the end.

The mating spline mortises on parts MM and NN can now be cut (using the router table) to the same length. Cut $1/4$ in. splines to fit the mortises, then dry assemble to make sure all parts fit well. It's important to remember to cut the splines so that the grain direction is at a right angle to the joint line. If the dry assembly is satisfactory, apply glue to the splines and mortises, then clamp securely.

The hood base ends (UU) and front (VV) can be made next (Fig. 24). You'll need a piece of stock that's about 41 in. long to make all three parts. Keep in mind that these lengths provide a little extra for later trimming.

The molding-head is used to cut the edge profile. Install the cutters (Sears 9-3212), then follow the procedure discussed in Part 1 to make the plywood inset and the auxiliary wood fence for the table saw. Once the table saw is properly set up, make the cut—but remember to do it in several passes, each pass removing a bit more stock.

Cut the 45-degree miter on the front end of parts UU, and on both ends of parts VV. To cut the spline mortises, use the router table jig shown in Fig. 25. Use a $1/4$ in. diameter straight bit set to a depth of $1/8$ in. Start the router and slowly lower the stock into the cutter. When the workpiece comes in contact with the table, push the workpiece forward so that the bit cuts the mortise as shown in Fig. 26. Continue making $1/8$ in. deep cuts until the full $1/2$ in. mortise depth is achieved.

In order to clamp parts UU and VV, you'll need to cut an $11^3/8$ in. long piece of scrap stock to serve as a spacer while the frame is glued.

Cut $1/4$ in. splines to fit the mortises, then dry-assemble to make sure all parts fit well. If the dry assembly looks good, apply glue to the splines and mortises, then add the scrap stock spacer and clamp securely with a web clamp. Check for squareness before setting aside to dry.

Next, lay out and mark the location of

the frame pin (MMM) holes in parts MM, NN, and UU. Bore the holes, then dry-assemble the hood case to the hood base frame (parts UU and VV) and check for squareness.

The two side spacers (WW) and the front spacer (XX) are next. After cutting the parts to length and width, use a compass to scribe the $5^7/8$ in. radius on part XX as shown in Fig. 27. As before, cut out with a band or saber saw then shape and sand to the line.

Parts WW can now be joined to the end frames with four $1^1/4$ in. by number 8 flathead wood screws. In order to allow the end frame to move with seasonal humidity changes, the screw holes through parts WW should be slightly oversized (about $5/32$ in. diameter). Note that the front edge of part WW is flush with the front edge of the end frame. Also note, as shown in Fig. 21, that the top edge of part WW is $1/2$ in. above the top edge of the end frame.

Part XX can now be added. Use glue and wood screws to secure in place. Note that its top edge is flush with the top edge of WW.

The scrollboard (ZZ) is made next. Cut $5/8$ in. thick stock to a width of $11^1/2$ in. and a length of 17 in. Both the width and length dimensions allow extra stock for later trimming. Set the table saw blade at 45 degrees then, cut the miter on one end. Measure across the front of the hood case to determine the needed length, then mark this dimension on part ZZ and cut the second miter.

With both miters now cut, temporarily clamp part ZZ in its proper position on the hood case. Note the bottom edge of part ZZ is flush with the bottom edge of part WW.

The two scrollboard sides (YY) can now be made. Cut $5/8$ in. thick stock to a width of $5^3/4$ in. and length of 11 in. The length dimension allows a little extra stock. Cut the 45-degree miter on the front end, taking care to insure that it results in a good fit with the mating miter on part ZZ. When satisfied with the fit-up, trim the back end flush with the case. Parts YY can now be joined to the hood case using glue and clamps. Remember, since part ZZ is only temporarily in place, don't apply glue to the miter joint.

Next, the left and right swan's neck molding (BBB) is made. Note that each

molding (Fig. 30) consists of two pieces: a $3/4$ in. by $3/4$ in. outside piece, and a $3/4$ in. by $1^1/4$ in. inside piece. These pieces are shaped individually, then joined with glue later on. You'll need two patterns (see Fig. 29) made from $1/2$ in. thick plywood—one measuring $3/4$ in. wide (for the outside piece) and the other measuring $1^1/4$ in. wide (for the inside piece). Fig. 29 shows the patterns oriented to make the left swan's neck molding. However, by simply flipping them, the same patterns are used to make the right swan's neck molding.

To make each plywood pattern, use a compass to scribe the radii (Fig. 29). Once scribed, use a band or saber saw to cut just outside the marked lines, then shape and sand exactly to the lines.

In order to make both the left and right swan's neck, you'll need four pieces of stock, each one measuring $3/4$ in. by 4 in. by 14 in. Start by making the outside pieces of the left side molding. Lay the $3/4$ in. wide plywood pattern on one of the boards, then trace the profile with a pencil. With a band or saber saw, cut just outside the marked line. Using double-face tape, secure the plywood pattern to the band sawn stock, then equip the router table with a laminate trimmer bit and trim the stock flush with the plywood.

The cross-sectional profile of the molding is cut using the router table and guide (Fig. 31). The guide is the same one used to shape the base panel (K) in Part 1. Equip the router with a $3/4$ in. core box bit and, with the plywood pattern still taped to the stock, make the cove cut as shown in Fig. 31. As always, don't make the cut in one step; do it in several passes, each one removing small amounts of stock. Once the cove is cut, use a $1/4$ in. roundover bit to make the $1/4$ in. round as shown. Follow the same procedure to make the outside piece of the right side molding—just remember to flip the plywood pattern.

To make the right and left inside pieces, repeat the above steps, but use the $1^1/4$ in. wide plywood pattern.

Now that the outside and inside pieces have been shaped, they can be joined using glue and clamps. Before adding glue, though, drive two or three small brads into one of the mating surfaces, then clip the heads off so that about $1/16$ in. is exposed. The brads will keep the

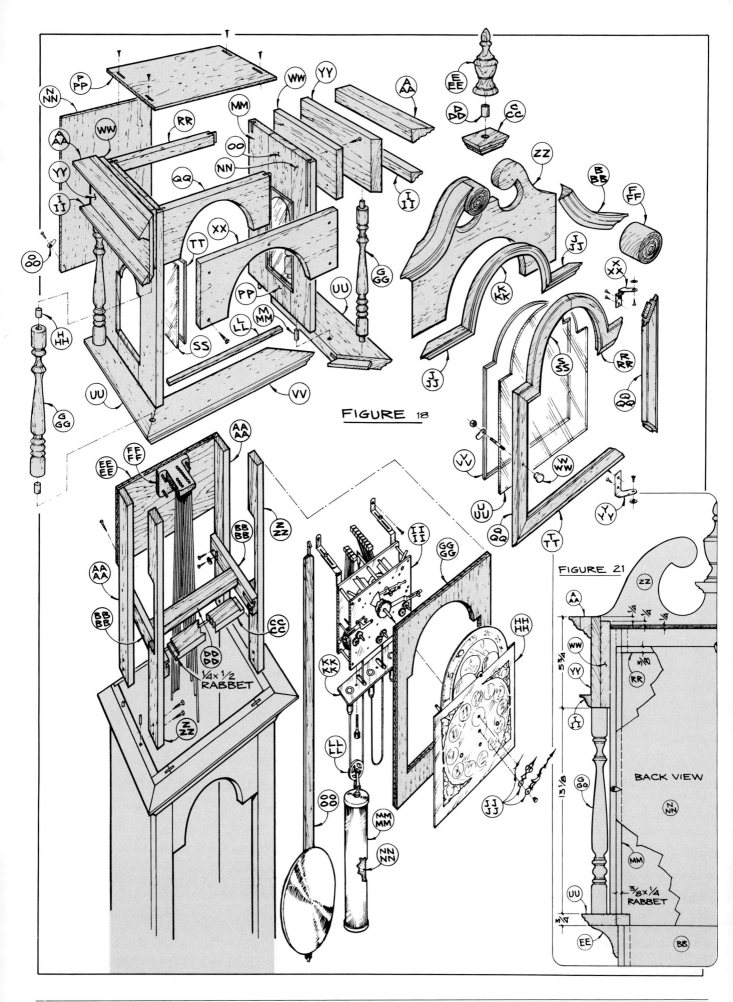

FIGURE 18

FIGURE 21

BACK VIEW

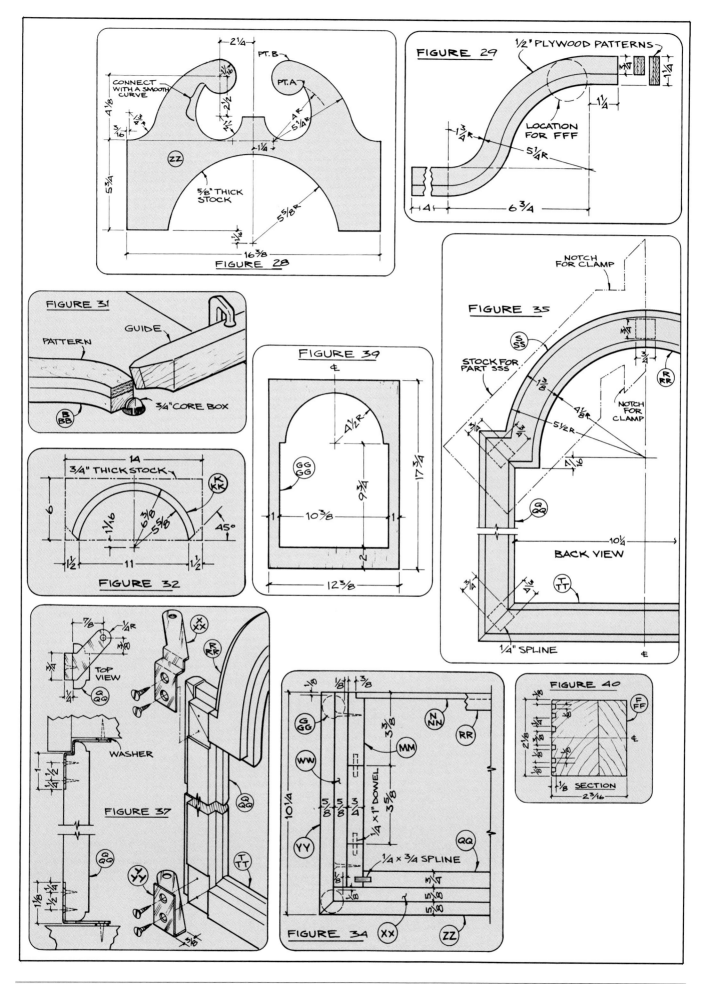

FIGURE 28

FIGURE 29
½" PLYWOOD PATTERNS

FIGURE 31
PATTERN
GUIDE
¾"CORE BOX

FIGURE 35
NOTCH FOR CLAMP
STOCK FOR PART SSS
NOTCH FOR CLAMP
BACK VIEW
¼" SPLINE

FIGURE 39

FIGURE 32
¾" THICK STOCK

FIGURE 37
TOP VIEW
WASHER

FIGURE 34

FIGURE 40
SECTION

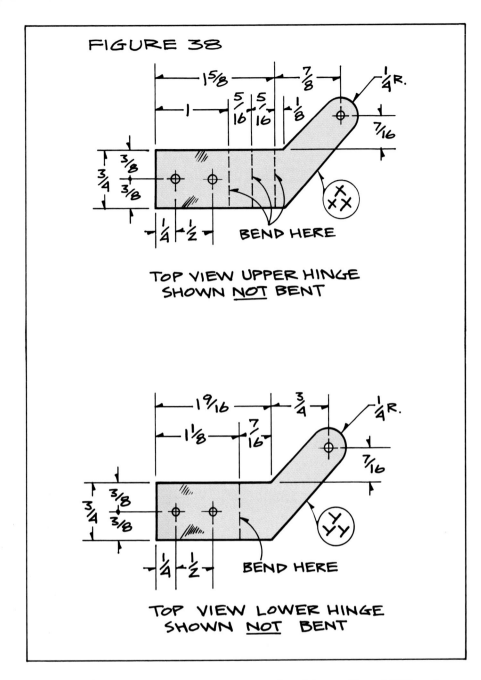

FIGURE 38

TOP VIEW UPPER HINGE
SHOWN NOT BENT

BEND HERE

TOP VIEW LOWER HINGE
SHOWN NOT BENT

BEND HERE

parts from sliding over each other when clamp pressure is added. And to keep the narrow (^{1}/8 in.) edge from denting as clamp pressure is applied, it's best to sandwich the molding between two boards.

The hood top end molding (AAA) is an extension of the swan's neck molding, and it has an identical cross-sectional profile. Follow the same procedure as was used to make the swan's neck, but use straight stock for the plywood patterns. From a practical standpoint, keep in mind that it makes sense to make parts AAA and BBB at the same time. This will save setup time and insure that the profiles match.

Next, referring to Fig. 28, lay out the profile of the scrollboard (ZZ) as shown. The swan's neck moldings can be used as templates to help with the layout. Cut out with a band or saber saw, staying on the waste side of the line. Don't sand smooth yet.

The rosette (FFF) can now be made (Fig. 40). Face-glue a piece of 1^3/4 in. thick stock, and a piece of ^{3}/4 in. thick stock, then trim to 2^1/4 in. square by 2^3/16 in. long. Attach the stock to a faceplate and turn on the lathe. Note that the rosette must have long grain on its turned end, not end grain. An end grain glue joint won't have enough strength.

Temporarily clamp parts BBB (in their proper position) to part ZZ. Referring to Fig. 19, transfer points A and B to

parts BBB, then use the rosette as a template to connect the points. Cut out with a band saw, but stay well on the waste side of the stock. A 2 in. diameter drum sander will do a good job of smoothing the cut to an exact fit. Work slowly, sanding a little at a time to insure accuracy. We found it helpful to undercut the molding at this point, so that just the front and top edge actually made contact with the rosette.

Next, the rosette can be glued and clamped to part ZZ. With the rosettes in place, locate parts BBB in their proper position and mark the location of the 45-degree miter cuts. Once the miter cuts are made, parts BBB can be glued in place. Use a piece of scrap stock to protect the narrow molding edge. When dry, use a laminate trimmer bit to trim the profile of ZZ (remember this was cut oversized) flush with parts BBB and FFF. Part ZZ can now be glued to the hood case.

Turn the four spindles (GGG) to the dimensions shown (Fig. 19), then bore the ^{1}/2 in. diameter by ^{3}/8 in. deep holes in each end to accept the spindle pins (HHH). Make sure the holes are square. Next, lay out and bore the four spindle pin holes in parts UU (Fig. 34).

Dry-fit the four spindles (with the four bottom spindle pins) on the hood base frame, then mark the proper location of the top end of the spindle. Because the top spindle pin holes are close to the hood case, a brace and bit must be used. Locate the bit at the centerpoint of the hole, crank the brace one-half turn, then ratchet back. Repeat the process until the hole is bored to a ^{3}/8 in. depth.

The scrollboard arch molding (KKK) is made next. Cut stock to the dimensions shown in Fig. 32, then cut the 45-degree miters as shown. Now, scribe the two radii and cut out with a band or saber saw. Shape and sand the edges to the scribed line. Next, use the router table and guide to cut the profile shown in Fig. 33.

To make the scrollboard side and end molding (III and JJJ), rip stock (about 36 in. long) to ^{3}/4 in. square. Cut the profile at the same time the profile for KKK is being cut.

Part KKK can now be glued and clamped to the hood case. When dry, parts III and JJJ can be added. Cut the 45-degree miters with care in order to insure a good fit.

The hood base frame (UU and VV) and the spindles (GGG) can now be assembled to the hood case. Apply glue to the mating surfaces, then clamp firmly and check for squareness.

When dry, use a router equipped with a piloted $^3/_8$ in. rabbet bit to cut the $^1/_4$ in. deep rabbet for the hood back (NNN). Use a chisel to square the two upper corners and to notch the back edge of parts UU.

Part NNN is made from $^1/_4$ in. walnut plywood (available from Constantine, 2050 Eastchester Road, Bronx, NY 10461). When buying the plywood, keep in mind that the base (P), and waist (BB) backs (shown in Part 1), and the dial board (GGGG) are also made with $^1/_4$ in. walnut plywood.

The finial base (CCC) is made as shown and glued in place. The finial (EEE) is then turned (Fig. 19) and glued using the finial pin (DDD) for added strength.

As the name implies, the movement support framework (parts ZZZ, AAAA, BBBB, CCCC, DDDD, and EEEE) serves to support the movement and its associated hardware. It is assembled as shown and secured to the inside of the waist side (X) with $1^1/_4$ in. by number 8 wood screws (Fig. 20). Each of the front mounting posts has a 1 in. by 8 in. notch in order to facilitate installation and to expose more of the movement (IIII) when viewed through the glass panel (SS).

To make the hood door right and left arches (RRR and SSS), cut two pieces of $^3/_4$ in. thick stock: each one measuring $3^1/_2$ in. wide by 11 in. long (Fig. 35). Cut a 45-degree miter on one end of each piece and temporarily join the two mitered ends with a spot of glue. Use a band or saber saw to cut the clamp notches.

Now, referring to Fig. 35, lay out the profile of parts RRR and SSS as shown. Also carefully lay out the location of the spline mortises.

Next, break the temporary glue joint and transfer the spline mortise location to the ends of the miter. Use a sharp

chisel to cut each one. Apply glue to the spline and mortises, then clamp the parts together with a pair of C-clamps.

When dry, use the table saw to cut the miter on each end, and the band or saber saw to cut the remaining profile. As always, cut just outside the marked line, then shape and sand.

Parts QQQ and TTT are now cut to size and mitered as shown. Again, lay out and mark the mortise location before cutting out with the chisel. Check for squareness before setting aside to dry. To cut the $^1/_4$ in. bead and back rabbet

Glass panel (SS) permits view of triple-chime movement.

(Fig. 36), follow the same procedure that was used to cut the waist door in Part 1.

The door hinges (XXX and YYY) are made from .032 in. thick brass stock (Figs. 37 and 38). Bend and shape as shown, then mortise the door and install.

The hood case can now be joined to the waist section. A pair of $^3/_8$ in. diameter by $^3/_4$ in. long dowel pins are used for added strength. Apply glue to the mating surfaces, then clamp firmly. Keep in mind that the upper waist side and front moldings (EE and FF) are not joined to the case yet. We showed how to make these moldings in Part 1.

At this point, apply three or four coats of a good penetrating oil to all parts.

The triple-chime cablewound movement (IIII), and moon dial (HHHH) were purchased from the Mason and Sullivan

Co., 210 Wood County Industrial Park, P.O. Box 1686, Parkersburg, WV 26102; tel. 1-800-225-1153. The movement comes complete with a chime block (FFFF), pendulum (OOOO), solid brass weight shells (MMMM), weight fillings (NNNN), winding crank (not shown), and hands (JJJJ). The movement will play Westminster, Whittington, or St. Michael chimes. Order part number 3232X.

The high arch moon dial (HHHH) measures 11 in. wide by $15^1/_2$ in. high. Its part number is 3902E.

When installed, the movement rests on the front and back seatboards (CCCC and DDDD). The notches cut in parts BBBB allow some vertical adjustment. For depth (in and out) adjustment, the movement can be moved on the seatboard parts. Make sure, however, that the cables do not contact the seatboard parts. If they do, you'll need to cut a small notch in parts CCCC or DDDD to allow free movement.

Along with their movement, Mason and Sullivan provides a booklet that explains, in detail, how to install it. The booklet also covers operation, troubleshooting, and maintenance. Their instructions take you through the process, from beginning to end.

The dial board (GGGG) can now be made (Fig. 39) using $^1/_4$ in. walnut plywood. It's glued to the front edge of parts ZZZ (Fig. 20). The bottom of the dial board rests on part VV, but the two parts are not glued. The cleat (LLL) is then glued to part VV, but not to the dial board.

The moon dial is now added. For installation instructions, refer to Mason and Sullivan's literature.

The brass latch (WWW), plastic glass retainer (TT and VVV), and back locks (OOO) can be ordered from The American Clockmaker (see Part 1 for their address and part numbers). You'll need to have the hood door glass (UUU) cut by a glass shop.

The installation of the hood back (NNN), hood top (PPP), and waist moldings (EE and FF) completes the project. ●

This mahogany tilt-top table is a reproduction of one built in Philadelphia in the mid-18th century. It is a fine example of how period furniture can mix practicality with elegance. Traditionally brought out for serving tea, tilt-top tables of this type feature a top that both pivots to a vertical position, and swivels around like a lazy Susan. With the top tilted vertically, the table could be stored flat against a wall or in a corner. This saves space yet allows the table to remain on dis-

play, showing off the elegance of its shapely legs and pedestal and its decorative figured top.

The tabletop with molded rim (A), known as a dish top, is glued up from wide mahogany planks and shaped on a lathe, as if it were a very large plate with a raised edge. The dish top can also be shaped by hand or with a router, though neither of these methods works as well as the lathe. We've included an alternate pattern for a flat top with a molded edge. Some tea tables from this period had flat tops, and the work saved in not shaping a dish top simplifies the project.

For either style of top, two cleats (B) are screwed under the top perpendicular to its grain. The cleats prevent cupping and are drilled to form the upper half of the tilting

18th Century
Tilt Top Table

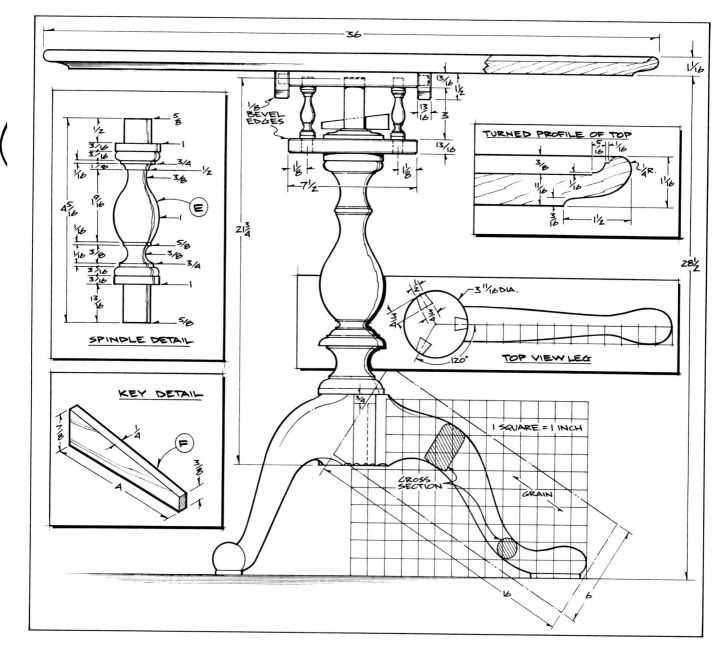

SPINDLE DETAIL

KEY DETAIL

TURNED PROFILE OF TOP

TOP VIEW LEG

CROSS SECTION

1 SQUARE = 1 INCH

GRAIN

BEVEL EDGES

mechanism's hinge. The top rests on a contraption usually called a birdcage (also gallery or crow's nest), which consists of two horizontal squares (C, D) drilled through their centers and separated by four small turnings (E)—the pillars at each corner of the cage. The birdcage serves three functions. It completes the tilt-top hinge, allows the swivel action, and fastens the top to the pedestal. A wooden key (F), resting on a turned washer (G), locks the top and birdcage to the base. The base consists of an urn-shaped pedestal (H) with three legs (I). The legs are attached with dovetails that slide up into the pedestal from below.

Begin the project by drawing all the table parts, except the top and key, full-size. Make patterns (out of stiff cardboard or 1/8 in. plywood) of the central pedestal, the cleats, the side profile of the leg, and the birdcage turnings. Also make a cross-sectional pattern of the table rim.

The 36 in. diameter dish top is turned outboard on the lathe. The larger a top is, the more vibration there will be when turning. A top this size requires an industrial lathe. The lathe should be bolted to the floor and wall. Additional diagonal

bracing will further help subdue the vibrations. Because the turning is done outboard, it requires a freestanding tool rest designed for the purpose.

The boards for the top should be chosen for their beauty. The tilting top is a natural show-off, so ribbony, richly colored mahogany is desirable. To obtain the 37 in. width, join two 18 1/2 in. wide pieces or three pieces that are each about 12 1/2 in. wide. Assemble the pieces so that the wood at the joint matches well and disguises the seams. If possible, arrange the boards to carry the grain from one to the next.

After the glue-up, the approximately 37 in. by 37 in. square blank for the top should be planed flat on the underside and rough cut with a jigsaw or band saw to a circular shape. Before turning this mahogany circle you need to cut an additional 3/4 in. thick plywood circle (Baltic birch is good) with a diameter of about 24 in. The bigger this circle the better, for it helps to support the mahogany during turning. Screw the outboard faceplate to the center of this circle, attach it to the lathe, and flatten (using scraping tools only) the face of the plywood. Now, off the lathe but still attached to the faceplate, glue the

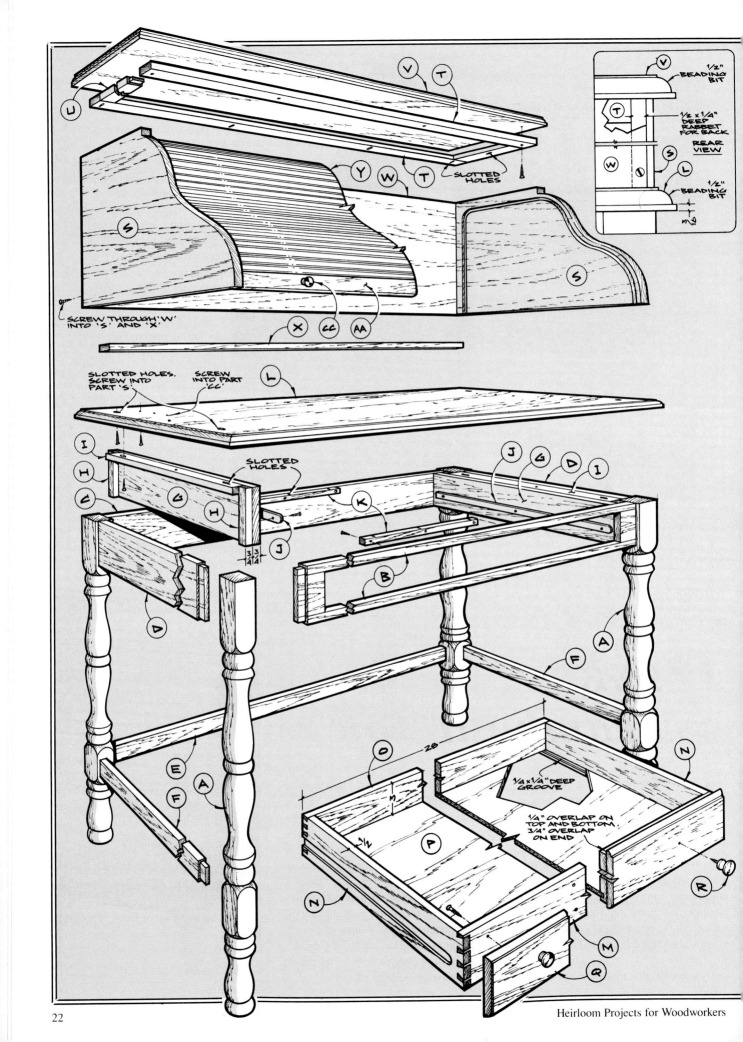

SLOTTED
HOLES

SCREW THROUGH 'W'
INTO 'S' AND 'X'

SLOTTED HOLES,
SCREW INTO
PART 'S'

SCREW
INTO PART
'CC'

SLOTTED
HOLES

¼ x ¼" DEEP
GROOVE

¼" OVERLAP ON
TOP AND BOTTOM,
¾" OVERLAP
ON END

½"
BEADING
BIT

½ x ¼"
DEEP
RABBET
FOR BACK

REAR
VIEW

½"
BEADING
BIT

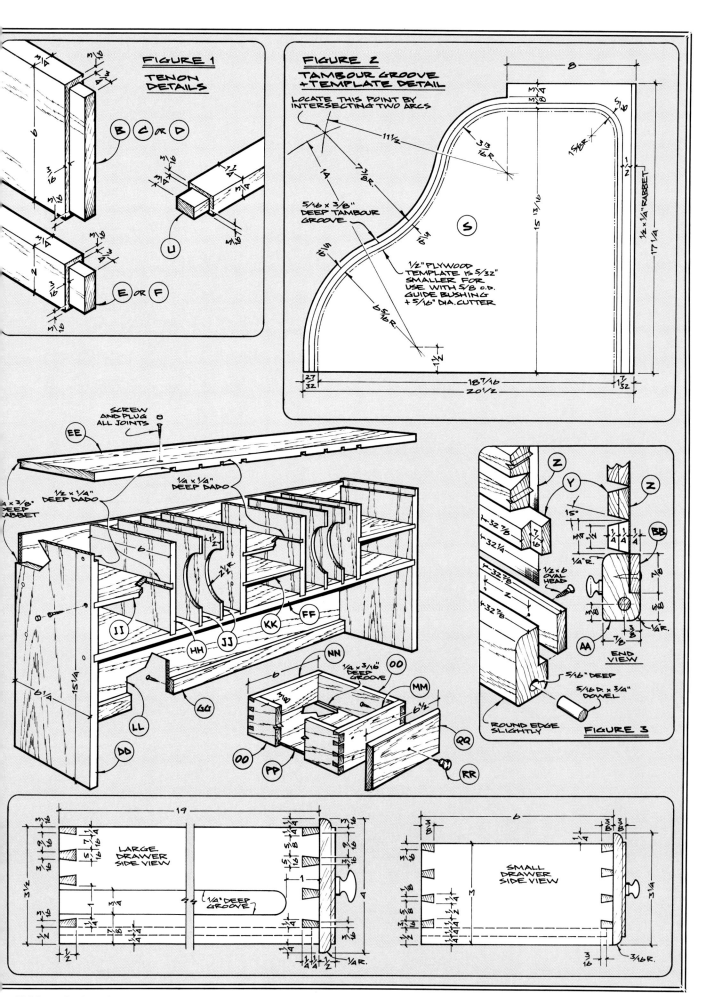

FIGURE 1
TENON
DETAILS

B C or D

U

E or F

FIGURE 2
TAMBOUR GROOVE
+TEMPLATE DETAIL

LOCATE THIS POINT BY
INTERSECTING TWO ARCS

8

3/4
3/8

5/16

11 1/2

3 13/16 R.

1 5/8 R.

1/2
1/2 x 1/4" RABBET

5/16 x 3/8"
DEEP TAMBOUR
GROOVE

S

15 13/16

17 1/4

1/2" PLYWOOD
TEMPLATE IS 5/32"
SMALLER FOR
USE WITH 5/8 O.D.
GUIDE BUSHING
+ 5/16" DIA. CUTTER

6 5/16 R.

1 1/2

27/32

18 7/16

20 1/2

1 7/32

SCREW
AND PLUG
ALL JOINTS

EE

1/4 x 1/4"
DEEP DADO

1/2 x 1/4"
DEEP DADO

1/4 x 3/8"
DEEP
RABBET

6

1 1/2

2 1/4 R.

2 1/4 R.

FF

II

JJ

KK

HH

15 1/4

6 1/4

GG

LL

NN

1/4 x 3/16"
DEEP GROOVE

OO

MM

3/16

6 1/2

QQ

OO

PP

RR

DD

Z

Y

Z

15°

1-32 7/8

7/16

1-32 1/4

1/4" R.

1/4 1/4

BB

1-32 7/8

1/2 x 6
OVAL
HEAD

Z

3/16

5/8

1/4 R.

AA

7/8
3/8

END
VIEW

5/16" DEEP

5/16 D. x 3/4"
DOWEL

ROUND EDGE
SLIGHTLY

FIGURE 3

19

3/16

7/16

3/16

3/4

1/2

1/4

3/8

1/4" DEEP
GROOVE

1 1/2

5/16

5 1/8

1

1/4 R.

1/4 1/4 1/2

LARGE
DRAWER
SIDE VIEW

3 1/2

4

6

3/8

1/4

3/8

3/8

SMALL
DRAWER
SIDE VIEW

3 1/4

3/16

3/16 R.

M

Bill of Materials
(all dimensions actual)

Part	Description	Size	No. Req'd.
	Base Section		
A	Leg	1³/₄ x 1³/₄ x 29¹/₂	4
B	Front Apron Assembly	³/₄ x 5¹/₂* x 32¹/₂**	1
C	Back Apron	³/₄ x 5 x 32¹/₂**	1
D	Side Apron	³/₄ x 5 18¹/₂**	2
E	Back Stretcher	³/₄ x 2 x 32¹/₂**	1
F	Side Stretcher	³/₄ x 2 x 18¹/₂**	2
G	Liner	³/₄ x 5 x 18¹/₂	2
H	Filler Block	³/₄ x ³/₄ x 5	4
I	Side Cleat	³/₄ x 1¹/₂ x 17	2
J	Drawer Guide	¹/₄ x ³/₄ x 18	2
K	Apron Cleat	³/₄ x ³/₄ x 12	2
L	Writing Surface	³/₄ x 22 x 36	1
M	Drawer Front	¹/₂ x 3¹/₂ x 28	1
N	Drawer Side	¹/₂ x 3¹/₂ x 19	2
O	Drawer Back	¹/₂ x 3 x 28	1
P	Drawer Bottom	¹/₄ x 27¹/₂ x 18³/₄	1
Q	Drawer Face	¹/₂ x 4 x 29¹/₂	1
R	Drawer Knob	brass, 1 in. dia.	2
	Top Section		
S	Side	³/₄ x 17¹/₄ x 20¹/₂	2
T	Front/Back Cleat	³/₄ x 1¹/₄ x 33	2
U	End Cleat	³/₄ x 1¹/₄ x 6³/₄**	2
V	Top	³/₄ x 9¹/₂ x 36	1
W	Back	¹/₄ x 17¹/₄ x 34	1
X	Tambour Stop	¹/₂ x 1¹/₂ x 33	1
Y	Tambour	¹/₂ x ³/₄ x 33³/₄	30
Z	Canvas	as needed	1
AA	Handle	⁷/₈ x 1¹/₂ x 32⁷/₈	1
BB	Backing Strip	¹/₄ x ⁷/₈ x 32⁷/₈	1
CC	Handle Knob	brass, ³/₄ in. dia.	2
DD	Organizer Side	¹/₂ x 6¹/₄ x 15¹/₄	2
EE	Organizer Top	¹/₂ x 6¹/₄ x 32¹/₂	1
FF	Organizer Shelf	¹/₂ x 6 x 32¹/₂	1
GG	Back Strip	¹/₂ x 1¹/₂ x 32	1
HH	Vert. Divider	¹/₂ x 6 x 7	4
II	Drawer Divider	¹/₂ x 6 x 6¹/₂	2
JJ	Separator	¹/₄ x 6 x 7	4
KK	Horiz. Divider	¹/₄ x 6 x 6¹/₂	2
LL	Divider Back	¹/₄ x 15 x 32¹/₂	1
MM	Drawer Front	³/₈ x 3 x 6	1/drawer
NN	Drawer Back	³/₈ x 2¹/₂ x 6	1/drawer
OO	Drawer Side	³/₈ x 3 x 6	2/drawer
PP	Drawer Bottom	¹/₄ x 5⁵/₈ x 5¹³/₁₆	1/drawer
QQ	Drawer Face	³/₈ x 3¹/₄ x 6¹/₂	1/drawer
RR	Drawer Knob	brass, ¹/₂ in. dia.	1/drawer

* Width allows extra stock.
** Length includes tenons.

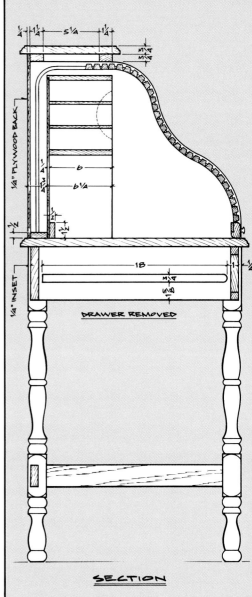

SECTION

¹/₄" PLYWOOD BACK

DRAWER REMOVED

¹/₄" INSET

turning points, you should have little difficulty keeping all four legs consistent. Remember to use sharp skews and gouges and to work carefully, since oak tears out rather easily. Final sand the legs while they are still on the lathe.

Next mill stock for the aprons and stretchers. The front apron (B) is made by ripping a 5¹/₂ in. wide board, cross-cutting the center section to create the drawer opening, and jointing the edges to obtain the two ³/₄ in. square strips and the two 3¹/₂ in. wide sections on either side of the drawer opening. The additional ¹/₂ in. on the part B width dimension allows for the saw kerfs and a light pass of each piece over the jointer. Glue and clamp the front apron parts and, when dry, cut the tenons on the ends using the table saw dado head. Make the back and side aprons (C and D) and the back and side stretchers (E and F), also cutting the tenons on the ends of these parts with the dado head (see Fig. 1 for tenon dimensions). Final sand parts A through F, test fit, glue, and assemble.

Now cut and fit the liners (G), filler blocks (H), side cleats (I), drawer guides (J), and apron cleats (K). Note the slotted holes in the various cleats to accept the top mounting screws. You may now machine and edge glue sufficient stock for the writing surface (L). (To save time, this could be done before starting on the base section.) When dry, cut the glued-up writing surface to overall length and width, and use a ¹/₂ in. bearing-guided beading bit to form the decorative edge on all four sides.

Make and fit the base drawer, consisting of parts M through Q, and final sand and finish all base and base drawer parts. The writing surface is not mounted now, nor are the slotted holes cut into it until after the tambour carcase has been completed.

To make the top section, start by gluing up stock for the sides (S). Then, referring to Fig. 2, make the template that you will use as a guide for the router to cut the tambour groove. Note that our template ⁵/₃₂ in. smaller all around than the groove inside, and is used with a ⁵/₈ in. outside diameter guide bushing and ⁵/₁₆ in. straight cutter. Use the radii shown in Fig. 2 as an aid in laying out for the template and groove. To find the centerpoint of the 3¹³/₁₆ in. radius top front curve, measure 8 in. from the back edge and 5¹/₄ in. down from the top edge. To find the 6⁵/₁₆ in. radius lower front curve, measure 1¹/₂ in. up from the bottom edge and 7 in. back from the front edge. The intersection of a 14 in. radius arc from this point and an 11¹/₂ in. radius arc from the previously located point will provide the centerpoint for scribing the 7³/₈ in. radius reverse curve. Remember that the template must be sized somewhat smaller than the groove, with the exact dimension depending on the particular router and guide bushing you use. More about routing the groove is included on page 128 of the Techniques section.

After the groove is complete, use the saber saw or band saw to cut the carcase sides to shape, and cut the ¹/₄ in. deep by ¹/₂ in. wide rabbet that will accept the back. Also cut the front and back cleats (T), and end cleats (U) that comprise a simple frame. Dimensions of the end

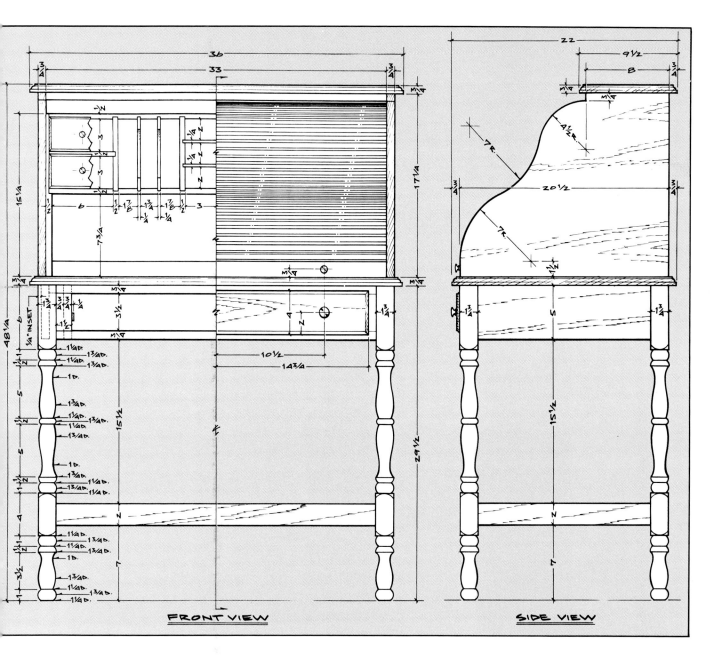

FRONT VIEW

SIDE VIEW

cleat tenons are shown in Fig. 1. Glue and assemble this cleat frame, and glue the carcase sides in place on either end. Make the top (V), applying an edge treatment with the $^1/_2$ in. beading bit, and mount the top as shown, fixed at the front edge with the slotted holes in the cleat frame permitting movement toward the back. Cut and fit the plywood back (W), making certain that the sides are parallel. Also glue the tambour stop (X) in place, as shown in the side view.

After making the top carcase, you must build the tambour front, consisting of the tambours (Y), the canvas (Z), the handle (AA), and the handle backing strip (BB). Again, refer to page 128 of the Techniques section for details on how the tambours are machined and laid up with the canvas.

The canvas is $32^1/_4$ in. wide to provide clearance on either side so that it will not come near or bind in the grooves. The canvas should be at least 28 in. long, providing overhang on the back end for tacking to the gluing fixture, and an extra $^7/_8$ in. on the front end for mounting the handle. After the canvas has been applied to the tambours, machine the handle and backing strip, and mount by sandwiching the canvas as shown in Fig. 3. Also, drill for and glue in place the location dowels in either end of the handle. *Note:* When making the tambour front, remember that dimensions may vary slightly, and the tambour must be sized to fit the tambour carcase.

The pigeon hole organizer (parts DD through LL) is made by milling $^1/_4$ in. and $^1/_2$ in. stock as needed, then cutting

to length and width and rabbeting and dadoing as required. Working from inner assemblies out, construct the organizer. Also make and fit the drawers (parts MM through QQ). *Note:* The organizer should be finished *before* its plywood back is applied.

After oiling and prefinishing all subassemblies, slide the tambour front into the tambour track. Then screw the writing surface to the tambour carcase. *Tip:* A spacer stick between the carcase sides will help keep them parallel. Next, insert the organizer and screw it to the writing surface. Finally, the entire top assembly is screwed to the base.

Mount the various drawer knobs (parts R and RR) and the tambour handle knobs (CC) to complete this project. ●

English *Cutlery Tray*

According to antiques dealer Weston Thorn, of Weston Thorn Antiques in Bantam, Connecticut, this cutlery tray was built of rosewood about 200 years ago and is of English origin. Although the insides of the tray bear myriad point pricks from the knives that were kept within, the tray is in remarkable condition for its age. Rosewood makes a lovely tray, but less costly domestic woods such as white oak, ash, cherry or walnut are also good choices.

Most of the work making the cutlery tray is in cutting the compound angle dovetails. Refer to the techniques article (page 108) for step-by-step instructions on cutting these dovetails.

Note that the scalloping along the upper edges on the sides (A) and ends (B), and the V-groove cuts on the inside faces of the ends, are made after the dovetails are cut but before the tray is assembled. You can use the router with a V-groove bit and a straightedge to cut the grooves, but since each groove is just $^1/_8$ in. deep, several passes with a sharp knife will work as well. Make your layout lines, cut one side of the V-groove, then complete the groove by cutting the opposite side. If you've made the tray from an exceptionally hard wood, you'll need a few more passes to achieve the full groove depth.

Next, lay out the scalloping from the full-size patterns, cut the profile with a

coping saw and round the edges by hand. Leave the corners square for now; you'll sand them after assembly.

Glue and assemble the sides and ends. When dry, cut the bottom (C) to size, round the edges and nail it in place. Use finish nails, and remember to pre-drill the nail holes. You can add a little epoxy to the nails to help anchor them. The nail heads should be set slightly; later you'll fill the holes with wood putty.

For the divider (D), try to select some quartersawn stock. Our antique cutlery tray used quartersawn stock for the divider, a sure sign that the maker was well aware of the characteristics of wood and the types of grain that are best for delicate parts. The advantage of using quartersawn stock is that it's unlikely to cup or warp, conditions that often occur on thin stock, especially boards that are elaborately cut out or carved.

Start with a board a little wider than the final desired size. Crosscut a 25-degree angle on each end, then establish the V-point along the length of the angle. The cuts to establish the V-point can be made on the table saw, but it's much easier and a lot less fuss to use a block plane. Make the layout lines for the V, clamp the divider securely in the vise, and use a sharp knife to back-cut the V at the edges. This prevents chip out. Several passes with the block plane should quickly form the two faces of each V. Test-fit the divider inside the tray and trim back the bottom edge as needed until the fit is right.

Now transfer the scroll pattern to the

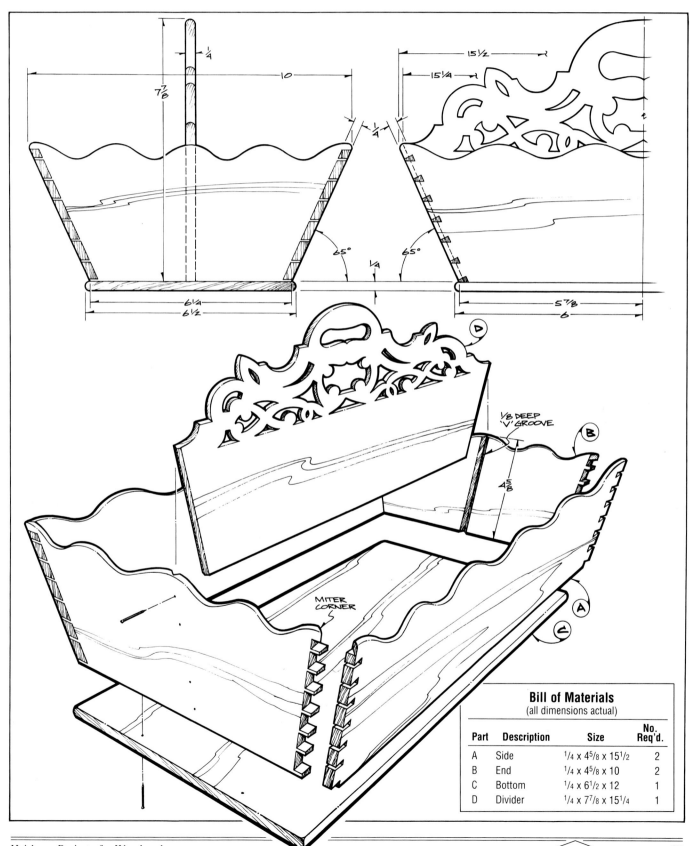

Part	Description	Size	No. Req'd.
A	Side	1/4 x 4 5/8 x 15 1/2	2
B	End	1/4 x 4 5/8 x 10	2
C	Bottom	1/4 x 6 1/2 x 12	1
D	Divider	1/4 x 7 7/8 x 15 1/4	1

Bill of Materials
(all dimensions actual)

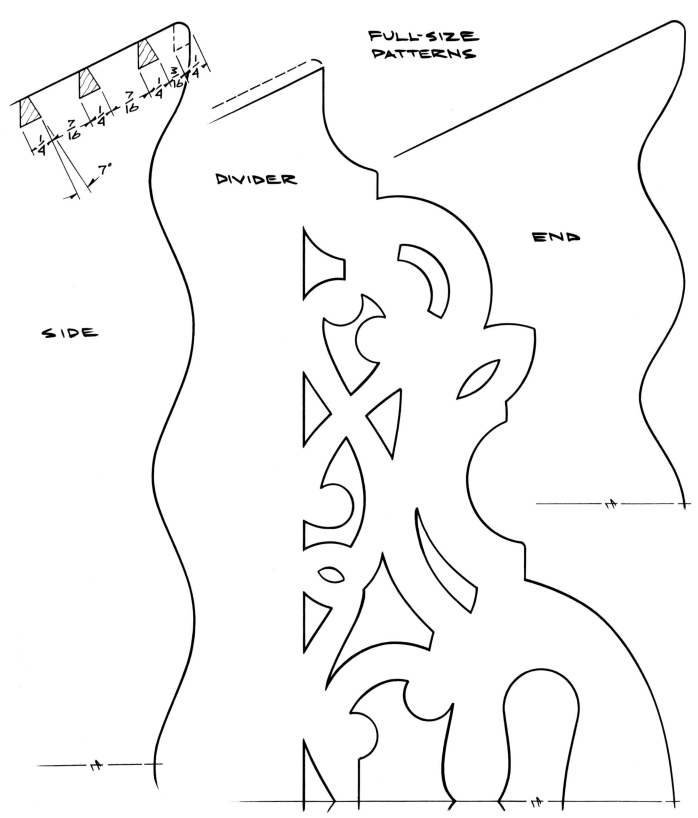

FULL-SIZE PATTERNS

DIVIDER

END

SIDE

divider using our full-size half pattern (both sides of the pattern are identical) and cut it out with a fretsaw or scroll saw. Drill starter holes for each of the inside cuts. A set of needle files is handy for cleaning up the blade marks that are left by the saw.

After final sanding, mount the divider. Use glue at the bottom edge of the divider where it meets the tray bottom,

and finishing nails through the ends at the V-groove joint and up through the bottom into the divider. Pre-drill for the nails, add a dab of epoxy and set them as before.

Apply a little colored wood filler or putty to fill the nail holes and any gaps at the dovetailed corners. Sand lightly, then wipe on at least three coats of Watco Danish Oil. Flood on the first

coat, wait about 15 minutes, then apply a generous second coat, adding extra finish to end grain and areas that are absorbing quickly. Once the wood seems saturated, wipe off the excess with a clean rag and let dry overnight. Lightly sand the surface with 360-grit wet-or-dry sandpaper, apply the third coat and buff with 0000 steel wool when dry.　●

Curio
Cabinet

O ver the years we've had a number of requests for curio cabinet plans. Well, good things take time to develop, so here finally is our full length curio cabinet. Since the design of this cabinet is neither traditional nor contemporary, falling somewhere in between, it should fit in well with most any room setting or style. Our cabinet is crafted of walnut, but oak, cherry, or mahogany will also look good. Use hardwood plywood parts that match the hardwood you select.

Start by milling sufficient stock for all parts. Note that all hardwood parts are $^3/_4$ in. thick. Keep in mind that because some plywoods are measured in millimeters, the edging (J, K) must be milled equal to the actual thickness of the plywood.

Be sure to joint and surface all stock. Select the clearest, straightest grain for the stiles (A, B, and E), since it's important that these parts remain stable and do not bow, twist, cup, or warp.

Now rip stock for all parts to approximate width. Our system is to rip the stock to the final width plus $^1/_{32}$ of an inch. We then move to the jointer and take a single $^1/_{32}$ in. pass to clean up the sawn edge and bring to final width. Of course, with each piece you must have one jointed edge to work off of.

These parts can now be cut to length. Mitered parts are left long since they will be cut to final length when the miters are cut. Use stops when cutting similar length pieces, such as the side and door rails, to maintain squareness when the side and door frames are glued up.

Next, cut all the spline mortises. We used spline construction in this project because it provided maximum strength while simplifying the assembly. Mortise-and-tenon construction could be substituted, though; just add the tenon length to both ends of the various rails.

Now cut out the rail profiles. Note that

the side rails have a $5^3/16$ in. radius, while the door rails have a $21^1/2$ in. radius. We use trammel points on a stick to scribe the radii. Also take note that the radii are centered on the rails and start 1 in. from either end.

Assemble and glue up the side and door frames. We left the mortises rounded on the ends, and rounded the splines to match, since this saves considerable labor. Always size the spline length slightly less than the combined depth of the two mortises to avoid bottoming and hydraulic back pressure from the glue, which might prevent the pieces being joined from butting up tight. As shown in the front elevation view of the curio cabinet, both the upper and lower splines are $1^7/8$ in. long, allowing about $1/16$ in. on either end given the 2 in. deep mortises.

When dry, rout the beaded detail all around the inner perimeter of both the side and the door frames. Note that we use a $3/16$ in. bearing-guided beading bit, as illustrated in the routing detail. Next, apply the $3/8$ in. by $3/8$ in. rabbet on the inside face of the door and side frames to accommodate the glass and keeper strip. You'll need to chisel the corners square where the router bit doesn't reach. Next, rabbet the back inside edges of both side frame assemblies to accept the plywood back panel. Be sure that you have designated right and left hand and top and bottom for the side frame assemblies.

You may now lay out and drill the holes for the brass shelf pin sleeves (U). After drilling these holes, and cutting the $1/4$ in. brass tube into $1/2$ in. lengths, epoxy the sleeves in place. We actually cut these sleeves about $17/32$ in. long and then sanded the brass flush with the wood after they have been epoxied in place. A countersink is used to apply the chamfer to the inside diameter of these sleeves. You can also cut the 1 in. brass shelf pins (V) to length from $3/16$ in. diameter brass rod at this time. If the pins are too tight a fit, they may require some sanding to slightly reduce their diameter.

Now cut hardwood plywood parts (H and I) to length and width. The lower part I does not show, so we simply used $3/4$ in. thick birch plywood here. If you have enough hardwood plywood, however, there is no harm in using it. Apply

the $3/4$ in. by 1 in. edging (J, K) to parts H and I, mitering the corners. About 18 feet of $3/4$ in. by 1 in. edging must be ripped in total. We cut and applied the front and side edging, letting the back ends of the side edgings overhang. They can later be trimmed off flush after the routed profiles have been applied. Be sure to use waxed clamp blocks to flush the edging with the plywood. Now apply the various routed details as illustrated. Note that the inner top, the top, and the inner bottom and the bottom profiles are perfect mirror images.

The continuous bracket foot base assembly, consisting of parts M, N, D, and L is made by following the step-by-step instructions provided in the article ''Making the Continuous Bracket Foot'' on page 122. The base back piece cannot be left square, since a small section of end grain would be visible. However, there is no need to band saw the cutout bracket profile.

All parts and subassemblies (the top, bottom, inner top, inner bottom, side frames, door frame and base) should now be final sanded. We next applied the final finish to all these parts, except the door frame. We used aerosol spray Deft clear lacquer to obtain a nearly flawless finish with no brush marks. Apply two coats, rubbing out with 0000 steel wool after the second coat. Then buff with a soft cloth to bring up the shine. Note that the back (L), which has not yet been cut, and the door frame are not finished until after they have been final sized and fit.

You are now ready to assemble the case. Start the assembly by screwing the

Bill of Materials
(all dimensions actual)

Part	Description	Size	No. Req'd.
A	Stile (front)	$3/4$ x 2 x 62	2
B	Stile (rear)	$3/4$ x $2^3/4$ x 62	2
C	Rail (lower)	$3/4$ x $3^1/2$ x $8^3/4$	2
D	Rail (upper)	$3/4$ x 3 x $8^3/4$	2
E	Door Stile	$3/4$ x 2 x 62	2
F	Door Rail (lower)	$3/4$ x $3^1/2$ x $14^1/2$	1
G	Door Rail (upper)	$3/4$ x 3 x $14^1/2$	1
H	Inner Top/Bottom	$3/4$ x $14^1/8$ x $18^1/4$	2
I	Top/Bottom *	$3/4$ x $14^7/8$ x $19^3/4$	2
J	Edging (cove) **	$3/4$ x 1 stock	102 in.
K	Edging (bead) **	$3/4$ x 1 stock	108 in.
L	Back	$1/4$ x 18 x 63	1
M	Base Front/Back	$3/4$ x 3 x 22	2
N	Base Side	$3/4$ x 3 x 16	2
O	Cleat	$3/4$ x $3/4$ stock	72 in.
P	Corner Block	1 x 1 x 2	4
Q	Side Glass	size to fit	2
R	Door Glass	size to fit	1
S	Keeper Strip ***	$1/4$ in. round	35 ft.
T	Shelf Glass	13 x 17	as req'd
U	Shelf Pin Sleeve ****	$1/4$ in. brass tube x $1/2$ long	4 ft.
V	Shelf Pin ****	$3/16$ brass rod x 1 long	as req'd
W	Hinge ***	$1^1/2$ x 2 brass	3
X	Double Ball Catch ***	brass	1
Y	Knob ***	$5/8$ in. dia. brass	1
Z	Leveler		4

* Bottom can be plain $3/4$ plywood.

** These edgings are plain $3/4$ in. x 1 in. stock. The molded details are not cut until after the edging has been applied.

*** All these parts are inlcuded as a kit from Mason & Sullivan, 210 Wood Country Industrial Park, P.O. Box 1686, Parkersburg, WV 26102-1686; tel. 1-800-225-1153. Order part no. H2344X.

**** Available from Allcraft Tool & Supply, 666 Pacific Street, Brooklyn, NY 11217; tel. 1-800-645-7124.

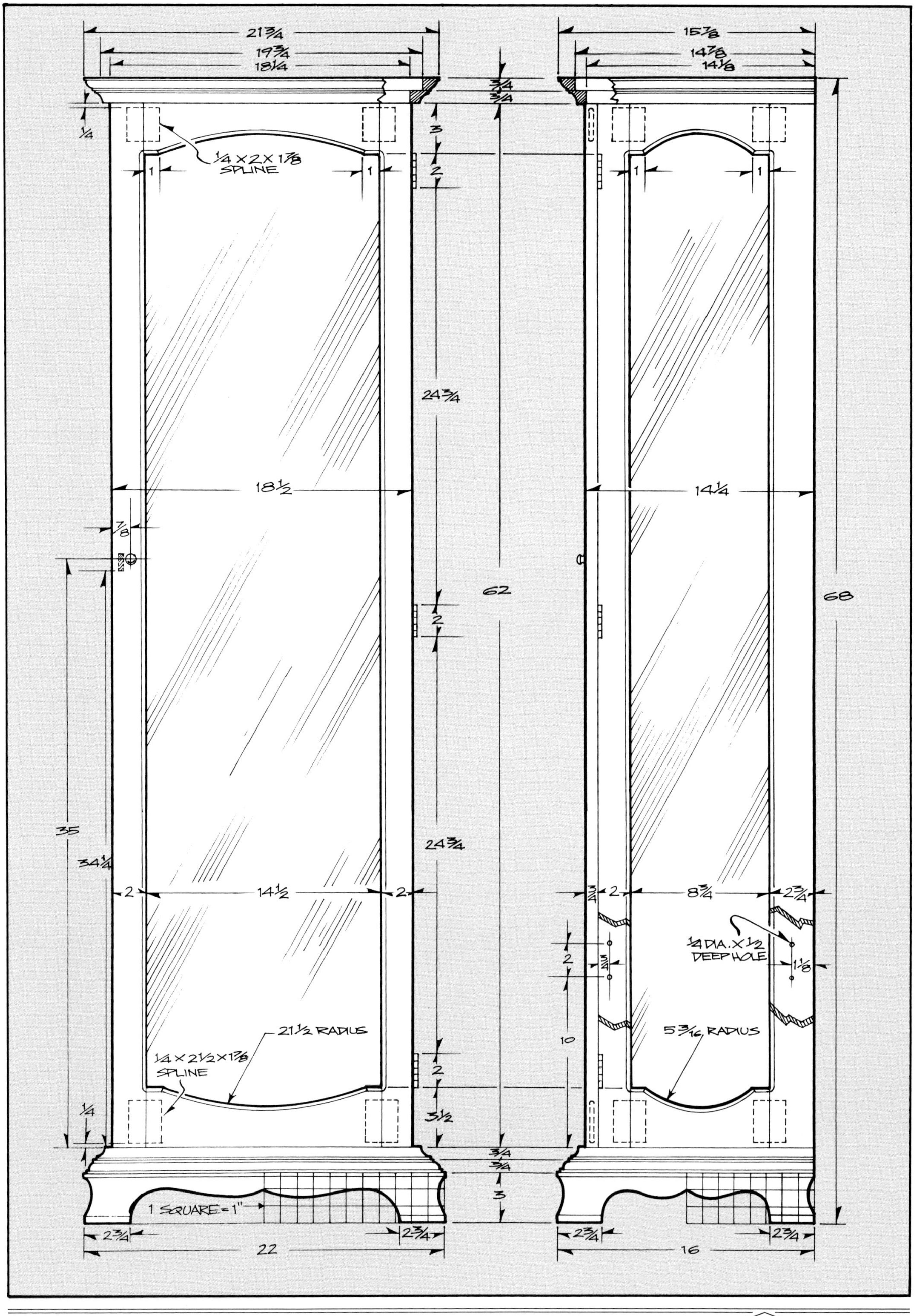
21¾
19¾
18¼
15⅝
14⅞
14⅛
¾
¾
¼
3
¼ × 2 × 1⅞
SPLINE
1
1
2
1
1
24¾
18½
14¼
⅞
62
68
2
35
34¼
24¾
2
14½
2
¾
2
8¾
2¾
¼ DIA. × ½
DEEP HOLE
2
¾
1⅛
10
21½ RADIUS
5 3/16 RADIUS
¼ × 2½ × 1⅞
SPLINE
2
¼
3½
¾
¾
3
1 SQUARE = 1"
2¾
2¾
2¾
2¾
22
16

3/16 X 1
INDEXING DOWELS

1/4 X 1/2 RABBET

1/4 X 1/2 RABBET

10

2

26 1/4

3/4

3/4

3/8 X 3/8 RABBET

1/4 X 1/2 RABBET

1 3/4 FLATHEAD SCREW

1 1/4 FLATHEAD SCREW

SCREW

E
G
I
K
H
J
B
A
U
V
X
R
Q
Q
S
T
L
A
Y
X
C
H
I
F
W
M
O
N
P
K
M
N

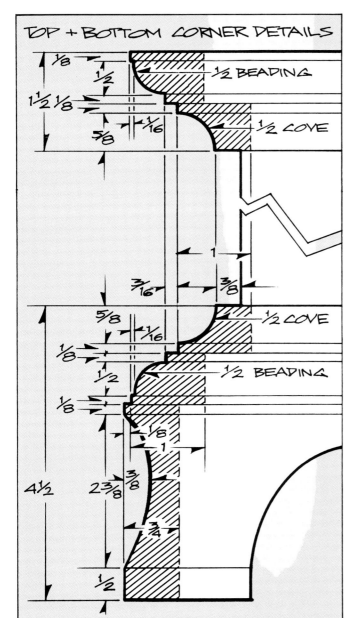

TOP + BOTTOM CORNER DETAILS

1/8 · 1/2 · 1 1/2 · 1/8 · 5/8 · 1/16
1/2 BEADING
1/2 COVE
1 · 3/16 · 3/8
5/8 · 1/16 · 1/2 COVE
1/8 · 1/2 · 1/8 · 1/8 · 1 · 1/2 BEADING
4 1/2 · 2 3/8 · 3/8 · 3/4 · 1/2

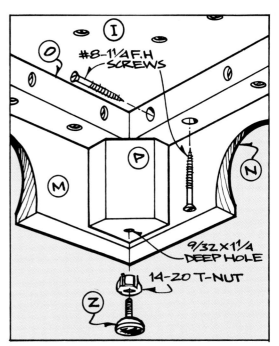

O · I
#8-1 1/4 F.H SCREWS
M · P · N
9/32 X 1 1/4 DEEP HOLE
14-20 T-NUT
Z

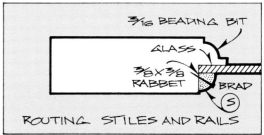

3/16 BEADING BIT
GLASS
3/8 X 3/8 RABBET
BRAD
S
ROUTING STILES AND RAILS

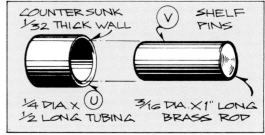

COUNTER SUNK 1/32 THICK WALL
V
SHELF PINS
1/4 DIA. X 1/2 LONG TUBING · U
3/16 DIA. X 1" LONG BRASS ROD

inner top and bottom to the side frames. Be sure to allow the 3/8 in. lip at the sides (see trim cross section), and keep the back edges flush. Now add the top and bottom. The top is glued, but not screwed, using indexing dowels to prevent slippage as clamp pressure is applied. The bottom can simply be screwed in place, after which the base assembly is screwed in position on the bottom, through the cleats as shown. Cut the 1/4 in. by 1/2 in. rabbet into the back edge of the inner top and bottom to accept the plywood back. The corners of these rabbets can be squared with a chisel, or you may leave them as a radius and round the corners of the plywood back to match.

Now size the plywood back. It is vital that the back be perfectly parallel and square, since it is the back that, when applied, will ultimately determine how

square the cabinet is. Temporarily install the walnut plywood back with four screws, then final size the door. We allowed 1/16 in. top and bottom on the door to permit a clear, free swing. To trim the top and bottom edges of the door, clamp a board as a straightedge across the door, and use the router with a bearing-guided trimming bit to trim the 1/16 in. off each end.

Now lay out and mortise for the hinges (W). Temporarily install the hinges, locate for the double ball catch (X) and mortise for it as required. Also locate and drill for the pull knob (Y). The catch and pull knob are not installed yet, however.

Next, remove the back and door, and finish them as you finished the other assemblies before installing the door and side glass (Q, R). We used a quarter-round flexible rubber keeper strip (S)

that is supplied with small brass brads (see Bill of Materials for source).

Use a utility knife to miter the keeper strip ends for a professional look. We started the brads with a pair of needle-nosed pliers, then used a large nail set with a cupped end to set the brads. The cupped end prevented the nail set from slipping off the brads.

Finally, reinstall the back and mount the door and all hardware. We purchased the door and side glass and the 1/4 in. thick shelf glass from a local glass shop. For accuracy we traced out paper templates to insure that the door and side glass would fit our frames. We recommend that you use the levelers (Z) to level the cabinet since a firm four-point stance is important, especially when the cabinet is filled. The levelers can be obtained locally from a hardware store.

●

Our photo of the Pencil Post Bed speaks far more eloquently of it than any description we might attempt. Suffice it to say that as handsome as it is in the photo, it is this and much more in person. It's a project that will make an impressive statement in any bedroom. The design is versatile enough to complement and fit comfortably with any number of different styles, from country and traditional to contemporary.

We selected cherry for this piece, because of its strength, workability and the rich warmth of the wood. Traditionally, pencil post beds were made of maple with wide pine stock for the headboard. Rope served both to hold the parts of the bed frame together and to support the mattress. Bed bolts, which became common around 1750, kept the bed frame rigid, even when the rope spring supports stretched and sagged. Noted bed builder Charles E. Thibeau

18th Century *Pencil Post Bed*

tells us that the wooden bed frame, called the bedstead, was valued far less than the bedclothes, covers, and hangings, which were called the "furniture." The tester frame, mounted on the ends of the pencil posts, supported the hangings, which consisted of a tester cover, valance, head cloth, head curtains, foot curtains and base. This bed furniture was an essential item in the small and poorly insulated homes of our forebears, where both warmth and privacy merited great value. The tester cover, head cloth, and valances are fastened to the tester frame with tack strips and tacks, although you could tack directly into the tester frame. Velcro also works well. The inset photo of the bed shows it dressed with base and valance curtains. We might add that the tester frame and the bed furniture are optional, and that the bed is just as handsome without all the trappings.

Thibeau also tells us that many of the original pencil post beds were finished with milk paint, although we shudder to think that anyone would consider covering a cherry bed with paint. If you decide

to paint the bed and you are a stickler for authenticity, milk paint can be ordered from The Old-Fashioned Milk Paint Company, Box 222, Groton, MA 01450.

We started by gluing up $^8/_4$ stock to get the required thickness for the four posts (A). If you have access to $^{12}/_4$ stock, you'll save some time here. You'll also need to edge-glue material to get the needed width for the headboard (D). Dimension stock for the rails (B, C) and tester frame (E, F) while you are waiting for the other parts to dry. Next, lay out the mortise locations on the posts. Note that you'll need to identify the left and right posts, and mark out the mortises for the headboard. As shown in the detail, the headboard mortises are $^1/_4$ in. longer than the ends of the headboard, which allows for possible expansion of the headboard as equilibrium moisture content changes. The top of the mortise starts 38 in. from the bottom end of the leg. Once these mortises are cut, drill the hole for the dowel pin at the top of the mortise. The dowel pin anchors the headboard flush with the top end of

the mortise, and directs movement down, so that any small gap remaining at the bottom end of the mortise will be less visible.

Next, using a 1 in. diameter Forstner bit, counterbore to a $^3/_4$ in. depth for the bed bolts (G). As illustrated, the end rail bolts are centered $20^1/_2$ in. from the floor, while the side rail bolts are centered $19^1/_2$ in. from the floor. This offset is important so the bolts don't intersect. Drill through with a $^{13}/_{32}$ in. brad-point bit to accept the bolt shanks, and chamfer the edge of the counterbore. The $^3/_8$ in. diameter tester-pin holes in the top ends of the posts are drilled next. Use a drill guide to insure squareness. We made ours from a block of wood.

You could establish the leg tapers now, but we found that it's best to first drill the bed bolt holes in the rails, cut all the tenons, and test-assemble the bed, since it's easier to make adjustments on the legs while they are square. Use a $^3/_4$ in. diameter Forstner bit to drill the $1^1/_8$ in. deep bed-bolt nut recess in the rails, then use a chisel to square the half of the

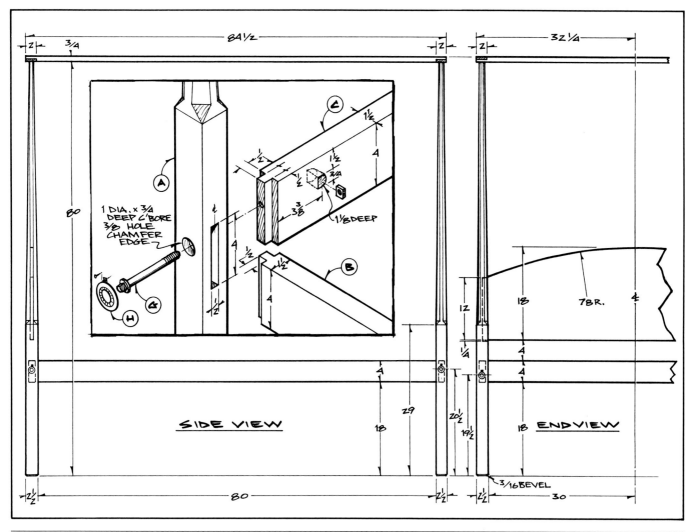

Heirloom Projects for Woodworkers

35

recess closest to the leg so it will accept the nut. Next, drill the bolt holes through from the ends using the jig shown. You'll need to make the guideblock $1\frac{1}{2}$ in. square, and drill a $^{13}/_{32}$ in. diameter hole through the center. This same type of jig, made with a $2\frac{1}{2}$ in. square block, could be used to drill the tester-pin holes. Finally, cut the tenons on the rail ends.

We outlined this sequence of steps since some woodworkers may not have a set of auger bits, but an auger bit will simplify drilling the bolt holes into the rail ends. Cut the tenons on the rail ends first, dry assemble the bed, and using the shank holes through the posts as a guide, continue these shank holes into the rails.

To establish the tapers on the posts, first lay out an octagon on the top end, and mark the point 29 in. from the bottom where the tapers end. Mark the first four tapers, which are on the same plane as the four sides of each post, and rough them in with the band saw. You'll need to shim under the end with one of your waste pieces to make the last band saw cut. Now, using a sharp jack or jointing plane, smooth these tapers down to the line. The next four tapers are cut on the corners. After laying the tapers out, mount the post in the jig as shown, establish a saw kerf, chisel out an area until you can use the plane, and plane and smooth these tapers until you are satisfied with the results. Then establish the 45-degree beveled shoulder with the chisel, as indicated, and very lightly bevel the top and bottom ends of the posts.

The easiest way to lay out the radius on the headboard is to mark the center point at the top edge, and points on either side 6 in. down, and $^7/_8$ in. from the ends. Then, with a pencil tied to a long string anchored with a nail, scribe the radius so you'll hit all three points. Our string was about 78 in. long, but you may need to adjust the length slightly to hit the three points. After shaping the headboard, drill the dowel-pin holes, and glue these pins into the posts.

If you decide to make the tester frame, select good straight quarter-sawn stock for the greatest strength. Half-lap the ends, and drill through for the $^3/_8$ in. diameter steel pins (I) that anchor the tester frame to the bedstead.

After sanding all parts up through 220

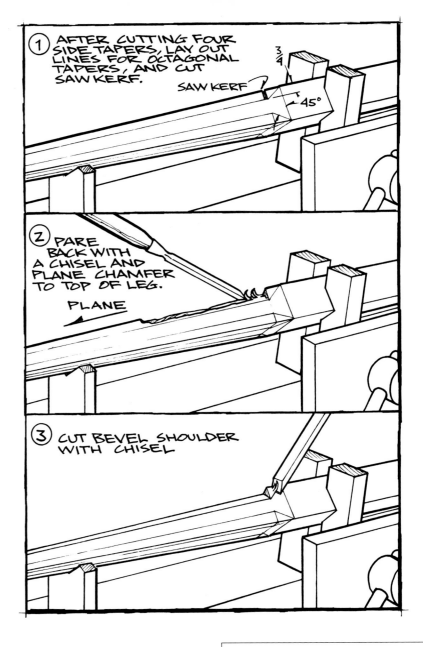

① AFTER CUTTING FOUR SIDE TAPERS, LAY OUT LINES FOR OCTAGONAL TAPERS, AND CUT SAW KERF. SAW KERF ¾ 45°

② PARE BACK WITH A CHISEL AND PLANE CHAMFER TO TOP OF LEG. PLANE

③ CUT BEVEL SHOULDER WITH CHISEL

grit, finish with three coats of tung oil. Locate for the hardware, and drill pilot holes for all screws and brads before mounting the angle-iron boxspring supports (J) and the bed-bolt covers (H).

We've arranged with the mail-order supplier, Paxton Hardware, to offer a package deal on all the hardware (except the tester frame pins) required to make one bed, at a substantial savings off the same parts ordered separately. Ordering information is provided in the Bill of Materials. The tester frame pins are cut from $^3/_8$ in. steel rod, sold at most hardware stores. Our bed is sized to accept a queen-size mattress and boxspring. No glue is used in the assembly of the bed, since all parts, including the headboard, should have knock-down capability to facilitate moving. ●

Bill of Materials
(all dimensions actual)

Part	Description	Size	No. Req'd.
A	Post	$2\frac{1}{2}$ x $2\frac{1}{2}$ x 80	4
B	Side Rail	$1\frac{1}{2}$ x 4 x 81	2
C	End Rail	$1\frac{1}{2}$ x 4 x 61	2
D	Headboard	$^3/_4$ x 18 x 62	1
E	Tester Frame Side	$^3/_4$ x 2 x $84\frac{1}{2}$	2
F	Tester Frame End	$^3/_4$ x 2 x $64\frac{1}{2}$	2
G	Bed Bolt	6 in. long*	8
H	Bed Bolt Cover	$1^7/_8$ in. dia. brass*	8
I	Tester Frame Pin	$^3/_8$ in. dia. x 2 long	4
J	Spring Support	3 x 8*	8

* Included in bed hardware package. Available from Paxton Hardware, 7818 Bradshaw Rd., Upper Falls, MD 21156; tel. (410) 592-8505. Order part no. 8700. If you don't have a 12-point mechanic's socket set, you'll need a special cast bronze bed-bolt wrench, also available from Paxton Hardware. Order part no. 6012.

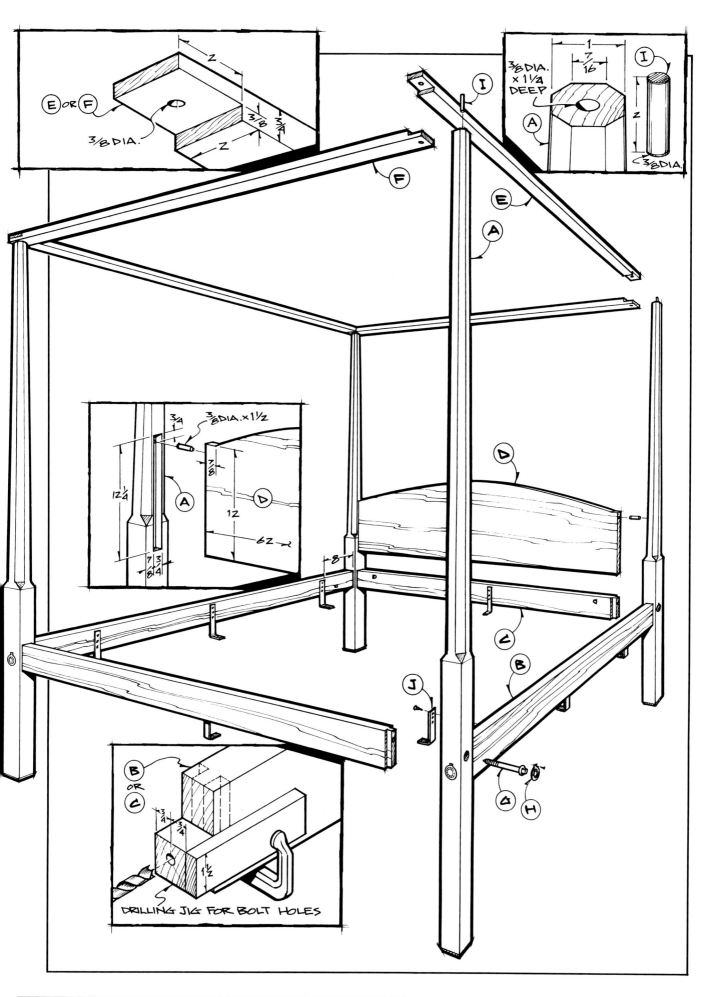

E OR F

2

3/8 DIA.

3/8
3/4

2

3/8 DIA.
x 1 1/4
DEEP

1
7/16

I

A

2

3/8 DIA.

I

F

E

A

3/4
3/8 DIA. x 1 1/2

12 1/4

7/8

A

D

12

62

7 3
8 4

8

D

D

D

C

B

J

A

H

B
OR
C

3/4
3/4

1 1/2

DRILLING JIG FOR BOLT HOLES

Connecticut River Valley
Highboy

The English refer to it as a high chest of drawers; we call it a highboy. By any name, it is certainly one of the most distinctive and beautiful pieces of furniture designed in the 18th century. The style of our piece is representative of the rural Massachusetts or Connecticut River Valley tradition. Crafted in cherry, it features graceful cabriole legs, a deeply scalloped apron, graduated drawers, a flat top with cornice, and carved sunbursts on the upper and lower center drawers.

We've opted for the flat top rather than the bonnet top that's found on some highboys. There are several reasons for this. First, the country cabinetmaker who probably would have built a piece like this would have also likely dispensed with the bonnet top, if for no better reason than his clientele had neither the cash nor desire for artifice and embellishment. But a more important reason is the scale of modern rooms. A bonnet top crowning a highboy of authentic proportions such as ours would hardly fit within the 8-foot high ceilings of most modern homes.

Building a piece of this size may seem like an impossible project; it is not. It is the result of methodically doing the same basic operations over and over. If you can build a dovetailed box, you can build this highboy. For builder Dennis Preston, this highboy was only his second effort at hand-cutting dovetails.

We've broken the highboy into two sections: the base and the upper section, or case. As in the originals, the upper section is actually a separate drawer case resting on a lower, or base, section. In addition to simplifying construction, this two-part design enables the highboy to be easily moved.

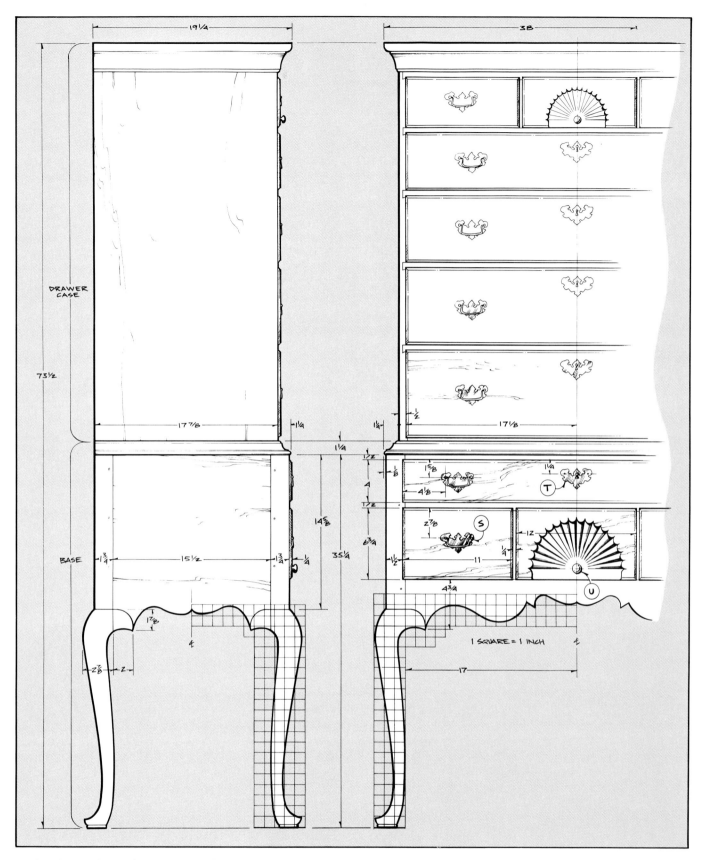

1 SQUARE = 1 INCH

If a highboy is not for you, just build the base section, omit the molding and add a top, and you'll have a handsome lowboy. In order for the lowboy proportions to be correct, though, you should scale down the legs so the overall height of the piece is between 29 in. and 31 in.

The Base

With any large piece, it helps to plan your approach. A good sensible approach with the base is to start by edge-gluing narrower stock to get the widths needed for the wider parts. The wide parts on the base are the sides (C) and back (D). If you build the piece from cherry, as we did, take care to match the grain on the sides carefully and rip away any of the white sapwood. Our highboy uses cherry only on those parts that are visible from the front and sides. The

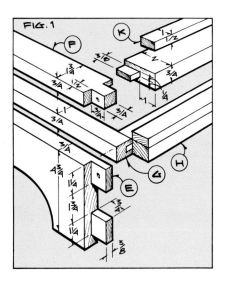

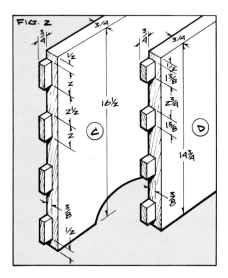

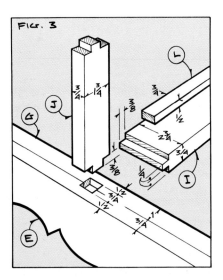

interior construction, including the back, is a secondary hardwood such as poplar.

While you're waiting for the sides and back to dry, get out stock for the legs (A) and the remaining base parts. We recommend first cutting all the base parts to size, and next laying out and cutting the various mortises in the square leg blanks. It's much easier to cut your mortises while the legs are still square. Then test-fit the entire assembly. The shaping of the legs isn't done until last, after you're certain everything fits as intended. When you're ready to shape the legs, refer to the techniques article, starting on page 115, where the procedure is detailed. Note that the ears (B) aren't added until later on.

Joining the legs and sides are an apron (E) and a series of open-ended frames. The upper frame consists of a front stretcher (F) and a pair of side rails (H). The middle frame is identical to the upper frame, but also includes a pair of center rails (I). The lower frame is identical to the center frame, except that a narrow bottom stretcher (G) replaces the wider front stretcher of the two upper frames. The bottom stretcher's 1 in. width, $^3/_4$ in. narrower than the $1^3/_4$ in. front stretchers, enables it to tuck neatly behind the $^3/_4$ in. thick apron. Fig. 1 shows the frame joinery details and the apron tenon dimensions. The center rail tenon dimensions are shown in Fig. 3. The bottom stretcher shown in both these details is technically an interior part, but you should make it from cherry to make the appearance of the three frames symmetrical (see photo).

By now your sides and back should be out of clamps, so you can cut the tenons on the ends of these parts (Fig. 2), and the matching mortises in the leg blanks. With these joints cut and test-fit, lay out for the scroll work that decorates the bottom edges of the apron and sides. The best way to transfer these profiles from the grid patterns shown on the elevations is to make full-size templates and then trace the patterns onto your stock using the templates. The profiles can be cut with a band saw, scroll saw, or a hand-held jigsaw.

Like the preceding joinery, the mortises for the dividers (J) are cut before any parts are glued and assembled. As shown in Fig. 3, the tenon on the bottom end of the dividers fits into a $^3/_4$ in. square by $^3/_8$ in. deep mortise that's cut on the line between the apron and bottom stretcher. Notch $^1/_4$ in. of the mortise into the apron and the remaining $^1/_2$ in. into the bottom stretcher. Don't neglect cutting the various mortises in the back for the side and center rails. These mortise-and-tenon joints support the frames at the back.

With all the joinery complete, now test assemble the base. Also, cut and fit the four side and two center guides (K, L). Mark each part for ease of reassembly, then take the base apart and cut and shape the legs, as per the instructions in the techniques article.

Assembly

There are several ways you can handle the final assembly, but here's a method we like that breaks the assembly into sections so you won't be working with too many parts at the same time. Start by gluing up the bottom stretcher and apron. Next, join that assembly to one of the front stretchers with the two dividers. Now take the stretcher/apron/divider assembly and the remaining front stretcher and join the two front legs. As a separate assembly, glue up the back with the two back legs. When these assemblies are dry, lay the back/leg section flat, glue the sides into the back legs and the rails into the back, and then add the front section. Check the base corners with a square and use clamp pressure or a clamp diagonally across the corners to make any adjustments.

Once the base is dry, add the guides and drill for and insert the pegs that lock

the various tenons. With modern adhesives, and assuming accurate joinery, the pegs are mostly a decorative detail. But if your mortise and tenon work isn't perfect, the pegs will add an important measure of mechanical strength.

All that remains of the base is the ears, drawers, molding (M) and filler strip (N). We used a 5-step procedure to cut the molding (see Molding Detail, page 43). When cutting complex moldings, it's often easiest to start with stock that's

larger than needed and then make ripping cuts to establish final size after the molding steps are completed. The extra stock is for ease of handling and to provide broader bearing surfaces.

The Molding

Start with a board that's 2 in. thick by 3 in. wide. Then, using the molding head equipped with a $5/8$ in. radius cove cutter, establish the cove. Start with the fence positioned so that only about $1/4$ in. of

BASE

Bill of Materials
(all dimensions actual)

Part	Description	Size	No. Req'd.
A	Leg	$3 \times 3 \times 35^{1}/_{4}$*	4
B	Ear	$1^{1}/_{4} \times 2^{1}/_{4} \times 2^{1}/_{4}$*	6
C	Side	$3/_{4} \times 16^{1}/_{2} \times 17$**	2
D	Back	$3/_{4} \times 14^{3}/_{4} \times 35^{1}/_{2}$**	1
E	Apron	$3/_{4} \times 4^{3}/_{4} \times 35^{1}/_{2}$**	1
F	Front Stretcher	$3/_{4} \times 1^{3}/_{4} \times 35^{1}/_{2}$**	2
G	Bottom Stretcher	$3/_{4} \times 1 \times 34$	1
H	Side Rail	$3/_{4} \times 2 \times 17^{1}/_{4}$**	6
I	Center Rail	$3/_{4} \times 2^{3}/_{4} \times 17^{1}/_{4}$**	4
J	Divider	$3/_{4} \times 1^{3}/_{4} \times 7^{1}/_{4}$**	2
K	Side Guide	$1/_{2} \times 1 \times 15^{1}/_{2}$	4
L	Center Guide	$1/_{2} \times 3/_{4} \times 16^{1}/_{2}$	2
M	Molding	See Detail	About 7 ft.
N	Filler Strip	$3/_{4} \times 3/_{4} \times 33^{3}/_{4}$	1

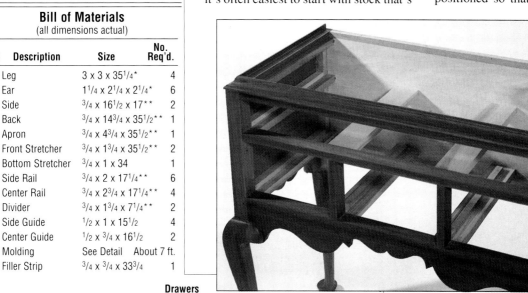

Drawers

Part	Description	No. Req'd Per Drawer	Top Drawer	Side Drawer	Center Drawer
O	Front	1	$3/_{4} \times 4 \times 34^{1}/_{2}$	$3/_{4} \times 6^{3}/_{4} \times 11$	$3/_{4} \times 6^{3}/_{4} \times 12$
P	Side	2	$1/_{2} \times 3^{3}/_{4} \times 18$	$1/_{2} \times 6^{1}/_{2} \times 18$	$1/_{2} \times 6^{1}/_{2} \times 18$
Q	Back	1	$1/_{2} \times 3^{1}/_{8} \times 34$	$1/_{2} \times 5^{7}/_{8} \times 10^{1}/_{2}$	$1/_{2} \times 5^{7}/_{8} \times 11^{1}/_{2}$
R	Bottom	1	$1/_{4} \times 17^{3}/_{4} \times 33^{1}/_{2}$	$1/_{4} \times 17^{3}/_{4} \times 10$	$1/_{4} \times 17^{3}/_{4} \times 11$
S	Chippendale Pull		$3^{7}/_{16} \times 2$ ($2^{1}/_{2}$ in. borings)*** 4		
T	Escutcheon		$3^{7}/_{16} \times 2$*** 1		
U	Knob		1 dia.*** 1		
V	Lock		$2^{3}/_{4} \times 2^{1}/_{4}$ (half mortise)**** 1		

   * Dimensions are before shaping
  ** Length includes tenons
 *** Pulls, escutcheon and knob (all solid brass) are available from Horton Brasses, Nooks Hill Rd., Cromwell, CT 06416; tel. (203) 635-4400. Order part no. H-34-S for the pulls (specify $2^{1}/_{2}$ in. borings), part no. H-34-SE for matching escutcheon, and part no. K-12 for the knob (specify 1 in. diameter, with machine screw for $3/_{4}$ in. thick drawer front). The hardware is available in a choice of finishes: antique, semi-bright, or bright polished.
**** Brass drawer lock is available from The Wise Company, 6503 St. Claude Ave., P.O. Box 118, Arabi, LA 70032; tel. (504) 277-7551. Order part number L01/56LC1.

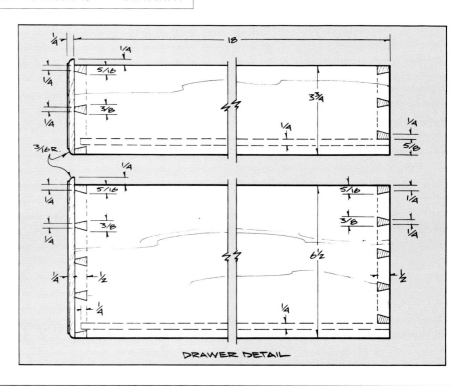

DRAWER DETAIL

stock is removed, then readjust the fence several times and make repeated passes until you've achieved the required $7/8$ in. depth and width of cut (Step 1). Since the stock is trapped between the molding head and the fence, you'll need feather boards to maintain steady pressure. Take extra care with the last pass; you don't want a slip here, as it would ruin the piece. Now switch to a $1/4$ in. radius roundover cutter in the molding head, relocate the fence, and establish the $1/4$ in. radius roundover at the top of the molding (Step 2). With that cut complete, relocate the fence once more and

cut the remaining roundover (Step 3). Switch to the dado head, set it for a $1/2$ in. deep by at least a $3/4$ in. wide cut, and plow the groove as shown (Step 4). Now all that remains is to make the ripping cuts to establish the final size of the molding (Step 5). Round the bottom edge of the molding, miter the ends, mount it with finishing nails, and then cut and glue the filler strip in place.

The Ears

For each ear, start with a $1\frac{1}{4}$ in. thick by $2\frac{1}{4}$ in. square block. Transfer the outside shape from our grid pattern, then

hold the block in position against the leg to transfer the side profile (Fig. 4). Now cut and rough shape the ear. Final shaping and sanding are done after the ears have been glued in place. Note that the ears are glued to the legs, but not to the sides or apron. This allows these parts to respond to seasonal changes, without risk of splitting off the narrow cross-grain sections at the bottom of the scroll profiles.

The Drawers

There are four drawers in the base: a full-width top drawer, two side drawers,

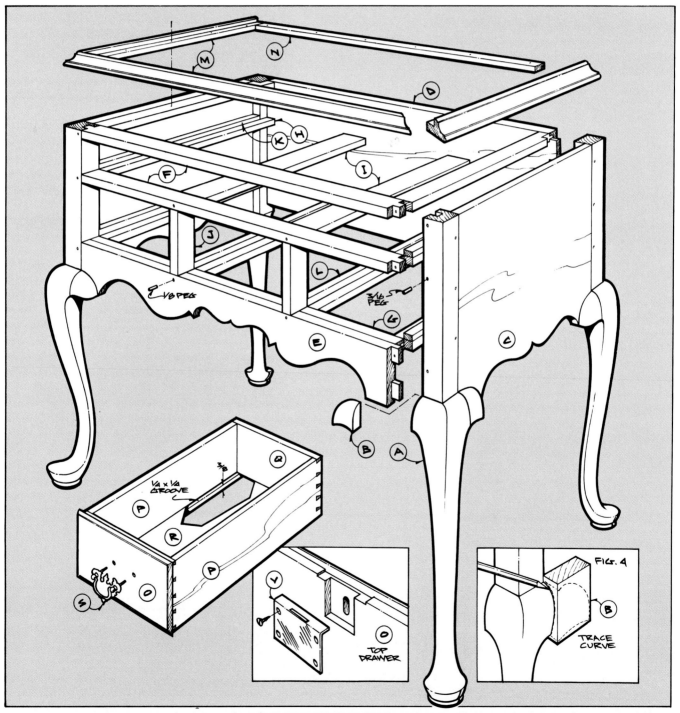

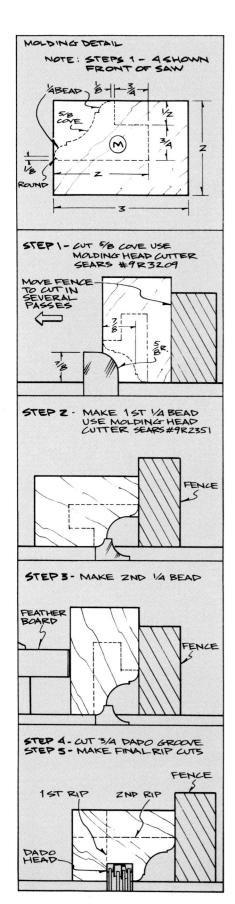

MOLDING DETAIL

NOTE: STEPS 1 - 4 SHOWN FRONT OF SAW

STEP 1 - CUT 5/8 COVE USE MOLDING HEAD CUTTER SEARS #9R3209

MOVE FENCE TO CUT IN SEVERAL PASSES

STEP 2 - MAKE 1ST 1/4 BEAD USE MOLDING HEAD CUTTER SEARS #9R2351

FENCE

STEP 3 - MAKE 2ND 1/4 BEAD

FEATHER BOARD

FENCE

STEP 4 - CUT 3/4 DADO GROOVE
STEP 5 - MAKE FINAL RIP CUTS

FENCE

1ST RIP   2ND RIP

DADO HEAD

and a center drawer that sports a handsome sunburst carving. All the drawers show traditional construction, with a molded front (O) joined with half-blind

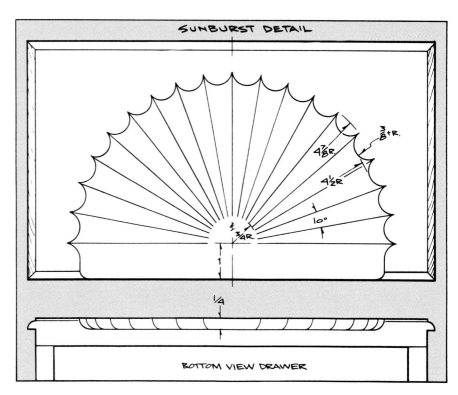

SUNBURST DETAIL

BOTTOM VIEW DRAWER

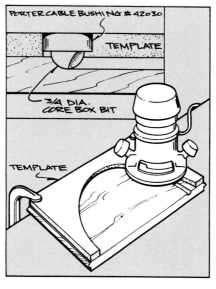

PORTER CABLE BUSHING #42030

TEMPLATE

3/4 DIA. CORE BOX BIT

TEMPLATE

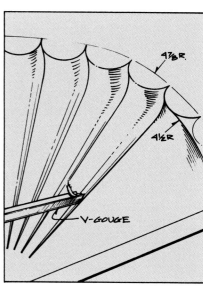

4 7/8 R.

4 1/2 R

V-GOUGE

dovetails to the sides (P). Through-dovetails join the sides and back (Q), and a bottom (R) slides under the back into grooves in the sides and front. Since this piece is not an exact copy of an original, we've used $1/4$ in. thick birch plywood for the drawer bottoms. You could substitute $1/2$ in. thick solid stock, beveled on the front and sides. The drawers are all sized to stop $1/4$ in. from the inside of the base back, with a $1/4$ in. wide lip on the top edge and ends of the drawer fronts serving as the stop. The Drawer Detail shows a suggested layout for the drawer dovetails. Note that a $3/16$ in. radius roundover is used to mold all four edges of the drawer fronts.

The Sunburst

The sunburst carving on the center drawer front is done after the dovetails have been cut and test-fitted, but before the center drawer is glued up and assembled. Here's an easy way to do this carving if you don't have any carving experience. With the center point of your compass located 1 in. up from the bottom edge of the drawer front, lay out the two radii, $4^{1}/2$ in. and $4^{7}/8$ in., as shown in the Sunburst Detail. Next, make a template to serve as a guide for your router, so that it will cut to the $4^{1}/2$ in. radius line. Clamp the template to the drawer front, chuck a $3/4$ in. diameter core-box bit in the router, set the bit for

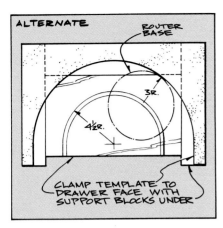

ALTERNATE
ROUTER BASE
3R.
4½R.
CLAMP TEMPLATE TO DRAWER FACE WITH SUPPORT BLOCKS UNDER

a ¹/₄ in. deep cut, and make several passes along the template edge (see detail). If your router doesn't include a guide bushing to fit a ³/₄ in. diameter core box bit, just make a larger template, cut some support blocks, and bear the router base directly against the template (see Alternate). Next, remove the template, switch to a ³/₄ in. diameter straight cutter, and waste away the remaining material at the ¹/₄ in. depth. Just be sure to start your cut at the center and work out toward the edges. You won't have any support for the router when you reach the center if you try working in toward the center from the edges. An oversize clear acrylic router base is helpful when routing large areas where there's not enough support for a normal-sized router base.

Now use scrapers to smooth the bottom of your sunburst. With the bottom reasonably smooth, divide the sunburst into 18 rays. Since the sunburst is essentially a half circle, an easy way to mark out the 18 rays is to just take a protractor and tick off a mark at every 10 degrees. Next, again using the compass, scribe the radii on the outside edge indicating where the rays terminate. The compass setting for these radii should be a little over ³/₈ in. Also scribe a 180-degree radius ³/₄ in. from the sunburst center point to designate

the point where the rays originate.

To create the individual rays, you'll use a V-gouge. The technique is simple: Just cut to about a ¹/₈ in. depth between the rays, then round the rays gently to approximate a radius. If you can't follow the ray lines accurately with the V-gouge, use a straightedge and an X-Acto knife to cut a shallow V-shaped guideline along each ray line. Deepen the points between the rays to touch the 4⁷/₈ in. radius line you scribed earlier, and fair the roundover here to meet the roundover on the rays at the bottom of the sunburst. After sanding you'll have a sunburst similar to the one shown.

Finishing Up

If you're building the project as a lowboy, it is now ready for finishing. We like a penetrating or tung oil mixture. No stain is needed as cherry will darken to a deep natural tone after exposure to sunlight over time. Sources for the solid brass Chippendale pulls (S),

matching escutcheon (T), knob (U) and lock (V) are listed in the Bill of Materials. Note that you'll have to specify one of three finishes for the brasses. We chose the bright brass.

The Case

Start by edge-gluing stock for the drawer case box. It's just two sides (A) with a top and bottom (B), all dovetailed together. The sides are solid cherry, but the top—which can only be seen from above—can be a secondary hardwood such as poplar. The bottom can also be a secondary hardwood, but as indicated in the dovetail layout detail (Fig. 1, page 47), you'll need a 1 in. wide strip of cherry along the front edge, to match the drawer frames. The tops of the dovetails are seen from the side, but the use of a secondary wood here is okay, since only about ¹/₄ in. of the tails is actually exposed when the drawer case is nested into the base.

Once your dovetails are complete, test-assemble the sides, top and bottom. While the dry assembly is together, mount a bearing-guided rabbeting bit in the router and cut the ¹/₄ in. deep by ³/₈ in. wide rabbet for the back (I). Square the corners with a chisel. Then disassemble the case and cut the various mortises for the drawer frame stretchers. Note that a ¹/₂ in. deep half-dovetail mortise houses the ends of the front stretchers (C), while a ³/₈ in. deep mortise is needed for the ends of the back stretchers (D). Appropriately, the front stretchers are ¹/₄ in. longer than the back stretchers. Note that except for the front stretchers and the two dividers (G), the remaining interior case parts can all be a secondary hardwood.

Now glue up and assemble the sides, top and bottom. When dry, cut and fit the front and back stretchers. Mortise these stretchers to accept the side rails (E),

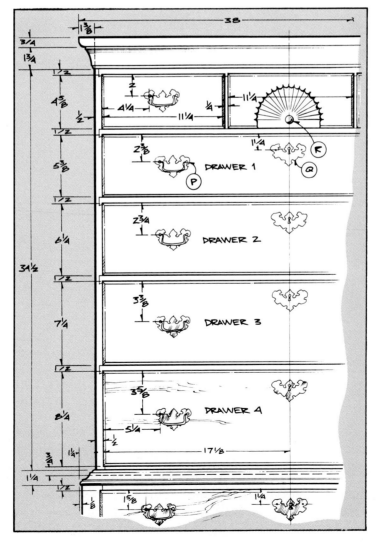

38
3/4
1¾
1³/₈
½
4⅝
½
2
4¼
11¼
¼
11¼
1¼
DRAWER 1
2⅜
1¼
K
P
Q
5⅜
1½
2¾
6¼
DRAWER 2
1½
3⅜
7¼
DRAWER 3
1½
3⅝
2¼
DRAWER 4
5¼
½
17⅛
34½
3/4
1¼
1¼
½
1/8
1⅝
1¼

adding the center rail (F) and divider mortises to the two uppermost front stretchers, and the center rail mortises to the two uppermost back stretchers. Joinery details for these mortises and for the tenons are shown in Figures 2 and 3. Test-fit the dividers, but don't cut the side and center rails yet.

Now apply glue to the ends of the two dividers, join the two uppermost front stretchers with them, and glue those stretchers into the case sides. Also glue the three remaining front stretchers in place.

Before you cut your side and center rails to length and tenon the ends, check the length dimensions in the Bill Of Materials. As indicated, the overall rail lengths, including the tenons, are a little shorter than the actual mortise-to-mortise dimension. When you assemble the rails and then add the back stretchers, this allowance should produce a $1/8$ in. gap between the rail tenon shoulder and the edge of the stretcher. The rails are *not* glued in place. They must float freely in order to allow for wood movement across the width of the sides. The $1/8$ in. gap allows the sides to contract $1/8$ in. If the wood you are using is dried to a moisture content that's greater than 7-8 percent, and you are building in the summertime when relative humidity is high, then you should probably increase the allowance for wood movement to about $1/4$ in. Don't exceed the $1/4$ in. allowance though, or the rails may drop out of the mortises.

With your rails sized, now lay the case face-down, mount the rails in the front stretchers, and add the back stretchers. Cut, fit and glue the guides (H) in place, then cut and mount the back (I).

The Molding

Now go to work on the cap and crown molding (J, K). The cap molding is just a length of $3/4$ in. thick by $1^3/8$ in. wide stock with a $3/8$ in. radius applied to one edge (see Molding Detail). For the crown molding, (Fig. 4), start with $8/4$ stock, establish the cove on the table saw, and then rip the stock in half. Note that you'll need at least five passes to get the final $7/16$ in. cove depth. Anything less and the blade is likely to burn. Also, if you use a blade that's not exactly 10 in. diameter, the angle of your fence must be altered to produce a similar cove. When we tried a 10 in. blade that after several sharpenings actually measured $9^3/4$ in. diameter, we found that an adjustment of several degrees in the fence setting was needed to get the same width cove.

Next, use the molding head (Sears cutter no. 9R2351) to mold the $1/4$ in. radius roundover. Here's where the extra thickness in your stock really pays dividends, since it provides an ample flat surface to gauge the stock off as you make the cut. Now resaw on the table saw to establish the final $3/4$ in. molding thickness.

Now miter and mount the moldings. The front cap molding is glued in place and glue blocks lend support to the front crown molding. Apply glue at the miters and along the first few inches at the sides. For the remaining side molding you'll use a mounting system that allows the case sides to expand and contract without restriction. To do this, fasten the rest of the cap molding with finishing nails angled down into the case sides from the top. The side crown molding sections are then glued to the bottom of the side cap moldings—a sound glue joint that doesn't interfere with the sides. Insert a few small finishing nails right at the step of the $1/4$ in. roundover; set and fill them. Pre-drill for the nails to avoid splitting the molding.

The Drawers

All that remains is the drawers. Each drawer is just a front (L), sides (M) and back (N), joined with traditional dovetail construction. The bottoms (O) are plywood, though bevel-edged solid stock bottoms are another option. Given the experience you've gained from the drawer work in the base, the drawers should be a snap. Suggested dovetail layouts are given in the Drawer Details. The sunburst carving that deco-

CASE

Bill of Materials
(all dimensions actual)

Part	Description	Size	No. Req'd.
A	Side	$3/4$ x $17^7/8$ x $37^1/2$	2
B	Top/bottom	$3/4$ x $17^7/8$ x $35^1/4$	2
C	Front Stretcher	$3/4$ x 2 x $34^3/4$*	5
D	Back Stretcher	$3/4$ x 2 x $34^1/2$*	5
E	Side Rail	$3/4$ x 2 x $14^1/4$*	10
F	Center Rail	$3/4$ x $2^3/4$ x $14^1/4$*	4
G	Divider	$3/4$ x 2 x $5^1/8$*	2
H	Guide	$1/2$ x $3/4$ x $15^1/2$	2
I	Back	$1/4$ x $34^1/2$ x $36^3/4$	1
J	Cap Molding	$3/4$ x $1^3/8$	7 ft.
K	Crown Molding	See Detail	7 ft.

* Length includes tenons or half dovetail. Note that the lengths of the side and center rails are $1/8$ in. less than the actual mortise-to-mortise dimension, the extra space being needed as an allowance for wood movement in the sides.

** Pulls, escutcheons and knob (all solid brass) are available from Horton Brasses, Nooks Hill Rd., Cromwell, CT 06416; tel. (203) 635-4400. Order part no. H-34-S for the pulls (specify $2^1/2$ in. borings), part no. H-34-SE for matching escutcheons, and part no. K-12 for the knob (specify $3/4$ in. diameter with machine screw for $3/4$ in. thick drawer front). The hardware is available in a choice of finishes: antique, semi-bright, or bright polish.

*** Brass drawer locks are available from The Wise Company, 6503 St. Claude Ave., P.O. Box 118, Arabi, LA 70032; tel. (504) 277-7551. Order part number L01/56LC1. Lock is not shown on upper section art. Refer to base art for details.

Drawers

Part	Description	No. Req'd Per Drawer	Three Small Drawers	Drawer 1	Drawer 2	Drawer 3	Drawer 4
L	Front	1	$3/4$ x $4^5/8$ x $11^1/4$	$3/4$ x $5^3/8$ x $34^1/4$	$3/4$ x $6^1/4$ x $34^1/4$	$3/4$ x $7^1/4$ x $34^1/4$	$3/4$ x $8^1/4$ x $34^1/4$
M	Side	2	$1/2$ x $4^3/8$ x $17^1/2$	$1/2$ x $5^1/8$ x $17^1/2$	$1/2$ x 6 x $17^1/2$	$1/2$ x 7 x $17^1/2$	$1/2$ x 8 x $17^1/2$
N	Back	1	$1/2$ x $3^3/4$ x $10^3/4$	$1/2$ x $4^1/2$ x $33^3/4$	$1/2$ x $5^3/8$ x $33^3/4$	$1/2$ x $6^3/8$ x $33^3/4$	$1/2$ x $7^3/8$ x $33^3/4$
O	Bottom	1	$1/4$ x $10^1/4$ x $17^1/4$	$1/4$ x $17^1/4$ x $33^1/4$	$1/4$ x $17^1/4$ x $33^1/4$	$1/4$ x $17^1/4$ x $33^1/4$	$1/4$ x $17^1/4$ x $33^1/4$

Hardware

Part	Description	Size	No.
P	Chippendale Pull	$3^7/16$ x 2 ($2^1/2$ in. borings)**	10
Q	Escutcheon	$3^7/16$ x 2**	4
R	Knob	$3/4$ dia.**	1
S	Lock	$1/2$ x $2^1/2$ x $1^7/8$ (half mortise)***	4

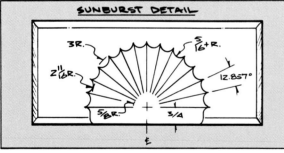

SUNBURST DETAIL

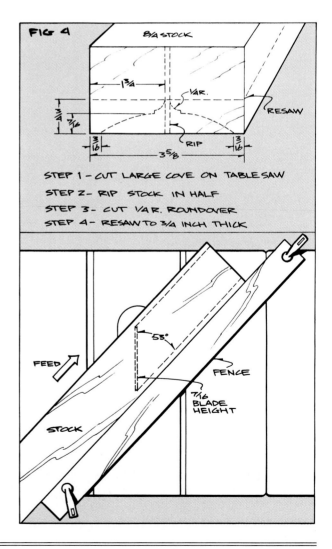

FIG 4

8/4 STOCK

STEP 1 - CUT LARGE COVE ON TABLE SAW

STEP 2 - RIP STOCK IN HALF

STEP 3 - CUT 1/4 R. ROUNDOVER

STEP 4 - RESAW TO 3/4 INCH THICK

rates the center drawer at the top is a smaller version of the sunburst on the center drawer in the base—with one exception. Instead of 18 rays, as the base drawer had, the top drawer sunburst has 14 rays. Use the same technique included with the base how-to, but employ a smaller template. The necessary radii and other dimensions are given in the Sunburst Detail.

Details

Naturally, your finish for the drawer case will match the base. The hardware is also nearly identical, with the Chippendale pulls (P), matching escutcheons (Q) and locks (S) all sized exactly the same. The only deviation is in the size of the center drawer knob (R)—$3/4$ in. diameter instead of the 1 in. diameter used on the somewhat larger base center drawer. By the way, if you'd rather not include locks on all four of the full-width drawers, don't. On our highboy, only the two lower drawers in the upper section actually included locks. A slip of black construction paper behind the escutcheon will pass all but the closest inspection.

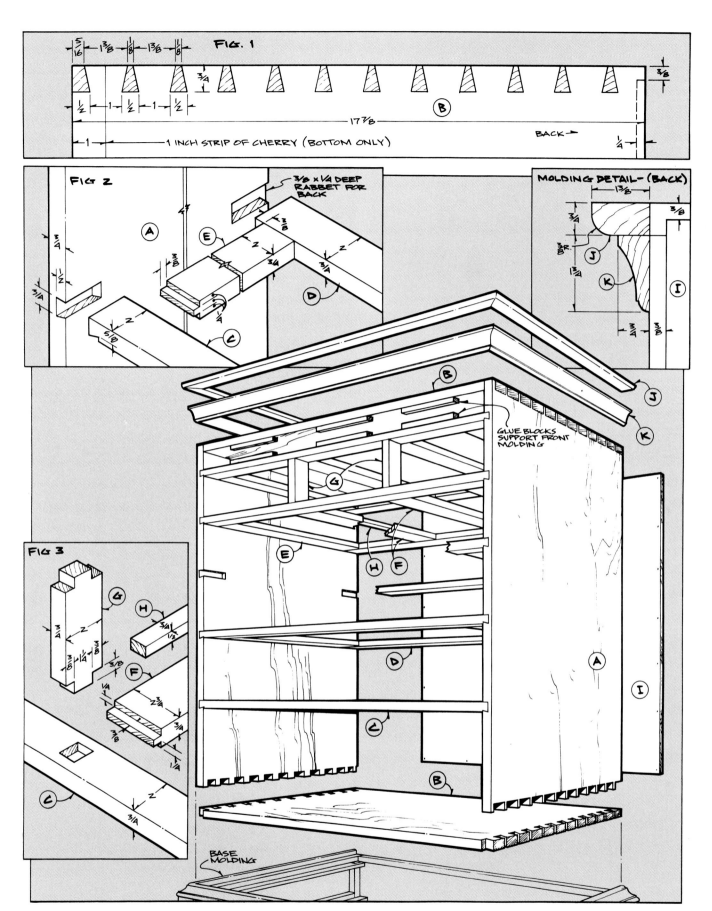

FIG. 1

5/16 1 3/8 1/8 1 3/8 1/8

3/4

3/8

1/2 1 1/2 1 1/2

B

17 7/8

BACK →

1/4

1

1 INCH STRIP OF CHERRY (BOTTOM ONLY)

FIG 2

A

E

3/8 x 1/4 DEEP RABBET FOR BACK

3/8

2

3/4

2

3/4

3/4

1/2

3/4

3/8

2

D

2

5/8

C

1/4

MOLDING DETAIL- (BACK)

1 3/8

3/4

3/8

3/8 R

3/4

J

1 3/4

K

I

3/4 3/8

B

J

K

GLUE BLOCKS SUPPORT FRONT MOLDING

G

E

H

F

A

I

FIG 3

G

3/4

2

3/4

3/4

1/4 3/8

3/8

H

3/4

1/2

F

1/4

2 3/4

3/4

3/8

1/4

D

2

3/4

C

C

B

B

BASE MOLDING

Although builder Dennis Preston did not include provision for a secret drawer or compartment, like much furniture of the period, there's ample room for these in the area above the top drawers. One option is to add a false top panel above the three top drawers, and incorporate several drop-down compartments. Or, devise a method for the front molding sections to slide up, revealing the hidden storage area and providing front access.

●

Jewelry Chest

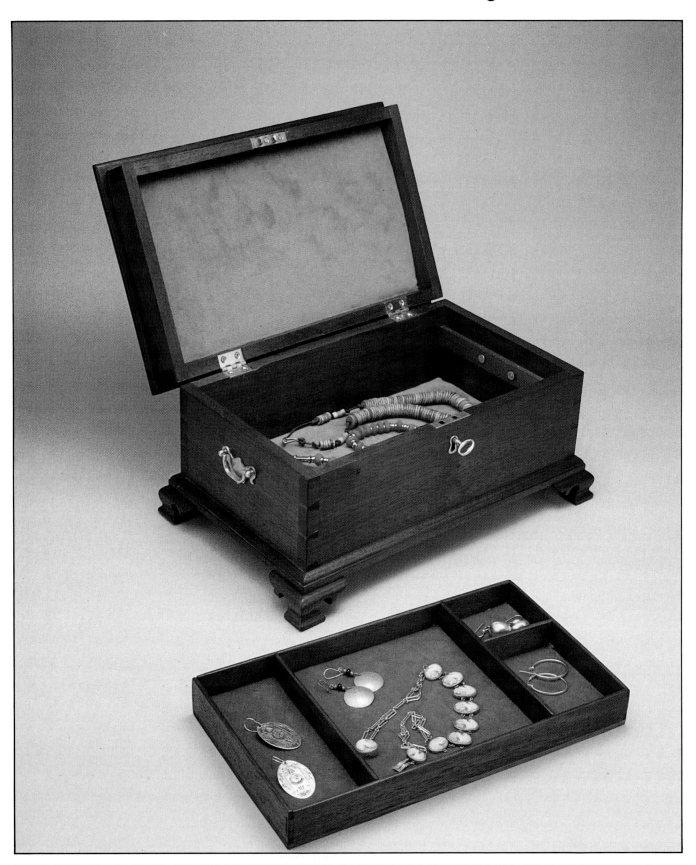

This classic jewelry box, designed and built by Connecticut woodworker Dennis Preston, features ogee bracket feet, dovetailed corners and delicate Chippendale hardware. For the distinctive feet, Preston used a router technique that eliminates most of the hassle of working with small pieces. This box is made from walnut, but any hardwood will work.

Start by preparing the stock. You'll need $^5/_8$ in. thick stock for the top (A), and $^1/_2$ in. thick stock for the bottom (B), front/back (C), and sides (D). The tray is made with $^1/_8$ in. thick stock for the front and back (H), the sides (I), and the partitions (J, K). The tray bottom (G) is $^1/_4$ in. thick plywood.

Cut the box front, back and sides so they're $^1/_8$ in. wider than the dimensions shown in the Bill of Materials. The extra width allows for the $^1/_8$ in. you'll lose when you cut the lid off the box. Then label the parts and lay out the dovetails as shown. Refer to page 104 for a step-by-step procedure on handcut dovetails.

Note that before gluing up the box, you'll need to mark the line where you'll separate the box from the lid. This is also a good time to rout out the lock mortise. The mortise is cut at two router settings, with a deeper cut for the thicker part of the lock mechanism. You'll need to

square up the router cuts with a chisel, but it's a good idea to wait until cutting off the top of the box for that operation.

Next, glue up the box and, when dry, separate the lid with a table saw cut. Then fit the lock, using the chisel to pare away the corners of the router mortise. Cut the top from a single piece of walnut. To establish the raised field, first make $^1/_8$ in. deep cuts along the edges of the raised portion. Then, with the workpiece on edge, use a table saw set $1^3/_4$ in. high to form the slight bevel, about 8

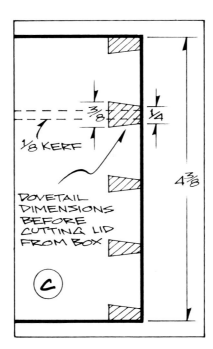

$^1/_8$ KERF

DOVETAIL DIMENSIONS BEFORE CUTTING LID FROM BOX

Ⓒ

Bill of Materials
(all dimensions actual)

Part	Description	Size	No. Req'd.
A	Top	$^5/_8$ x $7^3/_4$ x $12^5/_8$	1
B	Bottom	$^1/_2$ x $7^3/_4$ x $12^5/_8$	1
C	Front/Back	$^1/_2$ x $4^3/_8$ x 12*	2
D	Side	$^1/_2$ x $4^3/_8$ x $7^1/_8$*	2
E	Foot	as shown	4
F	Cleat	$^3/_{16}$ x $^3/_4$ x $6^1/_8$	2
G	Tray Bottom	$^1/_4$ x $5^3/_4$ x $10^5/_8$**	1
H	Tray Front/Back	$^1/_8$ x $1^1/_4$ x $10^7/_8$	2
I	Tray Side	$^1/_8$ x $1^1/_4$ x 6	2
J	Tray Partition	$^1/_8$ x 1 x $5^7/_8$	2
K	Tray Partition (small)	$^1/_8$ x 1 x $2^9/_{16}$	1
L	Hinge	1 x 1 as shown***	2
M	Lock	as shown****	1
N	Escutcheon	as shown****	1
O	Handle	as shown****	2

* Parts C and D start $^1/_8$ in. wider than final size to allow for cut separating the lid from the box.

** The walnut plywood for the bottom is available from Craftsman Wood Service Co., 1735 Cortland Ct., Addison, IL 60101; tel. 1-800-543-9367. They also sell the solid walnut in both $^1/_8$ in. and $^1/_2$ in. thicknesses.

*** The brass hinges are available at most hardware stores.

**** Parts available from Ball and Ball, 463 W. Lincoln Highway, Exton, PA 19341; tel. (215) 363-7330. The catalog numbers are: lock, TJB-055; handle, S24-044; escutcheon, L67-008.

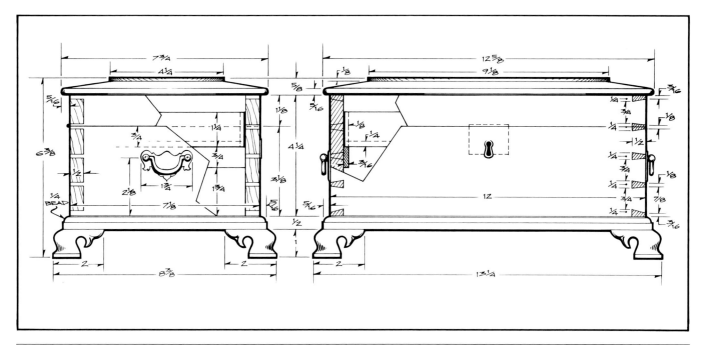

Making the
Bracket Foot

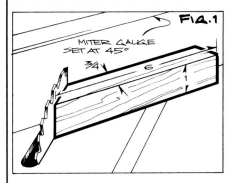

FIG. 1

MITER GAUGE
SET AT 45°

3/4

6

1

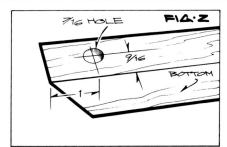

FIG. 2

7/16 HOLE

9/16

1

BOTTOM

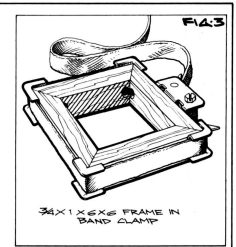

FIG. 3

3/4 X 1 X 6 X 6 FRAME IN
BAND CLAMP

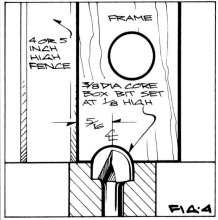

FIG. 4

FRAME

4 OR 5
INCH
HIGH
FENCE

3/8 DIA CORE
BOX BIT SET
AT 1/8 HIGH

5/16

¢

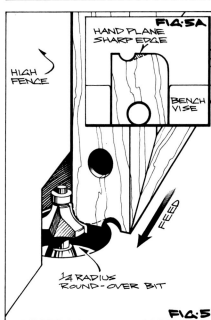

FIG. 5A

HAND PLANE
SHARP EDGE

BENCH
VISE

HIGH
FENCE

FEED

1/4 RADIUS
ROUND-OVER BIT

FIG. 5

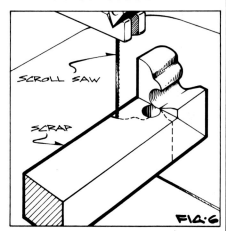

SCROLL SAW

SCRAP

FIG. 6

This bracket foot technique eliminates a lot of the handling of
small pieces, which is usually a
problem with making small feet. Most of
the shaping is done with the pieces glued
into a simple frame. Only for the last
step do you saw the individual feet apart.

To begin, rip out four pieces of walnut
3/4 in. thick by 1 in. wide by 6 in. long.
The length needn't be exact as long as
they're all the same; the idea is to make
the pieces long enough to handle easily.
Next, miter the ends at 45 degrees (Fig.
1), and locate and drill the 7/16 in.
diameter holes (Fig. 2). The holes later

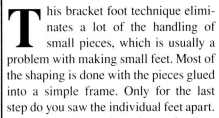

FULL-SIZE PATTERN

become part of the side profile. Now
glue up the frame using a band clamp
and corner blocks as shown (Fig. 3).

After the glue sets, shape the outside

of the frame with a router mounted in a
router table (Figs. 4 and 5). For safety
and stability, make sure you use a high
fence for this operation. The profile is a
combination of a 3/8 in. diameter core
box bit and a 1/4 in. diameter roundover
bit. The bits are available from MLCS,
P.O. Box 4053J, Rydal, PA 19046.
Remove the small area of transition
between the router cuts with a hand
plane or wood file (Fig. 5A).

Next, cut apart the feet and shape the
remainder of the profile with a scroll saw
(Fig. 6). Smooth the profiles with files
and sandpaper.

degrees. Use a high rip fence so there's
plenty of support for the workpiece. To
round the edge you can use a roundover
bit or a block plane and sandpaper.

Next, cut the bottom to size and shape
the edge with a router, using a 1/4 in.
radius beading bit. Note that when
routing the edges, it's best to shape the
ends first and then the front and back.
That way if the router tears out a chip
from the end grain—which it tends to

do—the subsequent passes with the
grain will remove the damage. After
finishing the bottom, make the bracket
feet (E) as shown in the sidebar.

To assemble, glue the feet to the
bottom and then screw the top and
bottom to the case. In both cases, use
"sloppy" or enlarged screw holes to
allow for seasonal wood movement. On
the bottom, you can drill up through the
workpiece into the case, countersinking

the holes. For the top, you'll need to drill
up through the case into the top. Drill
and counterbore those holes and hide
them with plugs. Make the counterbore
about 1/4 in. deep. Establish the sloppy
screw holes by elongating the shank
holes in the direction you want to allow
movement, which is across the grain of
the wood. The cleats (F) are glued and
clamped to the insides of the case.

With the case complete, make the tray

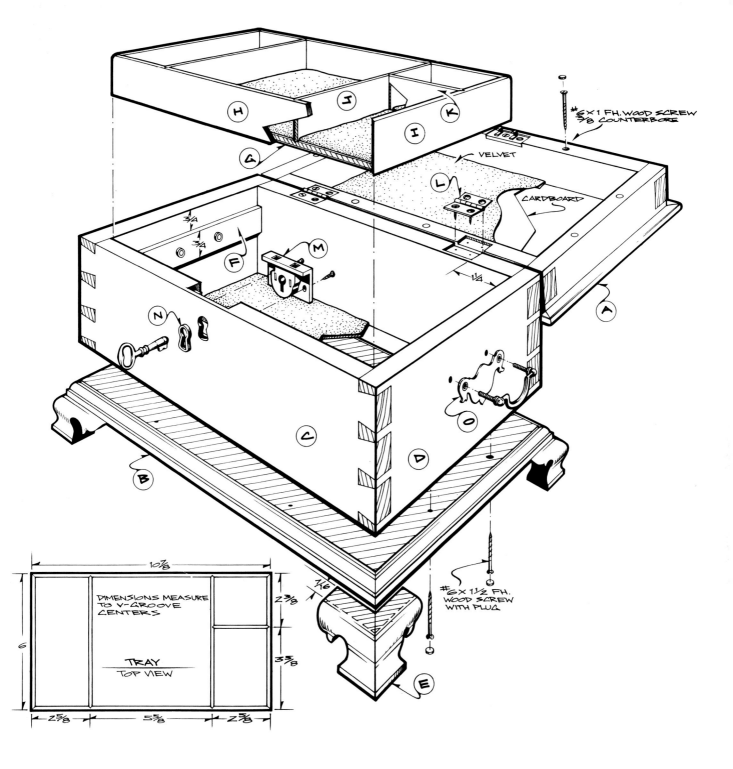

DIMENSIONS MEASURE TO V-GROOVE CENTERS

TRAY
TOP VIEW

6 X 1 FH. WOOD SCREW
3/8 COUNTERBORE

VELVET

CARDBOARD

6 X 1½ FH.
WOOD SCREW
WITH PLUG

to fit the actual dimensions of the inside, allowing about 1/8 in. for play. Cut the 1/16 in. deep V-grooves for the partitions with a router and V-groove cutter.

The tray front and back (H) and the tray sides (I) are mitered at the ends. The partitions (J and K) have beveled ends and fit into the V-grooves. They are held with glue along the bottom edges. You'll save time later if you sand the parts before assembling. The tray parts are

glued up around and on the plywood tray bottom (G). The bottom ties the assembly together.

Next, locate the handles (O) on the sides, and mortise in the hinges (L). Also mortise in the escutcheon (N). Use a sharp carving knife to establish the profile, cutting straight down to sever the top wood fibers. Once you have a clean line all around, you can remove the waste with a small chisel. After fitting

all the hardware, temporarily remove it so you can sand and finish the box.

The jewelry box is finished with several coats of shellac, which is rubbed out with pumice and rottenstone. A final coat of wax will help preserve the finish.

Finally, wrap the velvet around cardboard and glue it inside the compartment and into the lid and the bottom of the box. Also glue velvet to the bottoms of the feet. ●

Mission Style
Trestle Table

Here's a substantial table you'll be proud to serve dinner on. The dark oak and simple, sturdy construction are characteristic of the American Mission style popular in the late 19th and early 20th centuries.

We made the table from ⁵/₄ and ⁶/₄ stock to achieve a 1 in. thickness for the top (A), cleats (B) and legs (E), and the 1¹/₄ in. thickness for the shelf (C), spreaders (D) and feet (F).

Start by edge-joining boards for the wider parts of the table (the top and the shelf). After they are joined, plane or sand them to the final thickness.

Next, make the feet and spreaders, which are the same except for the cutout on the bottom of the feet. After making the parts to the size given in the Bill of Materials, cut the mortises. Lay them out carefully, using a marking gauge to insure they're all the same. Then drill a series of holes to establish the mortises, and clean them up with a chisel. Use a band saw to form the profiles.

Now cut the four legs to size, and form the 1¹/₄ in. long tenons. First establish the shoulders of the tenons by cross-cutting to the ¹/₄ in. depth all around the workpieces. Then use a tenon jig—or clamp the workpiece to a supporting piece of plywood—to remove the waste pieces. Don't try to run the workpiece through the saw on end without a support,

because the workpiece can twist and pull your hand into the saw blade. When making these cuts, it's best to try your setup with some scrap to insure the tenons fit tightly in the mortises.

Next, form the through-mortises in the legs, the matching tenons in the shelf, and the mortises in the shelf for the keys (G). Use a band saw to cut the profile and tenons on the ends of the shelf. Again, lay them out carefully with a marking gauge so that all the tenons are the same and they fit in the mortises.

Make the cleats from the ⁵/₄ stock and bevel the corners and drill the holes as shown. Note that one of the holes on each cleat is elongated to allow the screw to move slightly as the top adjusts to seasonal moisture changes. Also drill the holes for the 2¹/₂ in. by no. 10 machine screws that hold the spreaders onto the cleats.

The keys are cut on the band saw and filed and sanded to final shape. The chamfer on the ends of the shelf tenons is also established with wood files. Use a ³/₁₆ in. radius roundover bit in the router to soften the edges of the top.

Give all the parts a good sanding. Start with 120-grit paper and then use 150-, 180-, and 220-grit paper. Stain all the parts with a dark stain such as Minwax Jacobean. Then glue the legs into the feet and spreaders. Finish the piece with several coats of polyurethane varnish or lacquer. ●

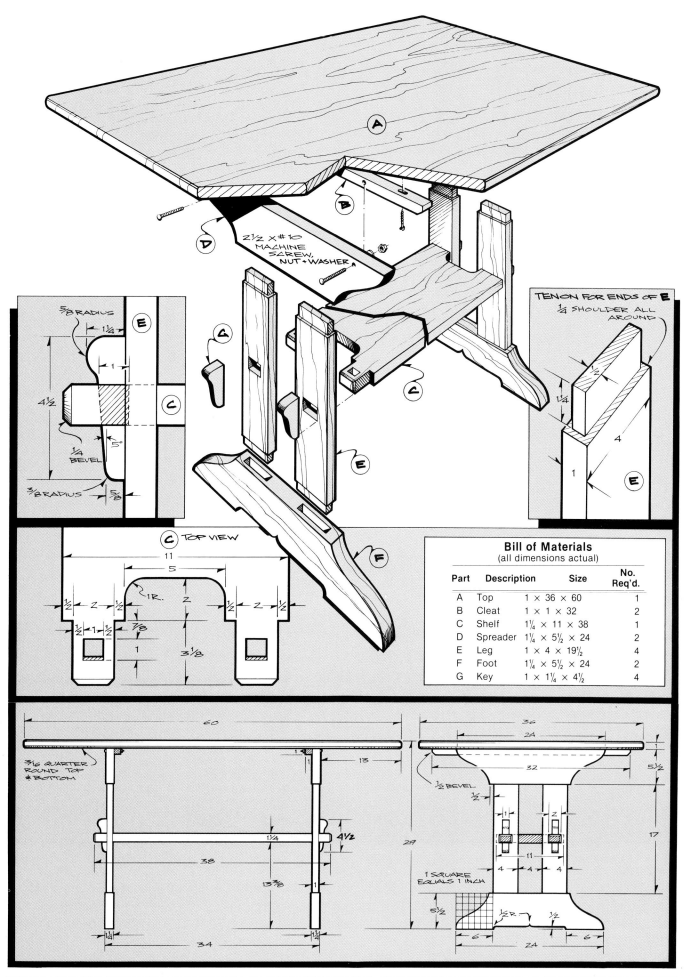

A

B

D

2½ × #10 MACHINE SCREW, NUT + WASHER

G

C

C

E

E

TENON FOR ENDS OF E
¼ SHOULDER ALL AROUND

½

1¼

4

1

E

⅝ RADIUS

1¼

E

1

4½

5°

¼ BEVEL

⅜ RADIUS

⅝

C TOP VIEW

11

5

1R.

½ 2 ½

2

½ 2 ½

½ 1 ½

⅞

3⅛

1

F

Bill of Materials
(all dimensions actual)

Part	Description	Size	No. Req'd.
A	Top	1 × 36 × 60	1
B	Cleat	1 × 1 × 32	2
C	Shelf	1¼ × 11 × 38	1
D	Spreader	1¼ × 5½ × 24	2
E	Leg	1 × 4 × 19½	4
F	Foot	1¼ × 5½ × 24	2
G	Key	1 × 1¼ × 4½	4

60

3/16 QUARTER ROUND TOP + BOTTOM

13

4½

1¼

38

13⅜

1

34

1¼

29

36

24

32

5½

½ BEVEL

½

1

2

11

4 4 4

1 SQUARE EQUALS 1 INCH

5½

17

½R

½

6

24

6

Gate-Leg Table

The gate-leg table is a classic furniture design, one that is characteristic of and first became popular during the William and Mary period. Although our table is not an authentic William and Mary antique, it is a fine turn-of-the-century reproduction in the William and Mary style. The table is from the collection of The Washington Historical Museum, a fascinating museum of Early American, Colonial, and period furnishings located in the picturesque little town of Washington, Connecticut.

Distinctive turnings and well-balanced lines make this table one of the nicest examples of the gate-leg style we have seen. Because of the number of turnings and the need for precision if the pieces are to fit accurately together, this project should only be attempted by experienced woodworkers with strong turning skills.

To make the table, you will need twelve 36 in. long 2 in. square turning blocks for the turned parts. All the remaining parts can be fashioned from 1

in. stock (which typically measures $^3/_4$ in. thick) except for the two small blocks (L) which can be made from the turning square cutoffs. Turning squares are available from a number of sources,

among them Constantine's, 2050 Eastchester Rd., Bronx, NY 10461. Although our table is crafted in mahogany, either cherry, maple, or walnut would also be a good choice.

Begin by laying out the various

turnings (parts A, E, F, G, I, J, and K) as shown in the turning details. You will need a single 36 in. long turning square for each of the four legs (A), the two side stretchers (F), and the two notched legs (I). The four short cross stretchers (E) are laid out and turned on a single 36 in. long turning square, and later separated. Using the same technique, one each of the two pivot legs (G), the two pivot stretchers (J), and the two fixed feet (K) are combined on the 36 in. turning squares, turned, and then separated. The one remaining turning square is an extra in case of some error in turning or perhaps a hidden defect in the wood. After all the turning is completed take care to accurately notch the legs (I) and the side stretchers (F) where they lap together.

The upper apron assembly (parts B and C), end rails (D), pivot rail (H), and the drawer guide support (M) and drawer guide (N) are all standard mortise and tenon construction. Refer to the apron and rail tenon details for the specific dimensions of these tenons and to figure the corresponding

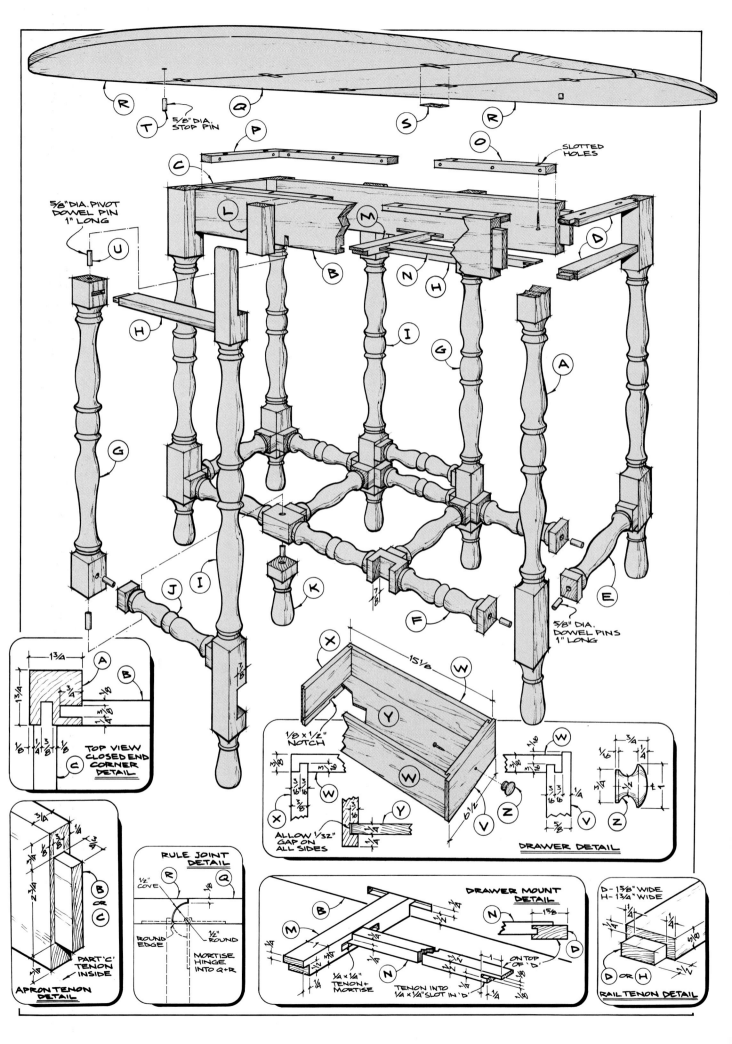

R T Q
5/8" DIA.
STOP PIN

S R O

SLOTTED
HOLES

C P

5/8" DIA. PIVOT
DOWEL PIN
1" LONG

U L M D

B N H

H

I G A

G

J I K F E

P

5/8" DIA.
DOWEL PINS
1" LONG

TOP VIEW CLOSED END CORNER DETAIL
13/4
13/4
3/4
3/8
1/8
1/8 1/4 3/8 3/16 1/8
A B C

APRON TENON DETAIL
3/4
1/4
3/16
3/8
2 3/4
B OR C
PART 'C' TENON INSIDE

RULE JOINT DETAIL
1/2" COVE
R Q
1/8
1/2" ROUND
ROUND EDGE
MORTISE HINGE INTO Q+R

DRAWER DETAIL
X W
15 1/8
Y W
1/8 x 1/2" NOTCH
3/16
3/16 3/16
3/16 3/16
3/8
X W
ALLOW 1/32" GAP ON ALL SIDES
Y
6 1/2
V Z
1/16
W
3/16
3/16 3/16
1/4
5/8
V
3/4
1/4
3/16
Z
1

DRAWER MOUNT DETAIL
B
M
N
N
1/4 x 1/4 TENON+MORTISE
TENON INTO 1/4 x 1/4" SLOT IN 'D'
15 5/8
ON TOP OF 'D'
D
1/4
1/4
1/16

RAIL TENON DETAIL
D - 1 5/8" WIDE
H - 1 3/4" WIDE
1/4
1/4
5/8
D OR H

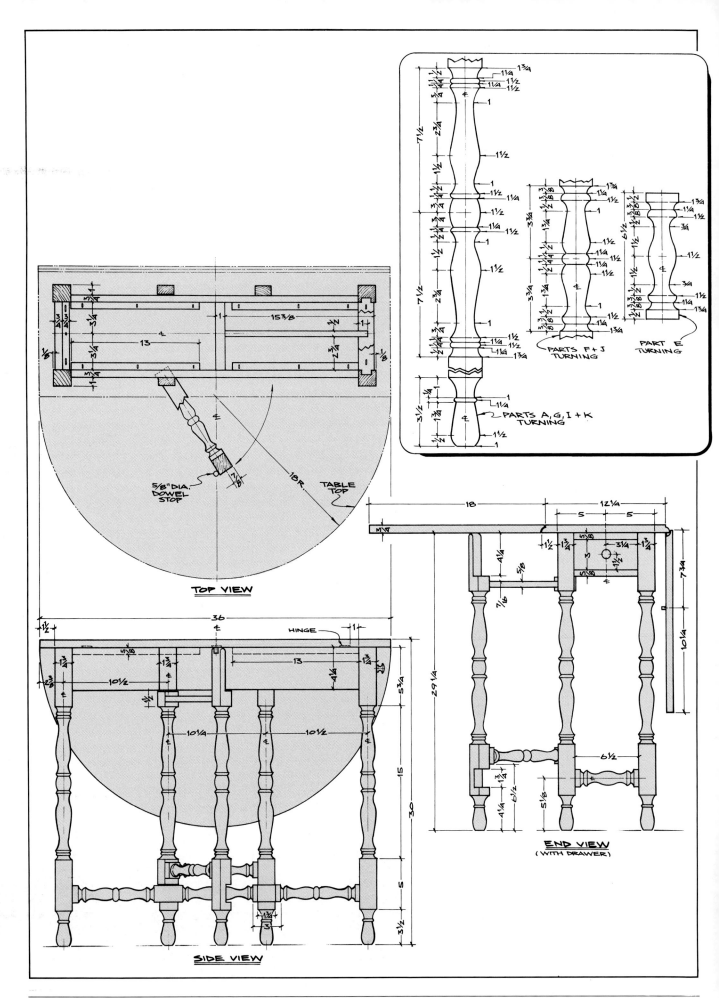

TOP VIEW

5/8" DIA.
DOWEL
STOP

TABLE
TOP

18R

PARTS F + J
TURNING

PART E
TURNING

PARTS A, G, I + K
TURNING

HINGE

SIDE VIEW

END VIEW
(WITH DRAWER)

mortises in the legs. When making the upper of the two end rails (D), note that several slotted and countersunk screw holes must be added in this piece, which also serves as a cleat for mounting the top. The top and leaves are made by gluing up stock, with the leaves then rounded out with a saber saw. Refer to the techniques feature on page 126 for detailed instructions on how to make the rule joint shown in the rule joint detail.

Build the drawer as shown in the drawer detail. Although the drawer bottom is dimensioned full width in the Bill of Materials, size it a little under 6 in. wide to accommodate any seasonal movement in the wood. Assemble the drawer and mount the wood knob, which is turned to the illustrated profile.

The various stretchers and legs are joined as indicated with $5/8$ in. diameter by 1 in. long dowel pins. In order to insure accuracy in the location of these pins a simple drilling guide jig can be made for this operation. Drill the dowel holes slightly long to prevent dowel bottoming and hydraulic glue back pressure during the final assembly process. Because the fit of all parts is so critical and must be exact, a dry-fitted test assembly of the entire table is a must.

For final assembly, begin by making the two end frame and the two pivot leg

Bill of Materials
(all dimensions actual)

Part	Description	Size	No. Req'd.
A	Leg	$1^{3}/4 \times 1^{3}/4 \times 29^{1}/4$	4
B	Side Apron	$3/4 \times 4^{1}/4 \times 31$ *	2
C	End Apron	$3/4 \times 4^{1}/4 \times 8$ *	1
D	End Rail	$5/8 \times 1^{5}/8 \times 7^{1}/2$ *	2
E	Cross Stretcher	$1^{3}/4 \times 1^{3}/4 \times 6^{1}/2$	4
F	Side Stretcher	$1^{3}/4 \times 1^{3}/4 \times 29^{1}/2$	2
G	Pivot Leg	$1^{3}/4 \times 1^{3}/4 \times 19$	2
H	Pivot Rail	$5/8 \times 1^{3}/4 \times 9^{1}/2$ *	2
I	Notched Leg	$1^{3}/4 \times 1^{3}/4 \times 29^{1}/4$	2
J	Pivot Stretcher	$1^{3}/4 \times 1^{3}/4 \times 8^{1}/2$	2
K	Fixed Foot	$1^{3}/4 \times 1^{3}/4 \times 4^{1}/4$	2
L	Block	$1 \times 1^{3}/4 \times 4^{1}/4$	2
M	Drawer Guide Support	$3/4 \times 1 \times 7$ *	1
N	Drawer Guide	$1/2 \times 1/2 \times 15$ *	1
O	Side Cleat	$5/8 \times 3/4 \times 13$	4
P	End Cleat	$5/8 \times 3/4 \times 6^{1}/2$	1
Q	Top	$3/4 \times 13^{1}/4 \times 36$	1
R	Leaf	$3/4 \times 18 \times 36$	2
S	Hinge	$1^{1}/2 \times 2^{7}/8$	6
T	Stop Pin	$5/8$ dia. $\times$ 1 in. long	2
U	Pivot Pin	$5/8$ dia. $\times$ 1 in. long	4
V	Drawer Front	$5/8 \times 3 \times 6^{1}/2$	1
W	Drawer Side	$3/8 \times 3 \times 15^{1}/8$	2
X	Drawer Back	$3/8 \times 3 \times 6$	1
Y	Drawer Bottom	$1/4 \times 6 \times 14^{3}/4$	1
Z	Knob	$3/4 \times 1$ in.	1
* Includes tenons.			

assemblies. Also join the two side stretchers with the two remaining cross stretchers. Now join the end assemblies, the lower stretcher assembly and the side aprons to make the table frame. Note that the grooves in these side aprons, cut to accept the drawer guide support, are purposely cut oversize (long). This is done so the guide support can be angled into place after the table frame has been assembled. The drawer guide is also mounted at this time, although it should not be permanently glued until the drawer has been test-fitted for smooth opening and closing. A little paraffin on the guide will reduce friction and wear.

To mount the pivot leg assemblies, first temporarily clamp the blocks (L) in place and drill the upper pivot pin holes. You will need to slightly tip the leg assemblies in order to mount them in the lower pivot pin holes. Glue on the blocks (L), locking in place the upper pins, and add the fixed feet (K).

Mount the top with screws inserted up through slotted holes in the five cleats and the upper rail. Add the two leaves, using three hinges for each leaf, as shown, and glue in place the dowel pins (T), which serve as a simple stop for the pivoting leaf supports. Final sand the table and finish by hand rubbing three coats of tung oil into the wood. ●

Vienna Regulator Clock

T he Vienna regulator clock was and still is considered to be one of the finest classic European clock designs. The style was developed and perfected in Austria and Germany during the 19th century, and has changed little over the years. This particular model is representative of a traditional Vienna regulator from the 1850's.

With thick beveled glass on the front and both sides, the Vienna regulator case is intended to fully expose the handsome solid brass movement, weight shells, and pendulum that characterized this design. While the model pictured was crafted in cherry, walnut would be an excellent alternate choice. We have arranged with the mail-order company Mason and Sullivan to provide a single kit including all the hardware, glass, and movement parts that you will need to build the clock exactly as shown (see Bill of Materials).

The construction of the clock case involves basic woodworking skills, however because of the need for precision, this is a project that is best undertaken by those with a moderate to advanced level of experience. It is strongly recommended that the hardware, glass, and movement (see Bill of Materials) be purchased *before* beginning the assembly to insure both availability and proper fit of all the parts.

The best method to build the case is to construct the individual assemblies of the side frames first. The stiles (A, B, C) and rails (D) are of a mitered molded type. First, use a $^3/_8$ in. radius ball bearing guided router bit to apply the $^3/_8$ in. radius detail, then cut the $^3/_8$ in. by $^3/_8$ in. rabbet for the glass. Tenon the ends of D and mortise A, B, and C to fit. Note that although the tongue cut on parts D which fits into the corresponding groove cut in parts F and E is stepped on the ends, this in no way affects the strength of the construction. Parts A and B are identical except in the hardware application, where A is mortised for the hinges, and B is mortised for the latches. After mitering the bead as shown (note that the stile bead must be mitered *and* cut back to accept the rails), glue and assemble the side frames. Now cut the parts for the base (E), top (F), upper

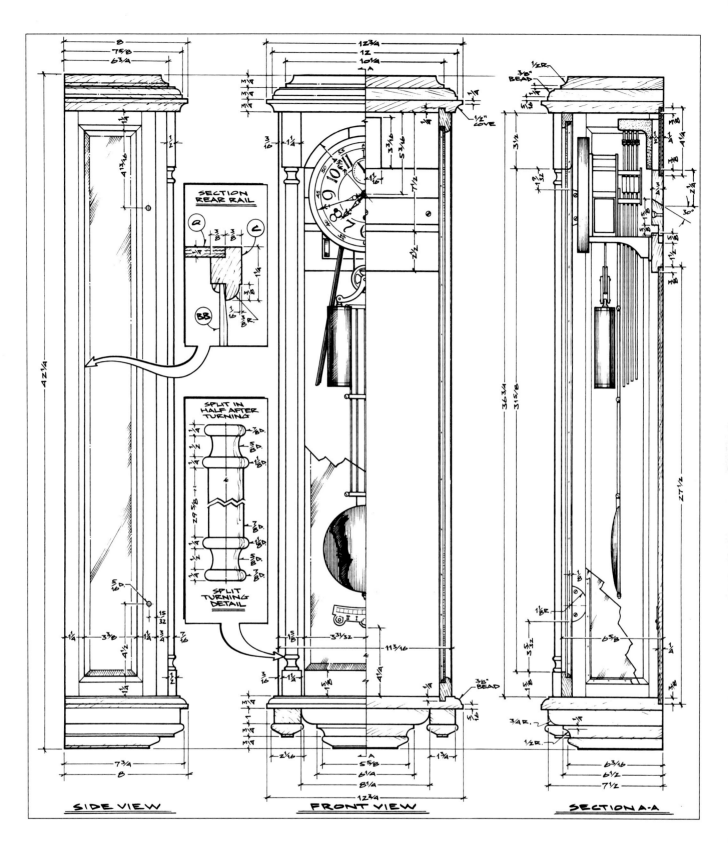

SIDE VIEW

SECTION
REAR RAIL

SPLIT IN
HALF AFTER
TURNING

SPLIT
TURNING
DETAIL

FRONT VIEW

SECTION A-A

top (G), crown (H), pediment base (I), lower pediment (J), pediment molding (K), base blocks (L) and base molding (M). A $^1/_2$ in. bearing guided cove cutter is used to profile parts H, F, and J, while a $^3/_8$ in. beading bit molds the edges of parts E and G. A $^3/_4$ in. radius roundover is applied to part I, and the simple four-step process shown in the molding detail is used to establish the pediment moldings on parts K and M. Don't forget to rout the $^3/_8$ in. by $^1/_4$ in. grooves in the base and top as

shown to accept the tongue on parts D.

Now assemble the case. Begin by mounting the base and top to the side frame assemblies. Bore, countersink and screw parts E and F to reinforce the tongue-and-groove glue joint. Screw part G to part H as shown, and then mount to part F. No glue is needed here, but all parts should be final sanded before assembly. The lower moldings and pediments are screwed in place, one over the other, as shown. Drill and countersink for all

Bill of Materials
(all dimensions actual)

Part	Description	Size	No. Req'd.
A	Right Side Front Stile	$3/4$ x $1^1/4$ x $36^3/4$	1
B	Left Side Front Stile	$3/4$ x $1^1/4$ x $36^3/4$	1
C	Rear Stile	$3/4$ x $1^1/4$ x $36^3/4$	2
D	Side Rail	$3/4$ x $1^1/2$ x $4^7/8$*	4
E	Base	$3/4$ x 8 x $12^3/4$	1
F	Top	$3/4$ x 8 x $12^3/4$	1
G	Upper Top	$3/4$ x $7^5/8$ x 12	1
H	Crown	$3/4$ x $6^3/4$ x $10^1/4$	1
I	Pediment Base	1 x $7^1/2$ x $8^1/4$	1
J	Lower Pediment	$3/4$ x $6^1/2$ x $6^1/4$	1
K	Pediment Molding	$3/4$ x $6^3/16$ x $5^5/8$	1
L	Base Block	1 x $1^3/4$ x $7^1/2$	2
M	Base Molding	$3/4$ x $2^1/16$ x $7^3/4$	2
N	Case Back Rail	$3/4$ x $2^1/2$ x $10^7/16$	1
O	Case Hanger	$3/4$ x $2^1/4$ x $10^7/16$	1
P	Wall Hanger	$3/4$ x $2^1/4$ x $10^7/16$	1
Q	Lower Back	$1/4$ x $10^7/16$ x $27^1/2$	1
R	Upper Back	$1/4$ x $10^7/16$ x $4^1/4$	1
S	Chime Spacer	$1/2$ x $2^1/8$ x $3^3/16$	1
T	Door Stile Right	$3/4$ x $1^5/8$ x $36^3/4$	1
U	Door Stile Left	$3/4$ x $1^5/8$ x $36^3/4$	1
V	Lower Door Rail	$3/4$ x $1^5/8$ x $9^{11}/16$*	1
W	Upper Door Rail	$3/4$ x $3^1/2$ x $9^{11}/16$*	1
X	Lower Stile Block	$1/2$ x $1^1/4$ x $1^5/8$	2
Y	Stile Turning	see Detail	split
Z	Upper Stile Block	$1/2$ x $1^1/4$ x $3^1/2$	2
AA	Door Glass (beveled)	$8^5/8$ x $34^1/16$**	1
BB	Side Glass (beveled)	$4^1/16$ x 35**	2
CC	Keeper Strip	$1/4$ x $1/4$**	20 ft.
DD	Hinge	$1^1/4$ x $1^1/2$**	2
EE	Latch	as shown**	2
FF	Catch	as shown**	2
GG	Regulator Plaque	$1^1/2$ x $3^5/8$ brass**	1
HH	Chime	Westminster**	1
II	Movement	solid brass, cable drive**	1
JJ	Hands	as shown**	3
KK	Pendulum	$5^1/2$ in. dia. brass**	1
LL	Lead Weight	as shown**	2

* Includes tenons.

** Parts AA–LL are all available as a kit from Mason & Sullivan, 210 Wood County Industrial Park, P.O. Box 1686, Parkersburg, WV 26102-1681; tel. 1-800-225-1153. Order part no. CO572X.

the screws, keep all edges flush at the back as indicated, and plug the screw holes in parts K and M.

Next, using the router equipped with a $3/8$ in. rabbeting bit, rabbet the case back to accept the various back and hanger parts. Square the rabbet corners with a chisel. Now cut and fit the lower and upper back (Q and R), the case back rail (N), case hanger (O), and wall hanger (P). Note that the case hanger and wall hanger are both beveled at 30 degrees. When complete, the case is lowered onto part P, which is mounted securely to the wall with toggle bolts or other screw type fasteners. The case back rail and case hanger are both glued and screwed in place, but the upper and lower back are secured only with screws. All these parts are best final mounted *after* the side glass has been fixed in place to provide clear access through the back for a drill.

The door, consisting of parts T, U, V, and W, is made as shown in the door tenon detail. Note that tenons on the ends of the upper and lower door rails fit into corresponding mortises in the stiles. The $3/8$ in. rabbeting bit is used to cut the $3/8$ in. by $1/2$ in. deep rabbet to accept the glass in the door rails and stiles. You will need several passes to achieve the $1/2$ in. depth. Make certain that you understand the door construction, and the fact that stiles T and U must be notched (see exploded view) to receive the top rail, before laying out and cutting the door parts. Assemble the door frame, and cut the upper and lower stile blocks (X, Z). The stile turning (Y) is a split turning. The stile blocks and split turnings are located and glued in place. *Note:*

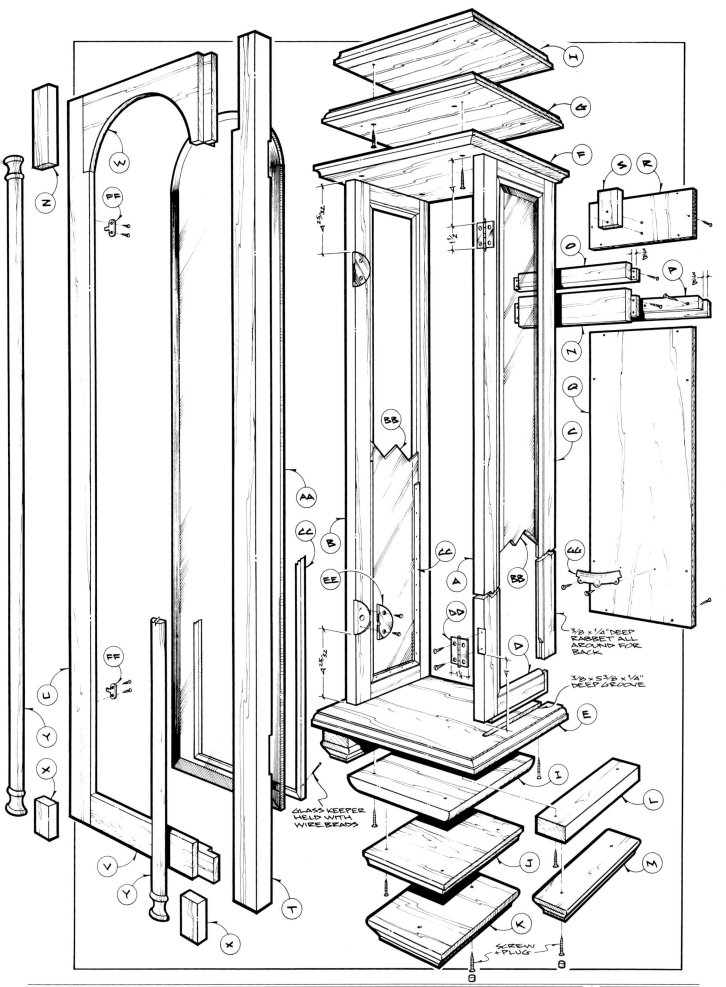

GLASS KEEPER
HELD WITH
WIRE BRADS

3/8 x 1/4" DEEP
RABBET ALL
AROUND FOR
BACK

3/8 x 5 3/8 x 1/4"
DEEP GROOVE

SCREW
+ PLUG

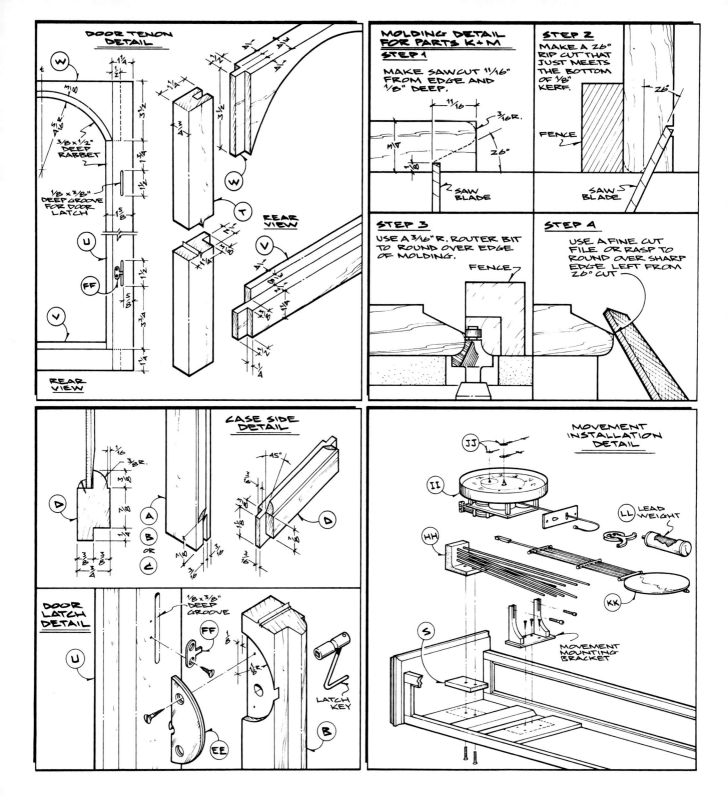

The 1/8 in. by 3/8 in. groove in part U to accept the door latch (see door latch detail) and the hinge mortises in part T are best cut before the stile blocks and split turnings are mounted.

The door and side panel glass (AA and BB) are secured with a plastic keeper strip (CC) that is included in the clock kit. You will need to pre-drill for the wire brads (also included) to avoid bending them or breaking the glass.

The clock movement (II) is mounted to the case back rail, and the chime assembly is mounted to the chime spacer (S), which has been screwed in place to the case back as shown. Further instructions on mounting and adjusting the movement are included in the kit.

Note: Final sanding of the clock case and door, and application of the finish should be accomplished before the glass is inserted and the movement mounted. Our clock was finished with several coats of a linseed oil/varnish mixture. Take care not to get finish on the area of the rabbets where the case back rail and case hanger will be glued in place. These parts, in addition to the upper and lower back and chime block, should be finished *after* they have been mounted. Touch-up finishing will probably be needed after the glass, door, and movement have been mounted. ●

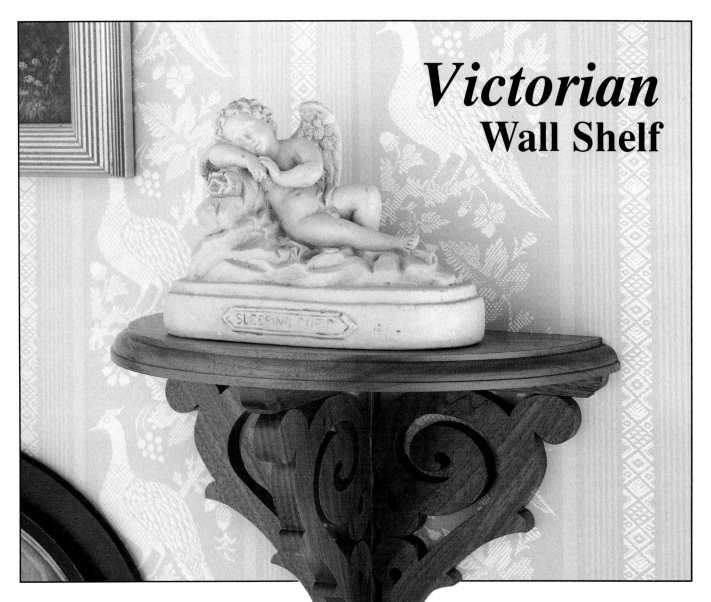

Victorian
Wall Shelf

Perhaps you've already imagined what you'd place on this little Victorian Wall Shelf. But if you haven't got a use in mind, no matter. The shelf makes a great gift, and only requires minimal stock. The scroll brackets look complex, but they are easily cut, either by hand with a coping saw or with a scroll saw. All three scroll brackets are identical, and they're simple to duplicate using the full-size pattern that's provided. We used walnut for our wall shelf.

This is a great one-board project. A single length of stock, $^3/_4$ in. thick by 7 in. wide by 42 in. long will yield all the parts. Note that while the top (A) is $^3/_4$ in. thick, the scroll brackets (B) and the cleats (C, D, E) are all $^5/_8$ in. thick. Cut a $13^1/_2$ in. length of board for the top, then reduce the remaining stock to $^5/_8$ in. thick. If you don't have a power jointer

or planer, a hand plane will quickly remove the extra $^1/_8$ in. of material.

Use a compass to lay out the $6^3/_4$ in. radius for the top, cut very carefully to the line with the band saw, and then use the router with a $^3/_8$ in. radius beading bit to establish the molded edge. Just be sure that your band saw cut is smooth before using the router. Any raggedness in the cut will be translated into unevenness in the molded edge.

Using a piece of carbon paper, trace our full-size scroll pattern directly onto

the bracket stock. But take note of the grain direction. The scrolls should be laid out so the grain runs as shown to give the brackets maximum strength. Also note that the scrolls have small flats where they contact the cleats. These flats provide some glue surface later on during assembly. You may find it easier to drill the various dowel holes in the brackets before cutting the scrolls.

Use as fine a blade as possible to cut the scroll brackets. A fine blade and careful cutting will mean less sanding or filing, which is difficult given the narrow open area within the scrolls. We used small flat and half-round files to smooth the interior curves.

The center cleat (C) joins the three scroll brackets, while the cross cleat (D) and back cleat (E) mount the scroll bracket assembly to the shelf. As shown in the exploded view, the cleats employ

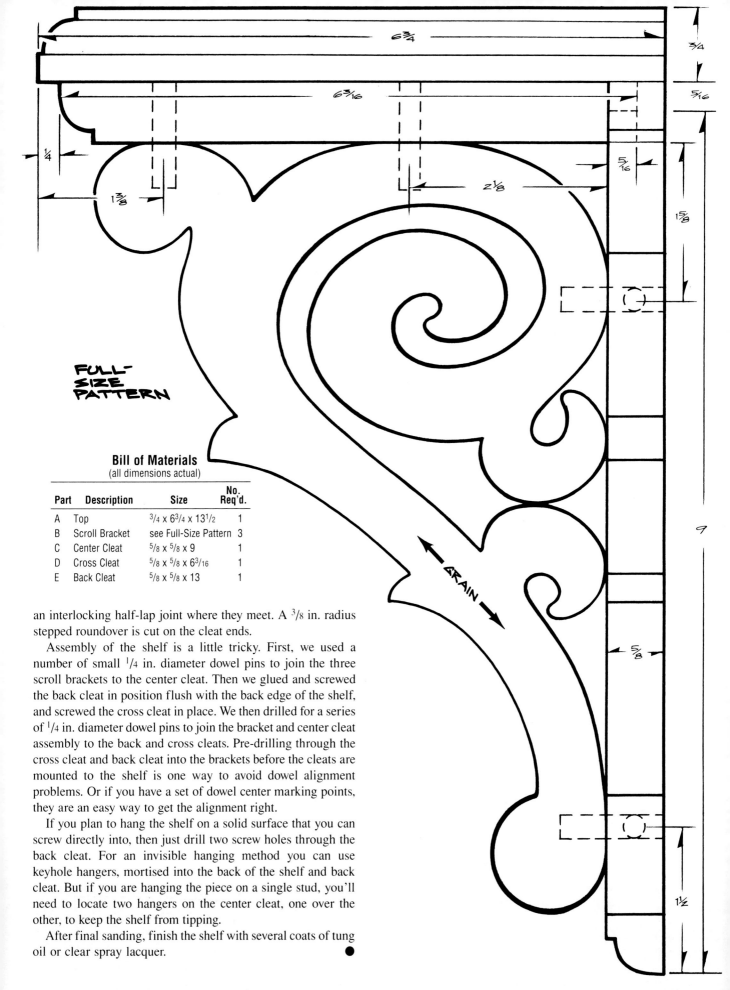

$6^3/4$

$3/4$

$5/16$

$6^3/16$

$5/16$

$1/4$

$2^1/8$

$1^5/8$

$1^3/8$

FULL-SIZE PATTERN

GRAIN

9

Bill of Materials
(all dimensions actual)

Part	Description	Size	No. Req'd.
A	Top	$3/4$ x $6^3/4$ x $13^1/2$	1
B	Scroll Bracket	see Full-Size Pattern	3
C	Center Cleat	$5/8$ x $5/8$ x 9	1
D	Cross Cleat	$5/8$ x $5/8$ x $6^3/16$	1
E	Back Cleat	$5/8$ x $5/8$ x 13	1

$5/8$

$1^1/2$

an interlocking half-lap joint where they meet. A $3/8$ in. radius stepped roundover is cut on the cleat ends.

Assembly of the shelf is a little tricky. First, we used a number of small $1/4$ in. diameter dowel pins to join the three scroll brackets to the center cleat. Then we glued and screwed the back cleat in position flush with the back edge of the shelf, and screwed the cross cleat in place. We then drilled for a series of $1/4$ in. diameter dowel pins to join the bracket and center cleat assembly to the back and cross cleats. Pre-drilling through the cross cleat and back cleat into the brackets before the cleats are mounted to the shelf is one way to avoid dowel alignment problems. Or if you have a set of dowel center marking points, they are an easy way to get the alignment right.

If you plan to hang the shelf on a solid surface that you can screw directly into, then just drill two screw holes through the back cleat. For an invisible hanging method you can use keyhole hangers, mortised into the back of the shelf and back cleat. But if you are hanging the piece on a single stud, you'll need to locate two hangers on the center cleat, one over the other, to keep the shelf from tipping.

After final sanding, finish the shelf with several coats of tung oil or clear spray lacquer. ●

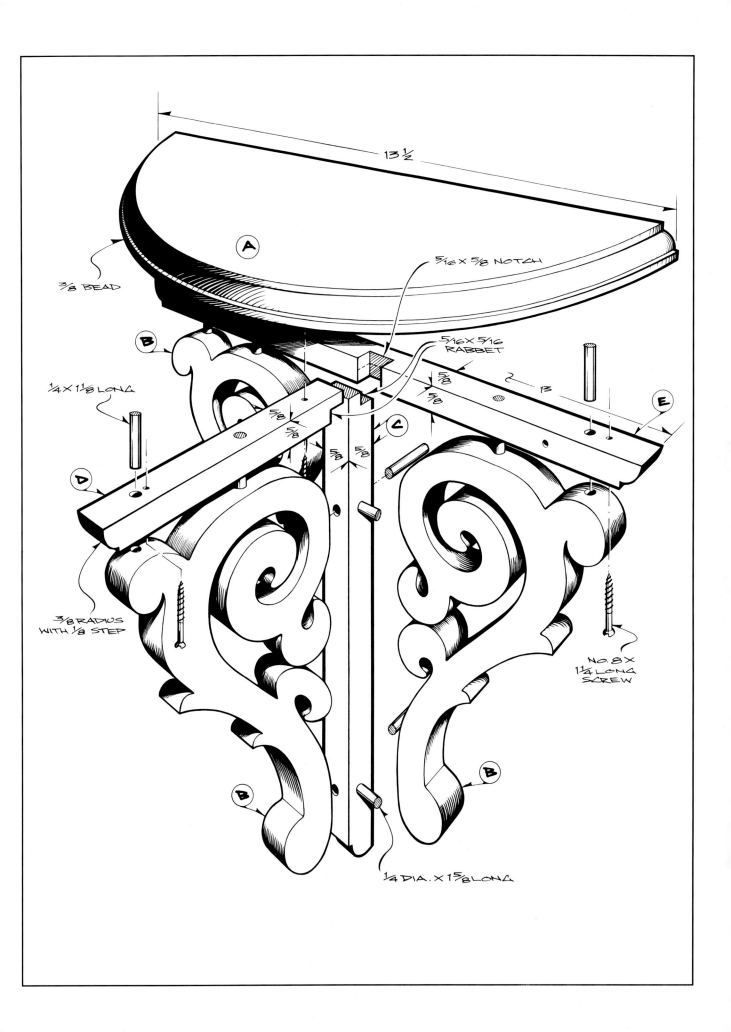

13½

A

5/16 × 5/8 NOTCH

3/8 BEAD

B

5/16 × 5/16
RABBET

¼ × 1⅛ LONG

5/8
5/8

13

E

D

5/8
5/8

5/8

5/8

C

3/8 RADIUS
WITH 1/8 STEP

B

B

NO. 8 ×
1¼ LONG
SCREW

B

¼ DIA. × 1⅝ LONG

Pennsylvania *Small Chest*

This small chest, by Massachusetts woodworker Paula Garbarino, is typical of the fine detail that woodworkers in the Pennsylvania area had achieved by the early 1700's. The combination of inlays, molded edges, and bun feet shows a strong William and Mary influence.

Walnut chests in this style were often used to hold books—such as the family bible—and valuable documents. Today it can be used as storage for just about anything, from a large jewelry collection to knitting. It could even make an elegant repository for reading matter in the living room.

With the exception of the line-and-berry and banding inlays (see the technique on page 118), the chest is rather simple to build. It's just a dovetailed, lidded box, nested in a molded frame and set on bun feet, with two shallow trays within. Our chest is walnut, though cherry or mahogany are other choices you may want to consider. By the way, if you like the chest, and would rather not fuss with all the inlay work, but still want some decoration, similar bandings are available from Constantine's, 2050 Eastchester Rd., Bronx, NY 10461; tel. 1-800-223-8087.

A good way to start is by edge-gluing stock for the wide parts—the chest front and back (A), ends (B) and lid (G). Once these parts are out of clamps, cut them to final length and width. Then refer to the Techniques article and do the inlays. The chest front has both a line-and-berry and banding, but the ends and back use the banding only.

Once the inlay work has been completed, use the table saw dado head to cut the $1/4$ in. deep by $1/4$ in. wide groove in the front, back and ends for the bottom (C), then lay out and cut the dovetails. If you haven't cut dovetails before, the techniques article on page 104 details an easy method for making hand-cut dovetails. The bottom panel is $1/4$ in. thick aromatic cedar. While you are at it, plane enough $1/4$ in. thick aromatic cedar to also yield the bottoms of the two interior trays. Test-fit the dovetails, then glue the chest front, back

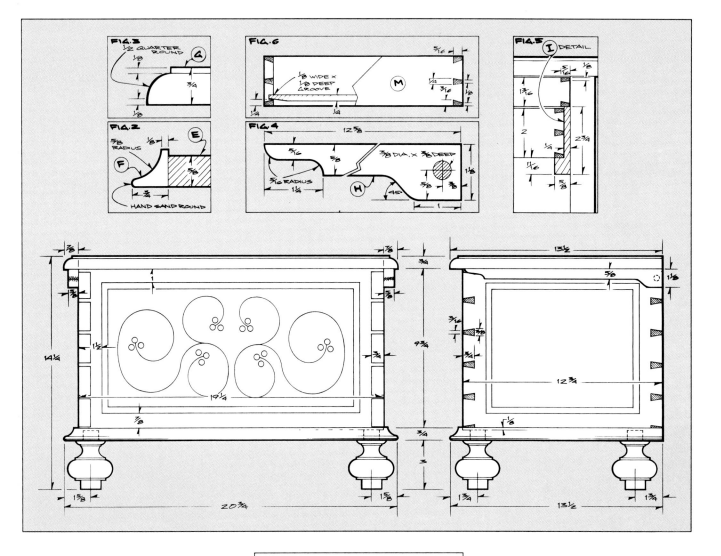

and ends up around the bottom. In practice, the bottom should be sized just a little under the groove-to-groove dimensions to allow for wood movement.

Next, make the frame. It's basically just two ends (D) and a front and back (E), mitered at the corners and joined with splines. The frame is 5/8 in. thick, which enables the chest to nest within the cavity that's created when the 3/4 in. square molding (F) is added. Naturally, the frame should be sized to fit the dimensions of your chest. The molding will cover the frame on the sides and front, but you should use walnut for the frame back, which is exposed. The 1/8 in. wide spline grooves are cut with the table saw, using a tenon jig to safely hold the stock. Be sure to cut the hardwood splines so the grain runs perpendicular to the joint (Fig. 1). Or you can use a biscuit jointer—should you have one—for the frame joinery.

The walnut molding is mitered and applied to the assembled frame as a 3/4 in. square strip, which makes the glue-up

Bill of Materials
(all dimensions actual)

Part	Description	Size	No. Req'd.
A	Front/Back	3/4 x 9 7/8 x 19 1/4	2
B	End	3/4 x 9 7/8 x 12 3/4	2
C	Bottom	1/4 x 11 3/4 x 18 1/4*	1
D	Frame End	5/8 x 2 1/2 x 12 3/4	2
E	Frame Front/Back	5/8 x 2 1/2 x 19 1/4	2
F	Molding	3/4 x 3/4 stock	4 ft.
G	Lid	3/4 x 13 1/2 x 21	1
H	Cleat	5/8 x 1 1/8 x 12 5/8	2
I	Tray Support	5/8 x 2 3/4 x 11 1/4	2
J	Upper Tray Front/Back	5/16 x 1 13/16 x 17 3/4	2
K	Upper Tray End	5/16 x 1 13/16 x 5 1/2	2
L	Upper Tray Bottom	1/4 x 5 1/8 x 17 3/8*	1
M	Lower Tray Front/Back	5/16 x 2 x 17 1/4	2
N	Lower Tray End	5/16 x 2 x 5 1/2	2
O	Lower Tray Bottom	1/4 x 5 1/8 x 16 7/8*	1
P	Foot	see full-size pattern	4

* Bottom panel widths should be sized a little less than actual groove-to-groove dimensions to allow for panel expansion.

easy. The router table with a 5/8 in. radius cove cutter is then used to mold the cove profile. Hand-sanding rounds the edge (Fig. 2). Once the frame and molding are complete, the frame is mounted to the chest with screws.

Now go to work on the lid. Use a 1/2 in. radius roundover bit to mold the front and ends of the lid (Fig. 3), then make the cleats (H). The cleat profile is shown in Fig. 4. Drill for the 3/8 in. diameter dowel pivot hinges, which fit in blind holes in the chest ends and on the inside face of the cleats. To mount the lid, first insert the pivot dowels, then add the cleats, and lastly screw the lid in place through the cleats. Note that the two frontmost holes in the cleats are slotted to allow for wood movement across the width of the lid. Test-fit the lid, but don't mount it permanently yet. That's not done until the chest is finished. Note that the top back edge of the chest is rounded to a 3/8 in. radius, which enables the lid to pivot smoothly without interference.

The two trays provide space for small

things inside the box. They rest on a pair of stepped supports (I), which are mounted with screws. To make the supports, notch some 5/8 in. thick by 2³/4 in. wide stock to give it an L-shape (Fig. 5). The upper tray (J, K, L) is 1/2 in. longer than the lower tray (M, N, O), but the lower tray is a little deeper. Suggested dovetail layouts for the trays are shown in Fig. 5. The tray sides and ends are constructed of 5/16 in. thick stock, a dimension that's yielded when 3/4 in. thick stock is resawed. You can resaw with the band saw or you can use a thin-kerf blade in the table saw. A good quality thin-kerf blade should produce a surface that needs minimal sanding.

The tray bottoms are cut from the same 1/4 in. thick aromatic cedar that you planed earlier. However, you'll need to bevel all four edges so the bottoms will fit within the 1/8 in. wide grooves in the trays (Fig. 6). The bevels are easily formed with a hand plane. The grooves are made with your 1/8 in. thick table saw blade, set for a 1/8 in. depth of cut.

All that remains are the bun feet (P). Actually, these are optional. If you intend the chest for a dresser top, you may want to dispense with the bun feet and just use four rubber feet to cushion the chest. If you opt for the turned feet, use our full-size pattern as a guide. Turned 1 in. diameter tenons on the upper ends of the feet fit within same-sized holes drilled in the frame.

Our chest sports a traditional French-polished lacquer finish. If you've never tried French polishing, a small chest like this makes an ideal practice project. We recommend Qualasole padding lacquer by Behlen. Called the modern French polish, Qualasole padding lacquer yields a French polish finish in about one-tenth the time required by traditional French polish methods. Qualasole is applied with cheesecloth, and both the finish and the cheesecloth can be ordered from Woodworker's Supply Co., 1108 North Glenn Road, Casper, WY 82601; tel. 1-800-645-9292.

Once your finishing work is complete, the lid can be mounted. The dowel hinge pins are glued into the chest, but the ends that fit into the cleats are waxed to reduce friction and wear. Make certain that the cleats pivot smoothly on the pins before you screw the lid in place. ●

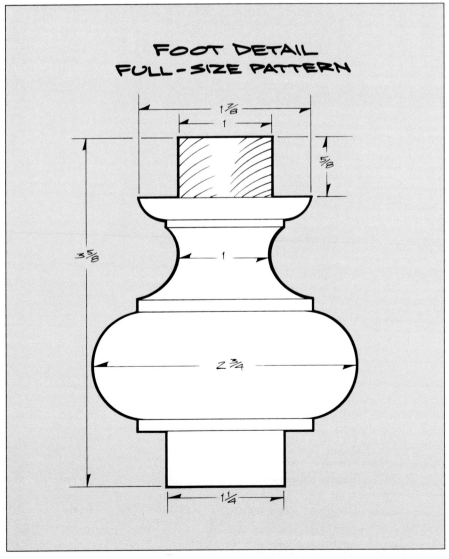

FOOT DETAIL
FULL-SIZE PATTERN

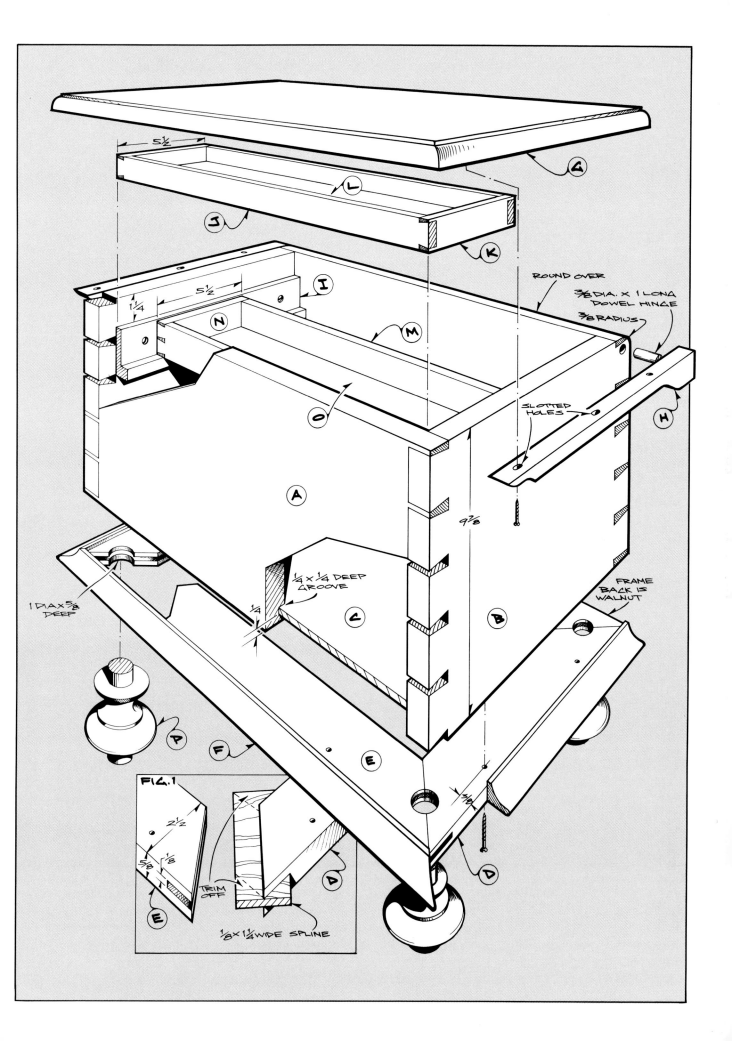

FIG. 1

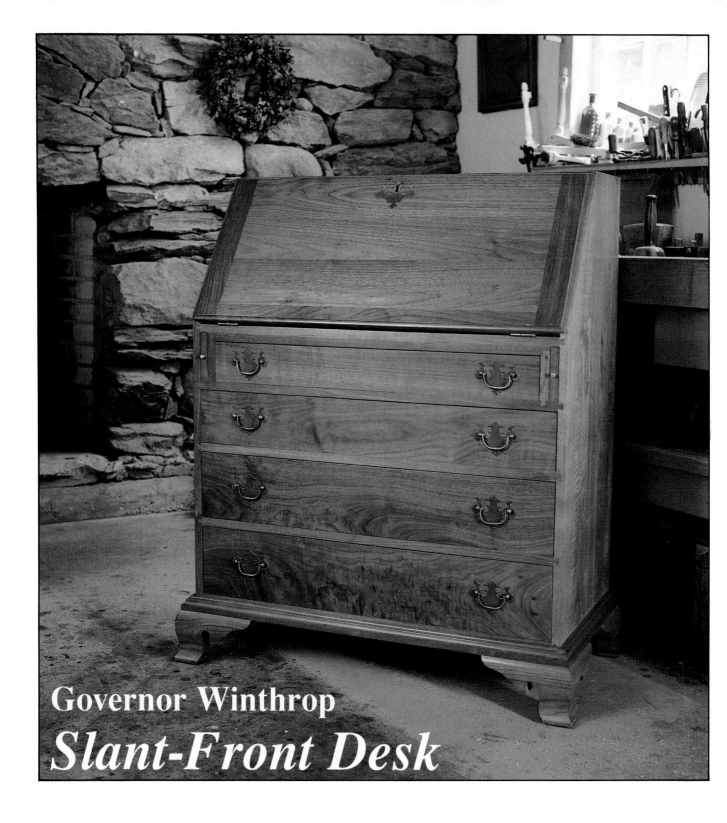

Governor Winthrop
Slant-Front Desk

his handsome desk is based on an original Wallace Nutting design from Berea College's Wallace Nutting collection. The collection has been housed at Berea College since 1945, when Nutting's widow bequeathed his furniture collection and blueprints to the school. The desk in the photo was built by the school's Woodcraft Furniture Division (see "Berea College: A Place To Learn and Earn").

For those of you who are wondering just who Wallace Nutting and Governor Winthrop were, here's a little background. The good Governor Winthrop, namesake of this desk, was one of the three famous 17th-century Governor Winthrops—father, son and grandson, all named John Winthrop. The first John Winthrop served as governor in the Massachusetts Bay Colony and the latter two served as governors of colonial Connecticut. We suspect, given the style of the desk, that the owner of the original was probably either the son (who served as Governor from 1657–1676) or the grandson (who served from 1698–1707).

Wallace Nutting was the famous eclectic pastor, collector, artist, and entrepreneur whose passion for Colonial furniture spawned much of the initial interest, early in the 20th century, in what was then a most neglected style. Traveling the New England countryside, searching through barns, attics and old homes, Nutting discovered many Colonial furniture treasures, and assembled a collection from which he built and marketed a line of reproductions. Although not an exact copy of the original (Nutting made a few changes to accommodate modern materials and techniques), this desk is faithful in size, proportion and detail to the original—right down to a very cleverly concealed secret drawer. As shown, the desk is crafted in walnut, though cherry or mahogany would also be good choices.

Can I Do It?

If you're like most woodworkers, there comes a time in your life when you step up from small or easy pieces to "serious" work. Perhaps this seminal moment was when you made your first cabinet door, hand-cutting mortises and tenons and discovering that the process really wasn't all that hard. Or perhaps the moment came when you first spent over $200 just for the wood to build a specific piece. Or maybe that moment came when you bought that long-sought, fully-adjustable dovetail jig, and savored the compliments as friends admired your dovetailed drawers that looked every bit like they'd been hand cut by the world's

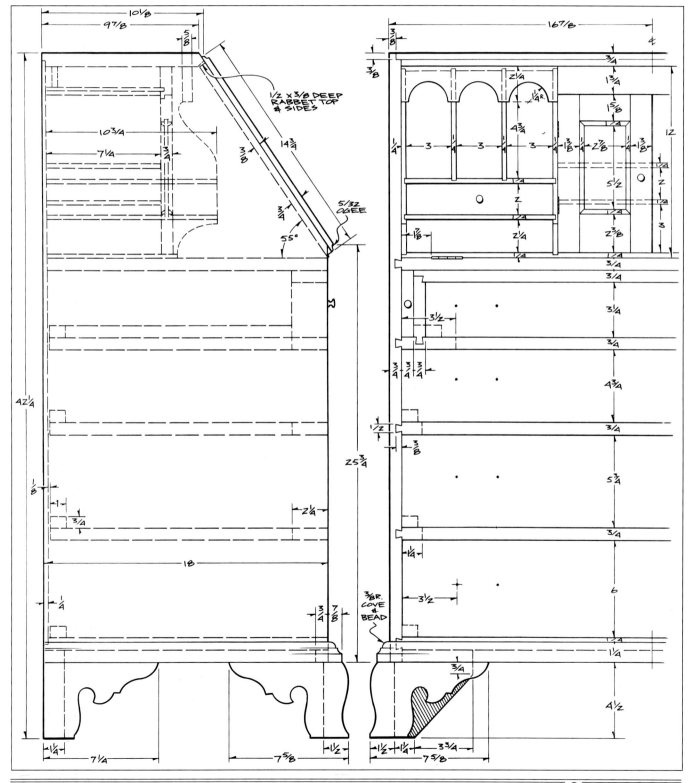

top craftsman.

We wouldn't suggest that you undertake this piece if you've never made a door or drawer, but if you've never made a piece this large, don't be scared off. Its important pedigree notwithstanding, the desk is basically just a box, with some drawers, a pigeonhole section, a slant front and bracket feet. If your shop is equipped with the basics—table saw, band saw, jointer, planer, router and a good selection of clamps—then you should have no problem making the desk.

What You'll Need

Whatever your choice of stock for the desk, take care with your board selection. Try to avoid any boards that would seem out of place (such as walnut with sapwood), especially for the front-facing surfaces such as the drawer fronts and slant front. Also, make certain that the stock you are using has been kiln-dried to a moisture content of no more than 6 to 7 percent. Although most of the stock is standard $^3/_4$ in. thick material, there are a number of other stock size requirements. If you don't own a thickness planer, you can usually find a local millwork shop that will plane your stock to size for a reasonable fee.

In addition to your hardwood, you'll need $^1/_4$ in. plywood for the back and drawer bottoms, and of course, the hardware. To simplify finding all the hardware, we've asked Aspen Kits (see Hardware Package) to put a kit together that includes all the hardware that you'll need. Although there are many sources for similar Chippendale-style brass pulls, the pulls shown in the photo are just about the finest we've ever seen, with exquisite detail. You could probably find brass-plated hardware that will save a few dollars over our solid brass hardware, but with a piece of this stature, it's pennywise and pound foolish to demean the finished product with less than top-shelf brasses. All the hardware in the Hardware Package is the exact same hardware as that used on the desk in the photo.

Let's Get to Work

As with any large case piece, the first order of business should be getting out stock, arranging boards so their grain matches as closely as possible, and

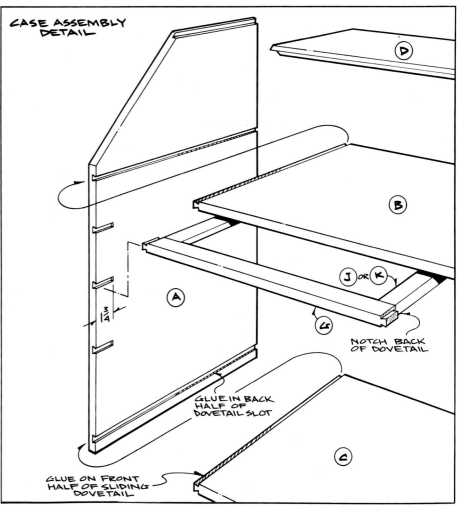

CASE ASSEMBLY DETAIL

GLUE ON FRONT HALF OF SLIDING DOVETAIL

GLUE IN BACK HALF OF DOVETAIL SLOT

NOTCH BACK OF DOVETAIL

jointing and edge gluing to make panels for the widest parts. For the desk, you'll likely need to edge-glue stock to yield the sides (A), desk surface (B), bottom (C), and slant front (E). Depending on what you have available, you may also need to edge-glue stock to yield the case top (D) and the pigeonhole tops (BB), bottom (CC), sides (DD), shelves (EE), (GG), and dividers (FF). All the $^1/_4$ in. pigeonhole stock can be resawed from thicker material. If you are resawing $^3/_4$ in. stock, that thickness should yield two $^1/_4$ in. thicknesses, taking into account a generous allowance for final thicknessing to the $^1/_4$ in. dimension.

Several of the parts are thicker than $^3/_4$ in. Although you could laminate several boards to yield the required thicknesses, it's better to just obtain the parts from thicker rough stock. Buy $^5/_4$ stock for the base moldings (R, S) and $^8/_4$ stock for the feet (T, U) and foot supports (V).

The easiest and the most logical way to build a piece like the desk is to divide the construction into a series of separate assemblies. In both our written instructions and in the Bill of Materials, we've

divided the desk into its component parts—the case, the case drawers, the pigeonhole section, and the pigeonhole doors and drawers. By tackling things one-at-a-time, you'll find that the desk isn't really all that complicated, after all.

The Case: Can You Make A Big Box?

As shown in the Case Assembly Detail, the case is basically just a big box. The main parts of the basic box are the two sides (A), the desk surface (B), the bottom (C), and the top (D). After cutting the above parts to length and width, set to work cutting the rabbets on the ends of the sides and top, and the various dovetail slots in the sides. These cuts are best made before you cut back the two topmost corners of the sides, establishing the slope of the slant front when the desk is in the closed position.

Cut the Dovetail Slots: There are a pair of through dovetail slots in each side, for the desk surface and bottom respectively, and three stopped dovetail slots in each side, to fit the dovetails cut on the ends of the drawer rails (G). As also shown in the Case Assembly Detail, these stopped dovetails are 1³/₄ in. long, or ¹/₂ in. shorter than the width of the drawer rails. Because the drawer rails and runners (J, K) are joined with a ¹/₂ in. long tenon, the dovetails on the drawer rail ends are notched back that same ¹/₂ in. A ¹/₂ in. dovetail bit set for a ³/₈ in. deep cut is used for all these dovetails.

Make The Slant Front Slope: Once the rabbets and dovetails are cut, you can cut back the corners of the sides to the 55-degree angle shown in the side elevation (note that the cut starts 25³/₄ in. from the bottom end of the sides). Also, cut back the front edge of the top at a matching 55-degree angle, and rip the bottom edge of the top to establish the right angle surface into which the rabbet on the slant front will fit.

Cut Sliding Dovetails: With the sides and top all cut, next you'll need to establish the sliding dovetails on the ends of the desk surface and bottom. Since these two parts will be a sliding fit into the dovetails in the sides, it's important that you don't make the fit overly tight. The best approach is to first cut the dovetails a little tight, and then make a light trimming cut until the desk surface and bottom dovetails can slide effortlessly into their mating dovetail slots. Don't forget to make certain that the desk surface is ¹/₄ in. less in width than the sides and bottom; this ¹/₄ in. allows the case back (W) to fit in place. You can cut and fit the sliding dovetails on the ends of the drawer rails now, but don't worry about assembling the drawer frames just yet.

Case Assembly Secrets: You are now ready to assemble the case. There's a simple secret (see Case Assembly Detail) to getting the long sliding dovetails that join the sides, desk surface and bottom to go together without a panic. (When we say panic, just remember how you felt the last time a long sliding dovetail that you were assembling seized up before the dovetail had been fully seated!) The secret to an assembly like this is apply glue *only to the back* ¹/₂ of the dovetail slot length and *only to the front* ¹/₂ of the corresponding sliding dovetail. By using this system you are able to slide the parts half-way together before you begin to encounter any resistance from glue. Work quickly, and

don't let any time pass between applying the glue and starting the assembly. The moisture in the glue will quickly swell the wood, and even a sliding dovetail that fit together effortlessly when dry may be impossible to assemble.

Assemble the sides and bottom first, then add the desk surface, and glue, counterbore, screw and plug the top in place. Face-grain plugs matched carefully to the grain of the top will help to make this joint all but invisible. If you are a stickler for authenticity, then use half-blind dovetails to join the top and sides.

Check Case for Squareness: Before the glue on the case assembly sets, you'll want to check the assembly for squareness, and make adjustments if needed.

Measure across the diagonals on the case back (from corner to corner). If the measurements aren't exactly equal, use a bar clamp and some blocks (so you don't mar the wood) to apply some pressure across the longer diagonal. Check the diagonals again and fine-tune the clamp pressure until the measurements are equal.

Cut Back Rabbet: Once the case assembly is dry, you can cut the rabbet in the sides, top and bottom for the plywood back. You can use a ball-bearing guided ³/₈ in. rabbeting bit, set for a ¹/₄ in. deep cut for most of the work. However, where the desk surface

interferes, you'll need to switch to a straight cutter and use the edge guide to guide the router. You can cut and fit the back, but don't mount it at this time. The back won't be mounted until after all the remaining work on the desk has been completed.

Make and Mount the Drawer Frames

Make three drawer frames, each consisting of one drawer rail and a pair of runners. The bottom two drawer frames are identical, but the topmost drawer frame has wider runners (K), to accommodate the connector (I) and guide (L), and to serve as runners for both the slides (N, O) and the narrow top drawer. Note that a stub tenon (¹/₄ in. by ¹/₂ in.

long) is used to join the runners to the rails on all three drawer frames, and that the back ends of the runners are drilled with slotted holes. These holes are for screwing the back end of the runners to the case sides, and the fact that they are slotted permits some seasonal wood movement in the sides. If the runners were permanently fastened to the case sides across the full width of the sides, there's a danger of the sides splitting should some shrinkage occur across the grain of such a wide piece.

The full dovetail on the bottom end of the connectors, and its mating dovetail rail slot are both 1³/₄ in. long—the same

Bill of Materials
(all dimensions actual)

Part	Description	Size	No. Req'd.
Case			
A	Side	3/4 x 18 x 37 3/4	2
B	Desk Surface	3/4 x 17 3/4 x 33 *	1
C	Bottom	3/4 x 18 x 33 *	1
D	Top	3/4 x 10 1/8 x 33	1
E	Slant Front	3/4 x 14 3/4 x 30 1/4 *	1
F	Slant Front End	3/4 x 2 3/8 x 14 3/4	2
G	Drawer Rail	3/4 x 2 1/4 x 33	3
H	Top Rail	3/4 x 2 1/4 x 30 3/4	1
I	Connector	3/4 x 2 1/4 x 4	2
J	Runner	3/4 x 1 1/4 x 15 7/8 *	4
K	Top Runner	3/4 x 3 1/2 x 15 7/8 *	2
L	Guide	3/4 x 3/4 x 15 3/8	2
M	Drawer Stop	3/4 x 1 x 1	8
N	Slide	3/4 x 4 x 16 1/4 *	2
O	Slide End	3/4 x 2 1/4 x 4	2
P	Slide Stop	1/2 x 3/4 x 2 1/2	2
Q	Filler	3/4 x 3/4 x 32 1/4	1
R	Base Front Molding	7/8 x 1 1/4 x 35 1/2	1
S	Base Side Molding	7/8 x 1 1/4 x 18 7/8	2
T	Front Foot	1 1/2 x 4 1/2 x 7 5/8	4
U	Back Foot	1 1/2 x 4 1/2 x 7 1/4	2
V	Back Foot Support	1 1/4 x 5 1/4 x 5	2
W	Back	1/4 x 33 x 36 1/4	1
Case Drawers			
(No's Req'd are per drawer)			
X	Front	See Chart	1
Y	Side	See Chart	2
Z	Back	See Chart	1
AA	Bottom	See Chart	1
Pigeonhole Section			
BB	Top	1/4 x 8 3/4 x 10	2
CC	Bottom	1/4 x 8 1/4 x 32 1/4	1
DD	Side	1/4 x 10 3/4 x 11 3/4	4
EE	Shelf	1/4 x 10 3/4 x 9 3/4	4
FF	Divider	1/4 x 10 3/4 x 7	4
GG	Center Shelf	1/4 x 7 1/4 x 12 1/2	2
HH	Front	5/8 x 2 1/4 x 10	2
II	Drawer Runner	1/8 x 1/2 x 6 1/2	2
Doors			
JJ	Stile	3/4 x 1 3/8 x 10	4
KK	Top Rail	3/4 x 1 5/8 x 3 7/8 *	2
LL	Bottom Rail	3/4 x 2 3/8 x 3 7/8 *	2
MM	Panel	1/4 x 3 3/4 x 6 1/2 **	2
NN	Trim Molding	1/4 x 1/4 about 8 ft.	
Pigeonhole Drawer			
OO	Front	3/4 x 2 x 9 1/2	2
PP	Side	3/8 x 2 x 10 1/2	4
QQ	Back	3/8 x 1 1/2 x 9 1/8	2
RR	Bottom	1/4 x 9 1/8 x 9 13/16	2
Secret Drawer			
SS	Front	3/4 x 1 15/16 x 12 1/4	1
TT	Side	3/8 x 1 3/4 x 7 3/4	2
UU	Back	3/8 x 1 1/4 x 11 7/8	1
VV	Bottom	1/4 x 7 1/16 x 11 7/8	1
Hardware*			
WW	Chippendale Pull	3 3/4 x 2 3/4	8
XX	Escutcheon	3 3/4 x 2 3/4	1
YY	Lock	1 3/4 x 2 1/2	1
ZZ	Knob	3/8 dia.	6
AAA	Slant Front Hinge	2 x 3	2
BBB	Butt Hinge	1 x 1	2
CCC	Bullet Catch	5/16 dia. x 3/8 long	2

 * Length includes tongue(s) or tenon(s).
 ** Panel width allows 1/8 in. for wood movement.

***Hardware Package

This hardware is of the very highest quality, with the Chippendale pulls, matching escutcheon, lock, knobs, and hinges all being solid brass. For current prices, write or call: Aspen Kits, 6 Hilltop Drive, Old Saybrook, CT 06475; tel. (203) 388-6179. Specify either antique or bright brass finish for pulls.

as on the rail ends and case—so as to not interfere with the stub tenon joining the rails and runners. Also at this time, make the top rail (H), and cut the interlocking half-dovetail on its ends and on the top ends of the connectors. Take care to test fit all these parts within the case.

If everything fits as intended, assemble the drawer frames and mount them in the case. The two bottom drawer frame assemblies will consist of just the drawer rails and runners. But the top drawer frame will include not only the drawer rail and the two runners, but also the connectors, top rail and guides. Use a framing square to make certain that the runners and rails meet at a perfect right angle. A small machinist's square is a handy way to make certain that the connectors are at a true right angle to the two rails that they connect. Once the drawer frame assemblies are out of clamps, apply glue and slide the rail dovetails into their mating stopped dovetails in the case sides. Measure carefully at the case back to insure that spacing between the drawer frames is the same at both the front and back, then screw through the slotted holes to secure the backs of the frames.

Slant Front and Sliding Supports
The slant front writing surface consists of the slant front (E) and the slant front ends (F), with a 1/4 in. by 1 in. long tenon on the slant front and a matching groove in the slant front ends joining these parts.. A 5/32 in. ogee router bit and a 1/2 in. by 3/8 in. rabbeting bit are used to mold the ogee profile and the rabbet around the top edge and ends of the writing surface, respectively. Mortise for and mount the slant front hinges (AAA) and lock (YY), and mortise for and mount the lock catch plate on the case top.

The sliding supports consist of the slides (N) and the slide ends (O). The grain direction of the slide ends is top-to-bottom, and a 1/4 in. by 3/4 in. long tenon and matching groove joins the slides and slide ends. Make and mount the slide stops (P), which prevent the supports from being pulled all the way out.

The sliding supports don't butt against a stop when in the closed position. Instead, they butt right against the case back. In theory, one might think that given the width of the case sides, and the possibility for wood movement, the slides might be sticking out 1/4 in. proud of the case front in winter, and be inset 1/4 in. during a humid summer. Theory, however, takes a back seat here to experience. Once your case is finished, and given the fact that you've taken special care to select only the best kiln-dried material, expansion and contraction should really be negligible. The best way to size the sliding supports is to cut them a little long for starters, and then make a final trimming cut at the back end just before mounting the case back. If some further adjustment is needed after several years of use, the supports can be easily removed by unscrewing the slide stops. Incidentally, for this same reason, when you mount the case drawers, it's a good idea to screw—but not glue—the drawer stops in place. This way, there's the opportunity for fine adjustment of the stops at some later date, just by unscrewing and removing the case back.

Make the Base
The base consists of the filler (Q), front and side moldings (R, S), front and back feet (T, U) and the back foot supports (V). The filler is just a 3/4 in. by 3/4 in. strip, glued in place between the sides and filling the space at the desk bottom. The moldings are easily profiled with a cove-and-bead or classical router bit.

The front and back feet will be the greatest challenge, but here too, we've worked out a simple system.

Start with a length of stock $1^1/2$ in. thick by $4^1/2$ in. wide by at least 4 ft. long. The traditional process to make a bracket foot, such as that on our desk, was to use a combination of hollow and round molding planes. The round sole planes established the concave portion of the molded foot, the hollow planes rounded the convex shape. The craftsman used a simple wooden template to check his profiles as the work progressed. Experienced craftsmen typically developed a "book" of such templates for their most commonly used shapes and molding profiles.

Traditional hollow and round molding planes are still quite common, and can be purchased for about $15 to $30. If you are lucky, you may even find a complete set of both hollows and rounds by the same manufacturer. However, a more modern approach to making bracket feet uses the table saw for most of the work.

In a perfect world, every 10 in. table saw blade measures exactly 10 in. in diameter, and detailing a setup for making a cove cut on the table saw requires that we simply provide a blade height and a fence angle setting for you

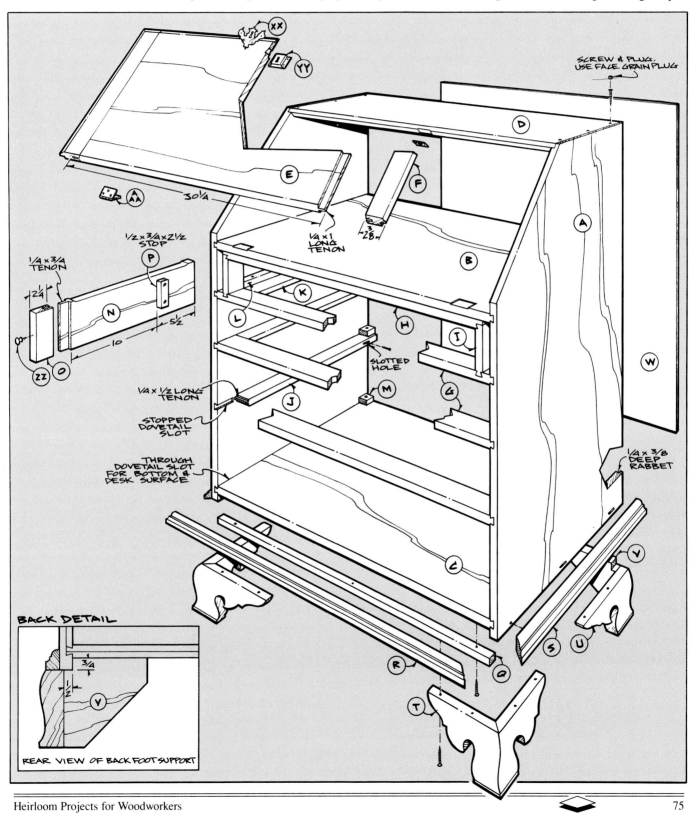

to duplicate on your saw. However, the problem with calling out a specific fence angle setting is that the angle will produce the desired cove only if your blade is an exact 10 in. diameter. If you have a 9 in. table saw, or if your 10 in. carbide blade has been resharpened several times and now measures 9³/₄ in., then the cove that you get with your blade won't be the same as the cove we achieved in our shop using a specific fence angle and our 10 in. blade.

A better method is to use a shop-built parallel arm jig to set the fence angle. The jig, as shown in Fig. 1, is easy to make. It's just a pair of parallel arms joined with a pair of connectors. We've used T-nuts in the arms and wing nuts for quick adjustment and ease of use, but whatever hardware you use to make this jig, keep in mind that the most important point is to have the holes in the arms and connectors drilled both on-center and identical distances apart. The holes in our 18 in. long arms are exactly 12¹/₄ in. apart, while the holes in the 10 in. long connectors are exactly 8³/₄ in. apart. This size parallel arm jig can be used to set up most coving operations with a table saw.

To use the jig is simplicity itself. As shown in Fig. 2, just set the jig so the parallel arms are a distance apart that's equal to the desired cove width (2³/₁₆ in. apart for our bracket foot cove), raise the table saw blade to the desired cove depth (³/₈ in. for our foot), and position the jig at an angle so the blade touches both of the parallel arms. Using a protractor, an angle finder, or whatever other tools you use to determine angles, now measure the angle of the jig to the blade. Remove the jig, set up a fence at the specific angle, locating it ¹/₄ in. from the blade (when the blade is raised to the full ³/₈ in. height) as shown in Fig. 3, and cut the cove in your 4 ft. length of foot stock. Just don't attempt to make the cove in a single pass. The usual procedure is to start with the blade raised about ¹/₈ in. and then raise the blade incrementally (about ¹/₁₆ in. to ¹/₈ in. at a time) until the full ³/₈ in. cove depth is achieved.

Once the cove is established, the roundover is made next. Our bracket foot's roundover is roughly a 2 in. radius. The simplest way to make this radius (if you don't have a hollow molding plane) is to use a jointing plane to gradually shape the radius. Make a

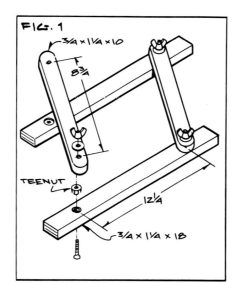

FIG. 1

3/4 × 1¹/4 × 10

8³/4

TEENUT

12¹/4

3/4 × 1¹/4 × 18

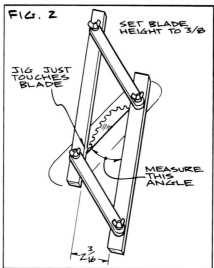

FIG. 2

SET BLADE HEIGHT TO 3/8

JIG JUST TOUCHES BLADE

MEASURE THIS ANGLE

2 3/16

FIG. 3

CUT COVE INTO 4 FT. LENGTH. MAKE CUT IN SEVERAL PASSES

1/4

SET UP FENCE AT SPECIFIC ANGLE

template from wood or stiff cardboard to gauge your progress. Once the radius is nearly complete, use sandpaper to final shape it and remove any of the lines left from the plane.

With the molded profile established, crosscut the board into the lengths required for the individual feet. Miter the

ends of the front feet, then transfer the foot shape (see full-size pattern) to the flat back surface of the feet, and cut out with a band saw or a hand-held jigsaw. Final sand the shape, then glue the front feet together at the miters.

Mount the Molding and Feet: The front molding is a good long grain-to-long grain glue joint, but the side molding is glued only at the miters and near the front of the case sides. The remaining molding length is fastened with screws inserted through slotted holes in the case sides, as shown in the exploded view.

The feet are glued and screwed to the molding and the bottom of the case. Note that the 1¹/₄ in. thick back foot support has a step cut into the top edge, to fit around the case sides and flush to the case bottom (see Back Detail).

The Case Drawers

Because of the explanation required with the rest of this piece, we won't go into great detail on the drawers. For a piece such as this, hand-cut dovetails—or machine cut dovetails made with a jig that allows for random spacing to yield a hand-cut look—are the best choice. Use half-blind dovetails to join the drawer fronts (X) with the sides (Y), and through dovetails to join the backs (Z) to the sides. The piece shown in the photo uses ¹/₄ in. plywood for the drawer bottoms (AA), though if you are a stickler for authenticity, bevel-edged drawer bottoms in solid stock could easily be substituted.

Our Case Drawer Chart shows the dimensions for the drawers, however, as with any case piece, you should make your drawers based on the actual dimensions from your case. The drawer depth should be sized to allow for the drawer stops (M). The best way to make the stops is to first make all the drawers, then cut and locate the stops so the drawers close flush with the case front.

The Pigeonhole Section

The pigeonhole section is cut, assembled and mounted in the case before the case back is added. The pigeonhole construction is basically just a box, with shelves, dividers, drawers and doors. The primary parts—the tops (BB), bottom (CC), sides (DD), shelves (EE, GG), and dividers (FF) are all ¹/₄ in. thick stock.

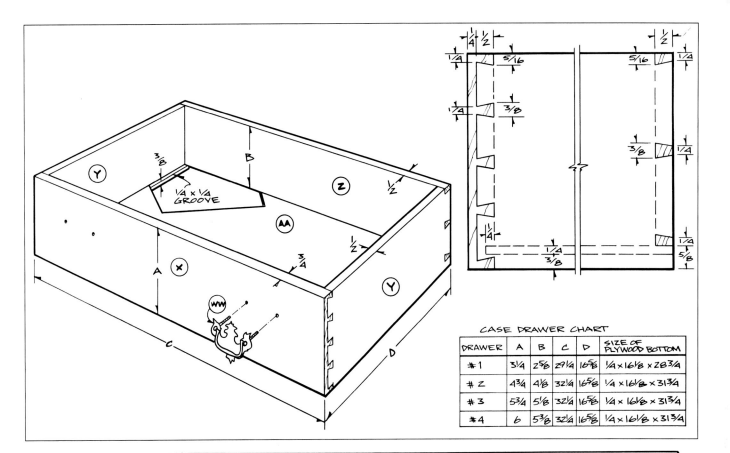

CASE DRAWER CHART

DRAWER	A	B	C	D	SIZE OF PLYWOOD BOTTOM
#1	3¼	2⅝	29¼	16⅝	¼ × 16⅛ × 28¾
#2	4¾	4⅛	32¼	16⅝	¼ × 16⅛ × 31¾
#3	5¾	5⅛	32¼	16⅝	¼ × 16⅛ × 31¾
#4	6	5⅜	32¼	16⅝	¼ × 16⅛ × 31¾

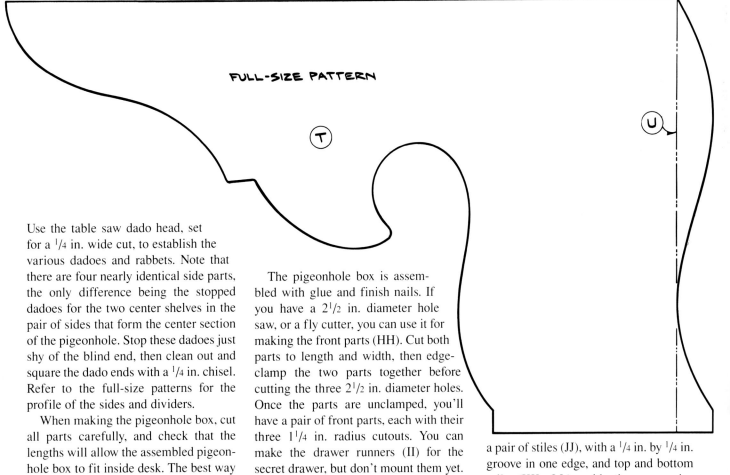

FULL-SIZE PATTERN

Use the table saw dado head, set for a ¹/₄ in. wide cut, to establish the various dadoes and rabbets. Note that there are four nearly identical side parts, the only difference being the stopped dadoes for the two center shelves in the pair of sides that form the center section of the pigeonhole. Stop these dadoes just shy of the blind end, then clean out and square the dado ends with a ¹/₄ in. chisel. Refer to the full-size patterns for the profile of the sides and dividers.

When making the pigeonhole box, cut all parts carefully, and check that the lengths will allow the assembled pigeonhole box to fit inside desk. The best way to avoid a problem is to dry assemble the box as you make it, checking regularly for the fit inside the desk.

The pigeonhole box is assembled with glue and finish nails. If you have a 2¹/₂ in. diameter hole saw, or a fly cutter, you can use it for making the front parts (HH). Cut both parts to length and width, then edge-clamp the two parts together before cutting the three 2¹/₂ in. diameter holes. Once the parts are unclamped, you'll have a pair of front parts, each with their three 1¹/₄ in. radius cutouts. You can make the drawer runners (II) for the secret drawer, but don't mount them yet.

The Pigeonhole Doors

The two pigeonhole doors are each just

a pair of stiles (JJ), with a ¹/₄ in. by ¹/₄ in. groove in one edge, and top and bottom rails (KK, LL), with the same size groove on one edge and tenons to fit the stile grooves. The panels (MM) on the

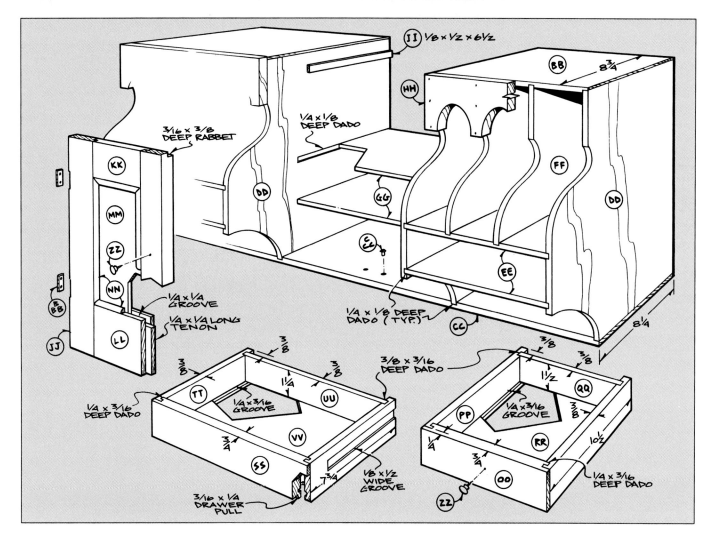

desk shown are bookmatched sections of crotch walnut. A $\frac{1}{4}$ in. by $\frac{1}{4}$ in. quarter-round molding (NN) trims out the panels. Note that this molding is glued to the door frames only, and not to the panels.

As shown on the exploded view of the pigeonhole section, a $\frac{3}{16}$ in. by $\frac{3}{8}$ in. deep rabbet is cut into the top back edge of the two doors. Don't neglect to include this rabbet; it interlocks the bottom lip on the secret drawer, making it impossible to open the drawer with the doors in the closed position. You'll need to mount the doors, though, before you mount the pigeonhole unit in the case—the hinges (BBB) must be screwed in place from the back of the pigeonhole. Also note that the hinges are mortised into the doors only, and not into the pigeonhole sides. Make the hinge mortises in the doors deep enough to accommodate the hinges in the folded (closed) position. Before final mounting the doors, you'll also need to drill for and mount the bullet catches (CCC). Since the holes for the bullet catches are

$\frac{3}{8}$ in. deep, they extend through the pigeonhole bottom and into the desk surface. You'll need to first drill through the pigeonhole bottom, then slide the pigeonhole unit into place, and mark through the holes and onto the desk surface before completing the holes.

Pigeonhole Drawers

We show a rabbeted construction on both the pair of pigeonhole drawers and the secret drawer. Make your drawers to fit the pigeonhole unit, using $\frac{3}{4}$ in. thick stock for the fronts (OO, SS), $\frac{3}{8}$ in. stock for the sides (PP, TT) and backs (QQ, UU) and $\frac{1}{4}$ in. plywood for the bottoms (RR, VV). The only real difference between the drawers is their size and the fact that the secret drawer includes a $\frac{3}{16}$ in. by $\frac{1}{4}$ in. lip on the bottom edge of the front, and $\frac{1}{8}$ in. deep by $\frac{1}{2}$ in. wide stopped grooves in the sides to accept the drawer runners (II). Note that the lip on the bottom edge of the front of the secret drawer doesn't run the full length of the drawer, but must be notched back on either end. The pigeon-

hole section is constructed so the secret drawer can only be removed when both doors are fully opened. The notched lip on the drawer front fits between the rabbets of the opened doors as the drawer is slid out. This is difficult to describe, but should be clear from the detail photo on page 79, which shows the secret drawer being opened.

The $\frac{1}{8}$ in. by $\frac{1}{2}$ in. wide stopped groove in the sides of the secret drawer is best cut with a $\frac{1}{2}$ in. diameter router bit, using the router table set up with a stop to limit the groove length to $6\frac{1}{2}$ in. Our illustration shows the groove and the runners as square-ended, so you'll need to use a chisel to square the groove ends. Back when the first Governor Winthrop Desk was made, routers weren't available (electricity had yet to be discovered). However, given our router-cut groove, an easier way is to just round the runner ends to match the radius at the groove ends. A pair of knobs (ZZ) completes the two pigeonhole drawers; the secret drawer, in keeping with its station, eschews the knob accoutrement. Instead, to open the secret drawer, one reaches under the drawer with both doors open, and the lip serves as a convenient finger pull.

Finishing Up

Needless to say, all the fine tuning and fitting of the drawers and doors for the pigeonhole section should be completed before the section is slid into the desk. When it finally comes time to mount the pigeonhole section, don't try to slide it into place from the desk front. That's a sure way to scratch the desk writing

The secret drawer lip rides in rabbets on the top of the doors.

surface. The pigeonhole section is slid into place from the back, before the plywood case back is screwed in place. Use a screw or two to fasten the pigeonhole section securely, so it won't move; no glue is needed here. And while we're on the matter of glue, don't use any on the case back either. There's always the possibility that at some future time you may need to remove the back to make some repair or adjustment.

For convenience sake, it's a good idea to finish the pigeonhole section, and its doors and drawers, before the unit is mounted in the desk. You could finish the desk with the pigeonhole section already in place, but it's a lot easier to get into corners, nooks and cubbies when there's easy access from all sides. Take care to set all finish nails, and fill the nail

holes on visible surfaces, such as the nails holding the front pieces, before applying the finish.

As for the final finish, you could really take your pick of several finishes, including penetrating oil, shellac and polyurethane. However, by far and away the best choice—and the finish used on the desk shown—is lacquer. A century or two ago, craftsmen used shellac in much the same way that lacquer is used today, but lacquer has several distinct advantages over shellac. It's durable, attractive, easy to maintain, and unlike shellac, it won't show a white ring from a moist glass that's left on the desk surface without benefit of a coaster. A spray finishing outfit is the best way to apply a lacquer finish, but if you don't have one, you can use brushing lacquer instead. Aerosol spray cans are another option, though on a project of this size your finishing budget will quickly be in the red if you're buying your finish in little aerosol cans.

The Chippendale pulls (WW), matching escutcheon (XX), and knobs (ZZ) should only be mounted after the desk has been finished. If you've pre-drilled for and already mounted some of the hardware, be sure to remove it before applying the finish. The hardware has it's own patina, and a layer of finish doesn't improve the look. ●

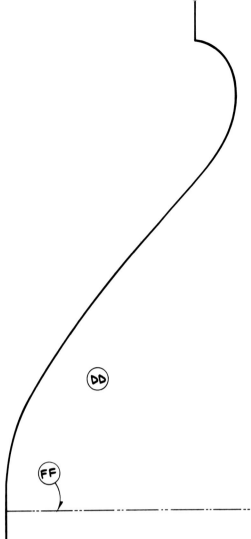

FULL-SIZE PATTERN

Federal Period Washstand

T his handsome washstand is part of the collection of the Washington Historical Museum in Washington, Connecticut. It is built of mahogany and features finely turned legs, and a small drawer with lion's head brass pulls. The museum original is very delicate, yet strongly constructed, and when we picked it up we were surprised by its extraordinarily light weight.

A good place to start this project is with the turned legs (A). Your turning stock should be about 2 in. longer than the $31^1/_2$ in. leg length to allow for mounting in the lathe. Refer to the turning detail for the turning layout.

Next, cut all the remaining wood parts, B through R. In the museum original, part G is a domestic hardwood while the apron facings (F) are mahogany. This unusual construction probably reflected the high cost of mahogany back in the early 1800's when it had to be shipped to America over great distances at considerable risk and expense. If you use mahogany throughout, simply increase the thickness of parts G by $^5/_{16}$ in., and dispense with part F.

Tenon the various apron and stretcher ends, referring to the appropriate tenon details, and mortise the legs correspondingly. As shown in Fig. 1, the aprons, facings, and stretchers are all inset $^1/_8$ in. Refer to the grid patterns for the profiles of parts B and L, and band saw them to shape. Cut the dovetails in parts L and M (see dovetail detail), tenon the shelf ends (see shelf tenon detail), and mortise parts L accordingly.

The washstand top features bowl and glass cutouts (see top view for size and location). However, if you intend alternate use for this piece, these cutouts need not be included.

Next, make the dovetailed drawer. The drawer side view shows the layout of these dovetails. Use a $^1/_{16}$ in. diameter veining bit (available from Sears) in the router to cut the $^1/_{16}$ in. grooves in the drawer front.

The original washstand is just glued

Bill of Materials
(all dimensions actual)

Part	Description	Size	No. Req'd.
A	Leg	$1^1/_2$ x $1^1/_2$ x $31^1/_2$	4
B	Upper Front Apron	$^5/_{16}$ x $1^3/_4$ x $17^1/_8$*	1
C	Upper Side Apron	$^5/_{16}$ x $1^3/_4$ x $13^1/_4$*	2
D	Upper Back Apron	$^5/_{16}$ x $1^3/_4$ x $17^1/_8$*	1
E	Stretcher	$^5/_8$ x $1^3/_8$ x $17^1/_8$*	2
F	Lower Side Apron Facing	$^5/_{16}$ x $3^1/_2$ x $11^3/_4$	2
G	Lower Side Apron	$1^1/_{16}$ x $3^1/_2$ x $13^1/_4$*	2
H	Drawer Runner	$^5/_8$ x $^1/_2$ x $11^3/_4$	2
I	Lower Back Apron	$^5/_{16}$ x $3^1/_2$ x $17^1/_8$*	1
J	Bottom	$^5/_{16}$ x $14^3/_4$ x $18^5/_8$	1
K	Top	$^5/_{16}$ x $15^1/_4$ x 19	1
L	End	$^5/_{16}$ x 6 x $14^3/_4$	2
M	Back	$^5/_{16}$ x 6 x $18^5/_8$	1
N	Shelf	$^5/_{16}$ x $2^1/_2$ x $18^1/_4$*	1
O	Drawer Front	$^5/_8$ x $2^1/_4$ x $15^5/_8$	1
P	Drawer Side	$^1/_2$ x $2^1/_4$ x $13^7/_8$	2
Q	Drawer Back	$^1/_2$ x $1^7/_8$ x $15^5/_8$	1
R	Drawer Bottom	$^1/_4$ x $13^5/_8$ x 15	1
S	Drawer Pull**	$2^1/_4$ long	2
T	Tabletop Fastener**	$^3/_4$, $^3/_8$ in. offset	16

 * Length includes tenons.
** Available from Constantine's, 2050 Eastchester Rd., Bronx, NY 10461. Pull is part no. KC25, fastener is part no. 96N4.

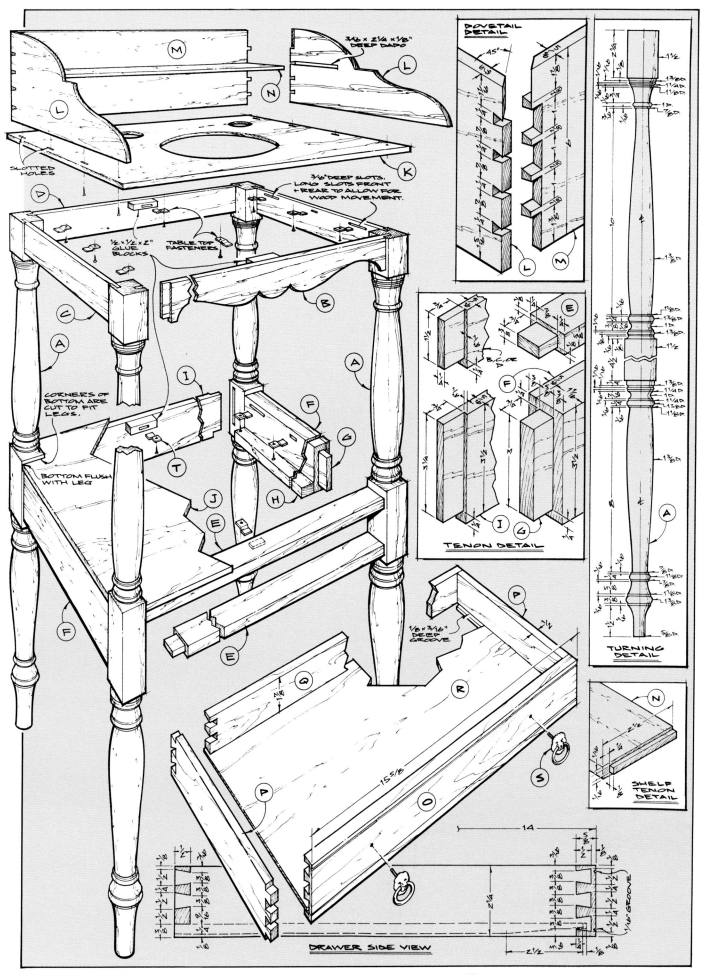

3/8 x 2¼ x ⅛"
DEEP DADO

DOVETAIL
DETAIL

SLOTTED
HOLES

3/16" DEEP SLOTS.
LONG SLOTS FRONT
& REAR TO ALLOW FOR
WOOD MOVEMENT.

½ x ½ x 2"
GLUE
BLOCKS

TABLE TOP
FASTENERS

CORNERS OF
BOTTOM ARE
CUT TO FIT
LEGS.

BOTTOM FLUSH
WITH LEG

TENON DETAIL

TURNING
DETAIL

1/8 x 3/16"
DEEP
GROOVE

SHELF
TENON
DETAIL

15 5/8

14

DRAWER SIDE VIEW

together, with no allowance made for movement in the top (K) and bottom (J). Many antiques were constructed this way, since before the age of central heating the wood didn't dry out like it does today. Furniture made today must take movement into account, so we've fastened the top and bottom using a series of tabletop fasteners, glueblocks, and slots. Tabletop fasteners are found in most hardware stores; size the slots to fit the fastener you buy.

When the washstand is assembled, parts L are screwed up through the slotted holes in K, and part M is glued to K. The completed top assembly is mounted to the leg/apron/stretcher assembly with the tabletop fastening system.

Fine sand the washstand and hand rub in three coats of tung oil, buffing with steel wool between coats. ●

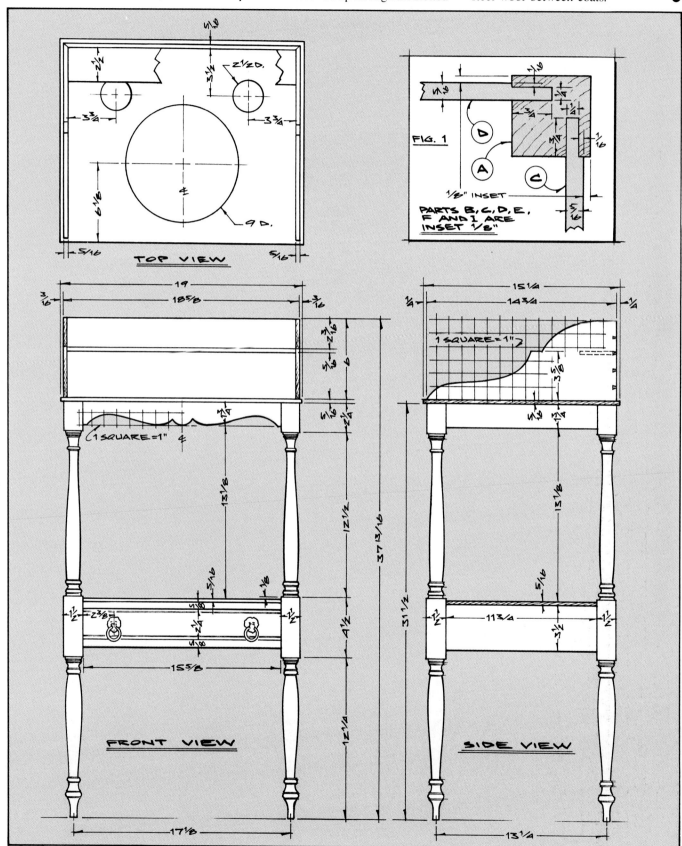

Tavern Table

Here's a simple table patterned after a piece commonly found in Early American taverns. Many a settler took stock of his fortunes and made plans for a new life seated at one of these small tables.

We made ours entirely from cherry. But the small tables were made from a variety of woods, usually what the local craftsman had on hand.

The construction is fairly simple, with trestle style legs that fit into chamfered feet. The joinery consists of double mortise-and-tenon joints that are pegged. The pegs add an interesting detail, and were commonly used instead of glue when these tables were originally made.

Start by edge-joining enough cherry boards to make the 18$\frac{1}{2}$ in. wide top (A). You'll probably want to make the panel for the top a little wider and longer than the finished size so you can square it up after gluing. Keep the boards as flat as possible during glue-up. One method of keeping the top flat is to clamp sturdy waxed blocks to one or both faces. (The wax prevents glue from sticking to the panels.) The blocks are clamped at right angles to the grain and go approximately from edge to

edge of the top.

While the top is in clamps, cut the remaining lumber to the sizes listed in the Bill of Materials. Note that the dimensions for the legs (B) and the top and bottom stretchers (C and D) include the lengths of the tenons.

Next, move on to the turnings, which can be difficult because of the square sections, called pommels, that break up the spindle profile. It's difficult to make the transition from the square to round sections without tearing out the corners. The easiest way to cut the pommels employs the skew chisel in a two-step process. For the first step, hold the skew with the long point down and slowly feed the point into the stock. To widen and deepen the groove, back out of the cut and enter the cut again a little to the side and from a slightly different angle.

When the grooves are all around the square, move on to the next step—a gentle paring of the shoulder to smooth the cut. Here, the skew is held with the long point up and well above the rotating workpiece. The cutting is done with the portion of the edge near the short corner of the skew. But it's important to cut only with the edge and not the corners. If either corner of the

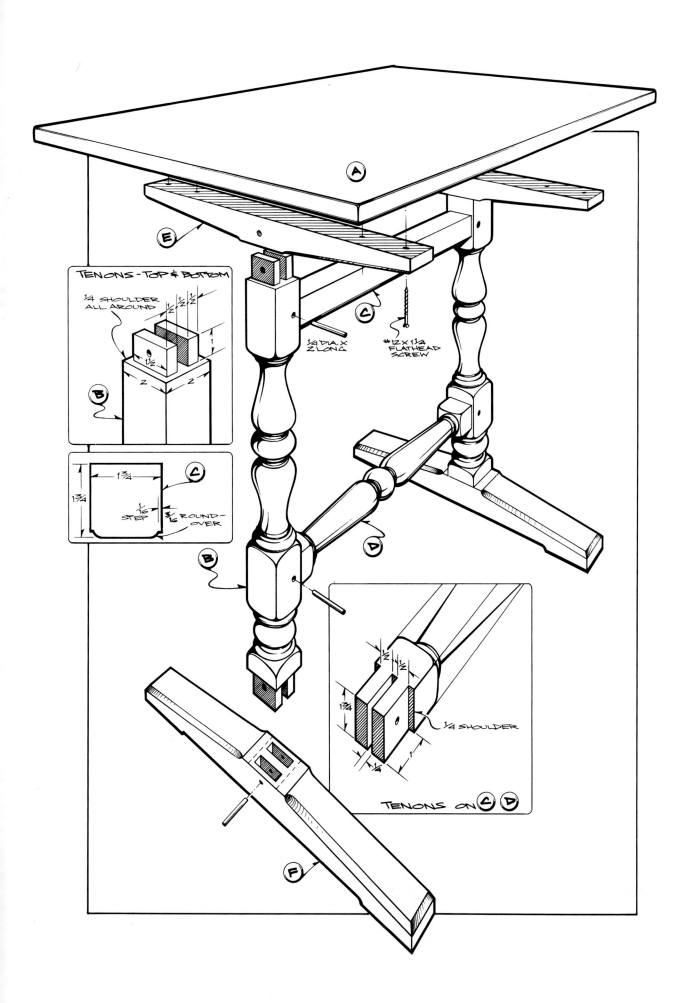

TENONS-TOP & BOTTOM

¼ SHOULDER
ALL AROUND

½ | ½ | ½

1

1½

2 | 2

B

A

E

¼ DIA. X
2 LONG

C

#12 X 1¼
FLATHEAD
SCREW

C

1¾

1¾

1/16
STEP

3/16 ROUND-
OVER

B

D

½ | ½

1¾

¼ SHOULDER

¼

1

TENONS ON C D

F

skew contacts the workpiece, you'll get a dig. Begin the cutting action with the flat of the bevel rubbing against the rotating workpiece. Then slowly change the skew angle to bring the cutting edge into contact with the workpiece. When the tool starts to cut, use a gentle rolling motion to smooth the shoulder.

This paring operation requires practice, so you may want to use sandpaper instead of the skew to smooth the shoulder.

Once the pommels are cut, the turnings are a straightforward combination of coves and beads around a double vase shape. First rough out the remainder of the cylinder with a gouge, then use the skew and gouge to cut the details. Making a full-size pattern from our drawings will help your accuracy in turning the parts. You can place the pattern behind the turning and refer to it as you work.

With the turning done, move on to the joinery. First, lay out and chop the mortises in the cleats (E) and feet (F). Use a drill press to establish a series of holes within the layout lines. Then square up the mortises with a chisel.

Next, cut the tenons on the ends of the legs and stretchers. You want to be sure of a snug fit, so use test cuts in scrap to make sure your setup is right before cutting the tenons on the turned pieces. Both the legs and the stretchers employ double tenons, but the legs have a $1/4$ in. shoulder all around, while the stretchers have the $1/4$ in. shoulder only on two sides.

For both, you establish the tenons in a two-step procedure. You first establish the shoulder with a crosscut on the table saw. (Remember to set the blade $1/4$ in. high.) You then cut away the rest of the tenon with the workpiece on end. Use a dado head set $1/4$ in. wide and 1 in. high. When cutting the workpiece on end, use a tenon jig high enough to accommodate two square sections.

After the joinery is complete, move on to the final details. Square up and sand the top, and taper and chamfer the feet and cleats. Also cut the profile along the bottom surfaces of the feet, establish the $3/16$ in. radius stepped roundover on the top stretcher, and drill for the pins in the mortise and tenon joints. It's best to clamp the workpieces together and cut these holes with a drill press. The pin will be forced in when you do the glue up. While you're boring holes, also drill the screw shank holes and counterbores in the cleats. The counterbores are a bit oversized to allow the top to move with seasonal moisture changes in the wood.

Next, give all the parts a thorough sanding, and dry fit all the parts one more time before gluing and finishing. The glue up is a two-step process. You first glue each leg into the foot and cleat. When each assembly is dry, you glue the two leg assemblies to the stretchers. Insert the pins while doing the glue-ups. Make them a little long and sand them flush.

After the glue dries, give the piece a final sanding and move on to the finishing, which imparts an antique flavor. We stained the piece with Minwax Colonial Maple, let that dry overnight, and then applied a coat of McCloskey's Walnut Varnish Stain. Right after brushing on the varnish stain we wiped the piece down with paint thinner, to highlight the turning crevices. We then applied two coats of orange shellac, rubbing the finish out with 0 steel wool between coats. After the second coat of shellac, which we also rubbed out with 0 steel wool, we applied a coat of Minwax Antique Oil Finish. As a final step, we rubbed the piece down with 000 steel wool and waxed the top. ●

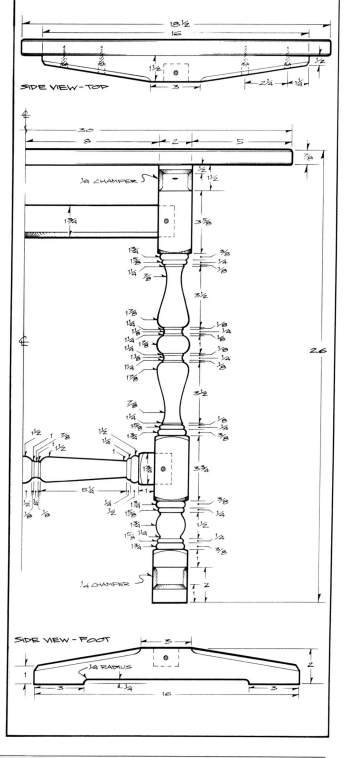

Bill of Materials
(all dimensions actual)

Part	Description	Size	No. Req'd.
A	Top	$7/8$ x $18^{1}/2$ x 30	1
B	Leg	2 x 2 x $23^{5}/8$ *	2
C	Top Stretcher	$1^{3}/4$ x $1^{3}/4$ x 18*	1
D	Bottom Stretcher	$1^{3}/4$ x $1^{3}/4$ x 18*	1
E	Cleat	$1^{1}/2$ x 2 x 16	2
F	Foot	2 x 2 x 16	2

* Length includes tenon.

SIDE VIEW-TOP

SIDE VIEW - FOOT

Cherry Lingerie Chest

Case Construction: Two Choices

Where case pieces are concerned, wood-workers using solid stock typically have two construction options. First, they can use wide boards (or edge glue several narrower pieces) to obtain the widths needed for the case sides, or second, they can use a frame-and-panel method of construction. Using a single wide board, or edge-gluing to yield a wide surface, may seem easiest, but there are several problems inherent with this method. First, if you do find a wide enough board, it may have some cup or twist. Edge-gluing narrower stock usually eliminates problems like this, but even with ideal stock, a wide flat surface may not be the most attractive option for your project. Also, with wide solid surfaces, considerable allowance for expected wood movement must usually be designed into the piece.

A frame-and-panel case may seem like considerably more work than solid board construction, but like much wood-working routine, once time for machine set-ups is factored out, there really isn't all that much more work involved. For our Lingerie Chest, the case is just three separate frame-and-panels, joined with tongue-and-grooves. The seven drawers are all identical, so you'll be able to mill all the drawer parts with a minimum of table saw settings. The eight drawer frames are also identical, so once again, a minimum of settings is required. Our chest uses cherry for all visible case parts, with the drawer boxes and drawer frames (excepting the front rail) being a secondary wood, such as poplar.

The Frame-and-Panels

The stock for all the frame-and-panel parts (excepting the $1/4$ in. plywood for the back panels) is $3/4$ in. thick. Rip and crosscut to yield the overall lengths and widths as listed in the Bill of Materials for the stiles (A, B, G) the rails (C, D, H, I, J), the side panels (E) and the facing (F). The overall dimensions include allowance for tenons and tongues.

All the tongue-and-groove joints are made with the dado head set for a $1/4$ in. wide cut, but note that the tongue on the front stile is offset to be flush with the inside edge, to avoid interfering with the bead that's cut on the front corner. With the exception of this offset joint, all the tongue-and-grove joinery can be accom-

If furniture trends can be determined by current furniture catalogs, then a traditional bedroom classic—the lingerie chest—is enjoying newfound popularity. Our chest is long and lean, and like its forebears, has a drawer for every day of the week. The chest is also an ideal introduction to a simple form of frame-and-panel case contruction, using tongue-and-groove joinery.

plished with just two rip fence settings (just make sure all stile and rail parts are identical thickness). As shown on the exploded view, the dado head depth-of-cut varies (the panel grooves in the frame stiles are $1/2$ in. deep; $5/16$ in. deep in the rails), but by organizing your work you can make all like cuts at one time.

The side panels are cut to size, then using the table saw set-up shown in Figure 1, the bevels are cut. The table saw blade is raised up through the Masonite, leaving a no-gap surface for you to run the panels across. Don't try cutting the bevels with your regular table saw insert—the gap may swallow the narrow $3/16$ in. edge, causing an accident. You'll need to do some sanding to clean up the cuts and square the bevel shoulder. A better choice for the cutting the raised panels is a dedicated panel raising router bit (see Sources). The bit leaves an even tongue to fit within the grooves in the stiles and rails, a distinct advantage over the beveled face of the table saw cut raised panel wedging into the

grooves. Also cut the birch plywood back panels (K).

Case Assembly

Glue the facings (F) to the front stiles (A), and check the assembly for squareness. When dry, glue and assemble the side and back frame-and-panels. Pin the raised panels on-center at the top and bottom to center them within the frame openings. Once these three separate frame-and-panel assemblies are out of clamps, lay out and make index marks on the inside of the side frames to locate the drawer frames. Then glue up the three frame-and-panels, as shown in the case assembly detail. The spacers across the front are needed to keep the entire assembly square. Take measurements across the case diagonals (the measurements should be identical) to insure squareness, then let dry.

Drawer Frames

There are eight identical drawer frames (the topmost frame is upside down),

each consisting of a rail (L), joined with a tongue-and-groove joint to a pair of runners (M). Take your rail length measurement—and the notches at the

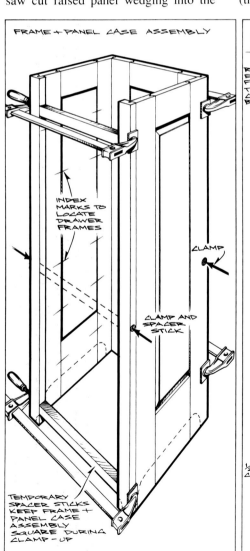

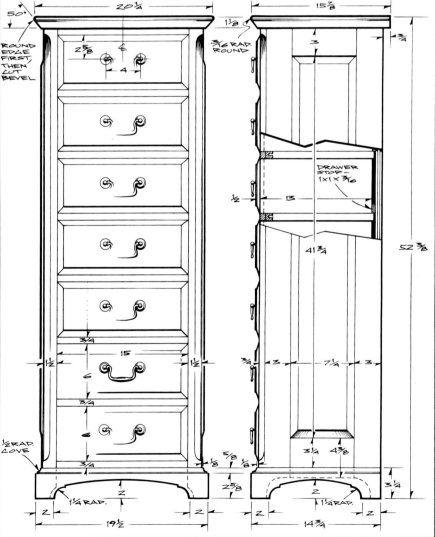

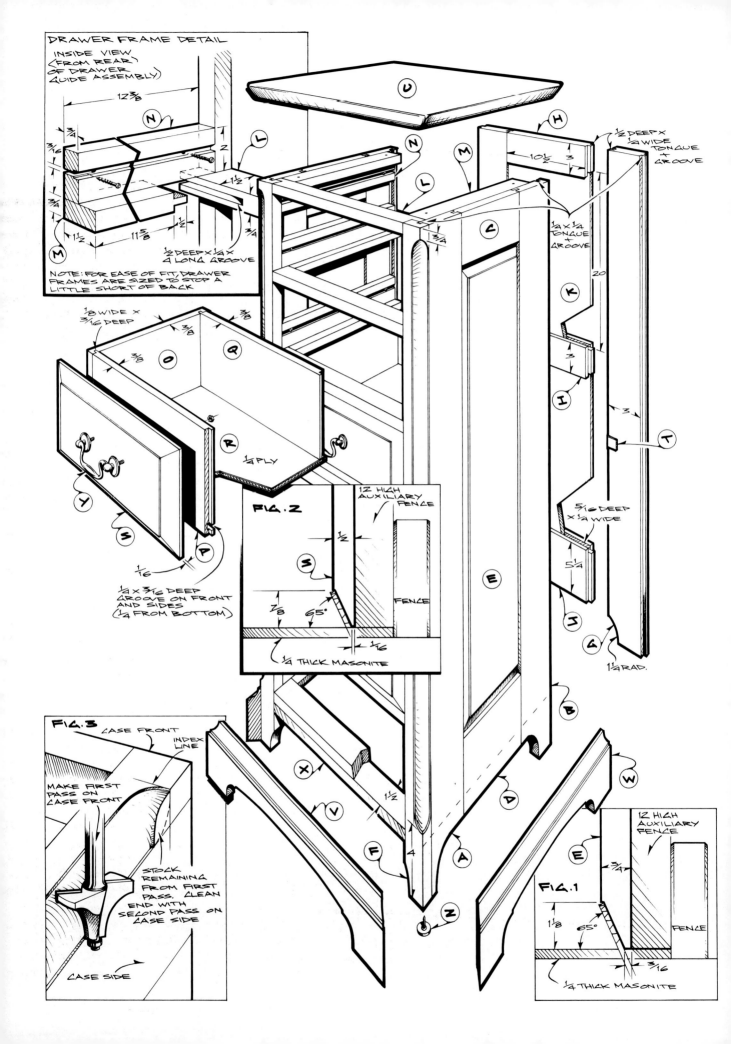

DRAWER FRAME DETAIL
INSIDE VIEW
(FROM REAR OF DRAWER GUIDE ASSEMBLY)

12 3/8

N

3/4
3/16

2

L

M

1 1/2
11 5/8
1/2

1/2 DEEP x 1/4 x 4 LONG GROOVE

NOTE: FOR EASE OF FIT DRAWER FRAMES ARE SIZED TO STOP A LITTLE SHORT OF BACK

U

H
10 1/2
3

1/2 DEEP x 1/4 WIDE TONGUE + GROOVE

M

L

N

C

1/4 x 1/4 TONGUE + GROOVE

K

3/4

20

1/8 WIDE x 3/16 DEEP

3/8

3/8

O

Q

I

3

5/16 DEEP x 1/4 WIDE

T

3

R

1/4 PLY

5 1/4

Y

S

FIG. 2

12 HIGH AUXILIARY FENCE

1/2

1/16

S

7/8

65°

A

1/16

FENCE

E

J

G

1 1/4 RAD.

1/4 THICK MASONITE

1/4 x 3/16 DEEP GROOVE ON FRONT AND SIDES (1/4 FROM BOTTOM)

FIG. 3

CASE FRONT

INDEX LINE

MAKE FIRST PASS ON CASE FRONT

STOCK REMAINING FROM FIRST PASS. CLEAN END WITH SECOND PASS ON CASE SIDE

CASE SIDE

X

V

1 1/2

D

B

W

F

4

A

N

12 HIGH AUXILIARY FENCE

E

3/4

FIG. 1

1/8

65°

3/16

FENCE

1/4 THICK MASONITE

rail ends—directly from the case assembly, while it's still in clamps. When joining the rail and runners, use a framing square to insure squareness. The guides (N) are glued and clamped to the runner/guide assembly. We show a groove for the screws, but they could just as easily be countersunk. By the

way, if you have enough foresight, you can cut the tongue-and-groove joint at the same time as the frame-and-panel joinery; just allow a little extra length on the rails so they can be trimmed later to fit the actual case. Our Drawer Frame Detail shows the groove in the rail as stopped about 4 in. from each end, since there's no need to run the groove along the full length. Once the drawer frames are out of clamps, notch the ends of the front rails to fit tightly between the case facings. Then install the drawer frames in the case (four screws for each drawer frame), using the marks for alignment.

Drawers

The seven drawers each consist of a pair of sides (O), a front (P), back (Q), birch plywood bottom (R), and face (S). We show a dado-and-groove joint, but use whatever joint you prefer. The bevel on our drawer face is cut using the set-up shown in Figure 2. It's similar to the side panel set-up, with the same blade angle, but different blade height and fence settings. As illustrated, we've sized the drawers a little short of the case back, and then used stops (T) glued to the case back to properly locate the drawer face bevel with respect to the case front. When positioned correctly, the bevel on the drawer face should be flush with the case front, as shown in the photo.

Details/Base/Top

Part of the charm of our chest is the 5/8 in. radius bead cut on the front corners. It's done with the router and a 5/8 in. radius beading bit (see Sources). Be sure to block the chest up so the side panels aren't resting on the floor. As shown in Figure 3, make index marks to indicate the cut ends, make a pass with the router on one face, then switch the router to the opposite face and make a second pass. This second pass is needed to produce a symmetrical form on the bead ends. Ideally, both passes will be indexed perfectly, but if you end up with a small step, some clean-up work with chisels may be needed.

Next up are the top (U) and base (V, W). The top is just solid boards, edge-glued to yield the 15 7/8 in. width. Round the edge with a 3/16 in. radius roundover bit (see Sources), then, using the table saw, cut a 50-degree bevel on the sides and front. The base parts are cut from a

single board about 50 in. long. Use a 1/2 in. radius cove bit (see Sources) to mold one edge of the board, then use miter cuts to establish final length. Lay out the base profiles as indicated, joining the 1 1/4 in. radii with long, gentle curves. Before adding the base parts, use a hand-held jigsaw to cut back the case bottom at the front, back and sides. The base is glued and finish-nailed to the case, with a long glue block (X) providing additional support for the base front. The top is screwed in place through the upside down uppermost drawer frame.

Finishing Touches

Our cherry chest has a Minwax cherry stain, topped with two coats of clear shellac and finally one coat of McClosky's Heirloom Satin Varnish. The solid brass bail pulls (Y) are from Horton Brasses (see Sources). The levelers (Z) were purchased from a local hardware store.

Assembly Tip

It may be tempting to try to get all your tongue-and-groove joinery exact (with tongue length identical to groove depth), but in practice, it's a good idea to trim a hair from the tongue (or tenon) length—or make the grooves (or mortises) just a bit deeper. This insures that shoulders along the joints close up good and tight during assembly. ●

Provincial Four-Poster Bed

If you've checked the furniture store circulars that usually come with the Sunday paper, chances are you know just how costly beds can be. Canopy-top four posters like ours usually sell for about $1,000, and that's for the bed only, without the mattress and box spring.

For our bed, your materials expense should be considerably less than that.

You can use no. 2 pine for the bed, but avoid boards with loose knots.

Our bed accepts a standard queen size box spring and mattress. Though we don't show a headboard and footboard, if you'd like to include these, just come up with a pleasing profile matching the canopy top, leave a sufficient flat on the posts for mounting hardware, and order an extra set of bed rail fasteners.

Start by making the four posts. As shown in the Corner Detail, each post is actually a right angle formed by two 3/4 in. thick pine boards joined with a simple tongue-and-groove joint. Although our Bill of Materials lists the two pine boards as a post side (A) and post end (B), the orientation isn't important. Once assembled, the joint that's formed won't be easily seen.

To make the post, rip $3/4$ in. thick pine to $4^1/2$ in. wide for the post sides, and to 4 in. wide for the post ends. Using the table saw and dado head, cut the dado in the post sides and the rabbet in the ends to form the matching tongue. Check your table saw setups on some scrap first, before committing your project stock. With the tongue-and-groove joint cut, apply glue and clamp securely. Use several 90-degree waxed blocks to keep the parts at a true right angle along their entire length.

Once the posts are dry, lay out the $3/4$ in. radius bead on the corner, the ogee on the edges, and the foot profile. As shown on the Corner Detail, the $3/4$ in. radius bead, once cut, falls $1/16$ in. past the joint line. Don't worry about this. After the finish is applied, the joint line won't be noticed. Note that the bead is stopped $3^1/2$ in. from the top of the post. The ogee starts 14 in. from the bottom end of the posts and runs to the top. Later, the top portion of the ogee is removed when the post edge is cut back and mitered to fit the top rails. Use the grid pattern shown on the end view to transfer the foot profile.

For the router work, you'll need a router with a $1/2$ in. collet capacity. That's because the required $3/4$ in. radius ball-bearing guided router bit is only available with a $1/2$ in. shank. Establish the roundover and ogee molded edges, then cut the foot profile with a hand-held jigsaw. Sand to smooth the jigsaw cut on the foot profile, then cut the corner blocks (C) and glue in place.

Next, cut the rail stock to length and width. The bottom rails (D, E) are square edged, but both top rails (F, G) are shaped and molded. We cut the top rails to length and width and established the miters where the ogee molded edges

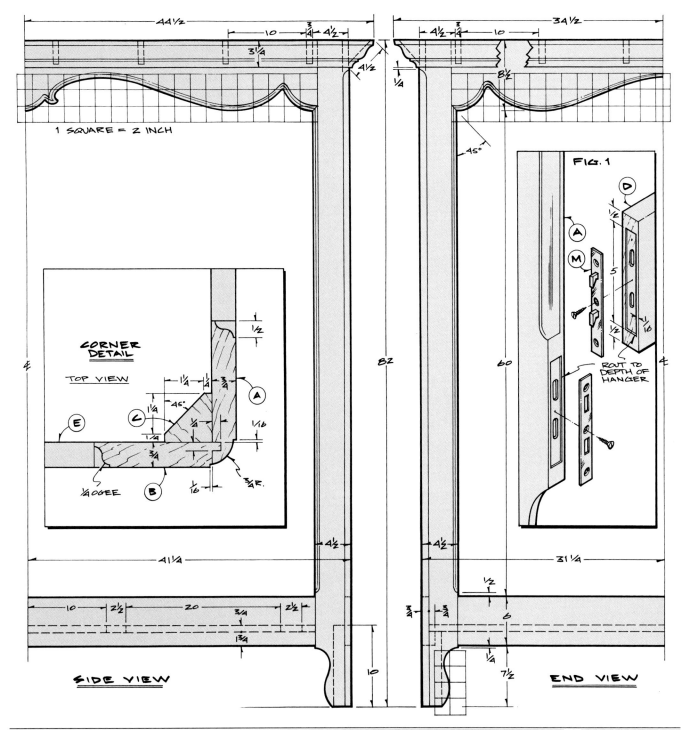

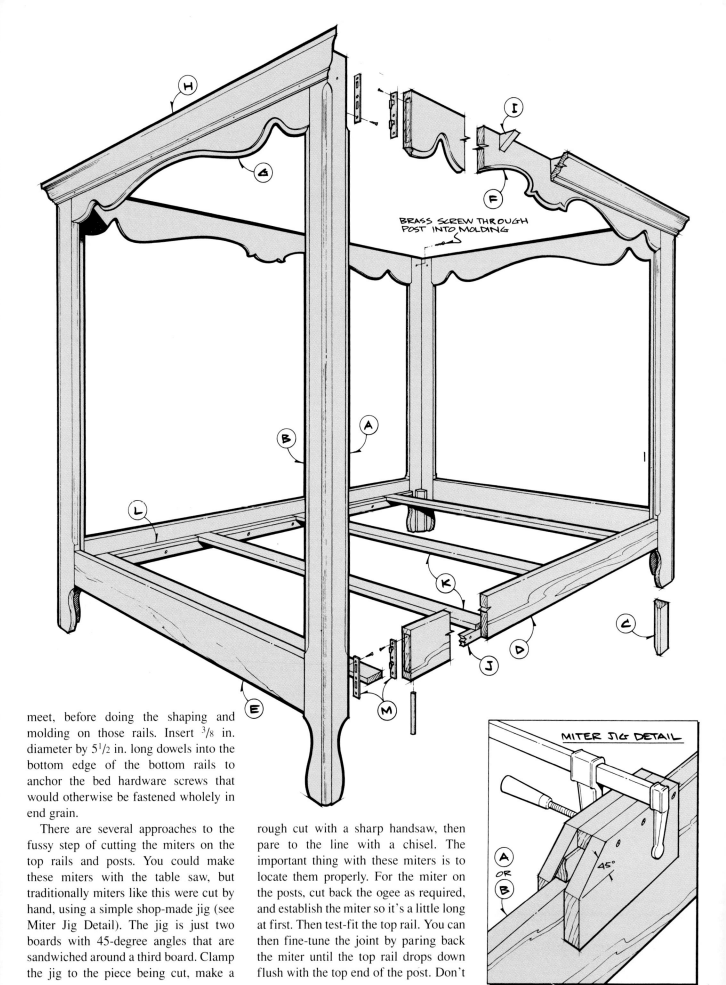

BRASS SCREW THROUGH POST INTO MOLDING

MITER JIG DETAIL

45°

A OR B

meet, before doing the shaping and molding on those rails. Insert $^3/_8$ in. diameter by $5^1/_2$ in. long dowels into the bottom edge of the bottom rails to anchor the bed hardware screws that would otherwise be fastened wholly in end grain.

There are several approaches to the fussy step of cutting the miters on the top rails and posts. You could make these miters with the table saw, but traditionally miters like this were cut by hand, using a simple shop-made jig (see Miter Jig Detail). The jig is just two boards with 45-degree angles that are sandwiched around a third board. Clamp the jig to the piece being cut, make a

rough cut with a sharp handsaw, then pare to the line with a chisel. The important thing with these miters is to locate them properly. For the miter on the posts, cut back the ogee as required, and establish the miter so it's a little long at first. Then test-fit the top rail. You can then fine-tune the joint by paring back the miter until the top rail drops down flush with the top end of the post. Don't make the mistake of trying to get it right the first time. Remember, you can always cut back a little more stock, but once the stock is gone, it's a monumental task trying to stretch that board out!

To shape the top rails, transfer the profiles from the grid patterns and cut out with the jigsaw, then use rasps, files and sandpaper to smooth. Smoothing is an important step since the ball-bearing guided ogee bit will follow any bumps or gouges, causing the irregularities to be reproduced in the ogee molding. Take extra care with the router when you reach the miter on the top rails. If you let the bearing follow the miter at the end of the board, you'll round the end and ruin your crisp miter cut. An easy way to avoid this problem is to just guide the router off the end in a straight line. Or you can stop the ogee cut short of the miter and use files and sandpaper to continue the ogee profile to the miter.

With your rails shaped and molded, you'll need to cut the mortises for the bed rail fasteners (M) that hold the rails and posts together. Our bed is all knock-down, so every rail-to-post joint uses one of these fasteners, which

Bill of Materials
(all dimensions actual)

Part	Description	Size	No. Req'd.
A	Post Side	$3/4 \times 4^{1}/_{2} \times 82^{*}$	4
B	Post End	$3/4 \times 4 \times 82$	4
C	Corner Block	$1^{1}/_{2} \times 1^{1}/_{2} \times 10$	4
D	Bottom Side Rail	$3/4 \times 6 \times 73^{1}/_{2}$	2
E	Bottom End Rail	$3/4 \times 6 \times 53^{1}/_{2}$	2
F	Top Side Rail	$3/4 \times 8^{1}/_{2} \times 74^{1}/_{2}$	2
G	Top End Rail	$3/4 \times 8^{1}/_{2} \times 54^{1}/_{2}$	2
H	Crown Molding	$5/8 \times 4^{1}/_{2}^{**}$	28 ft.
I	Molding Block	$3/4 \times 2^{1}/_{2} \times 2^{1}/_{2}$	28
J	Cleat	$3/4 \times 1^{3}/_{4} \times 73^{1}/_{2}$	2
K	Box Spring Support	$3/4 \times 2^{1}/_{2} \times 61$	4
L	Filler Strip	$3/4 \times 3/4$	11 ft.
M	Bed Rail Fasteners	$5/8 \times 5^{***}$	16

 * Width dimension before corner shaping.
 ** When buying, specify $4^{1}/_{2}$ in. crown molding. Note that the profile and dimensions of the molding your local lumberyard carries may differ slightly from that shown.
 *** Available from Constantine's, 2050 Eastchester Rd., Bronx, NY 10461; tel. (800) 223-8087. Order part no. 96J10 for a set of four (you'll need four sets).

amounts to 16 in all. With so many mortises to cut, you'll be well advised to build a simple jig (see Working with Bed Rail Fasteners) for your router or

laminate trimmer.

With the fasteners mounted and the bed assembled, add the crown molding (H). Most lumberyards carry a $4^{1}/_{2}$ in. crown molding similar to the profile shown. We glued molding blocks (I) to the crown molding and rails, and then inserted a brass screw through each post side and end to pull the miters up tight. The screws must be removed to disassemble the bed. Strips of wood, temporarily clamped to the top rails and even with the bottom edge of the crown molding, are an easy way to position the molding correctly while you are working on mounting it.

Next, add the cleats (J), box spring supports (K) and filler strips (L). The cleats and filler strips are glued and screwed in place, but the box spring supports just nest in the pockets between the filler strips.

The bed must be disassembled to apply the finish. We used three coats of orange shellac followed by a single coat of McCloskey Heirloom Satin Varnish. The orange shellac adds just the right amount of color to the wood, making a stain unnecessary. ●

Working with Bed Rail Fasteners

Before locating for the bed rail fastener mortises, you should take the hardware and see how the parts lock together. Note how the holes in the plate side of the hardware are offset toward the top. This little detail insures that both plates will be on the same plane when in the locked position. On most bed constructions, getting both parts of the hardware on the same plane isn't all that critical, since if you miss by $1/8$ in., no one will notice. But that's not the case on the top rail-to-post joints for our bed. If both parts of the fastener aren't close to or exactly on the same plane, you could end up with an unsightly gap at the miters where the ogees meet. To insure a tight miter, cheat the prong side of the hardware (the half that's mounted to the top rails) up just a hair. Also, to avoid a fastener that locks tight before the prongs are fully seated, test-assemble each fastener before mounting. A few taps with the hammer will seat the prongs.

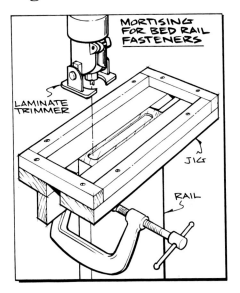

Mortising for bed rail fasteners may seem as easy as drawing a breath, but what looks easy can also be deceptive. We recommend that you use a jig (see Mortising For Bed Rail Fasteners detail) to rout the bed rail fastener mortises. Once located and clamped in

place on the respective post or rail, the jig insures an accurate, foolproof mortise for the fasteners. Given the narrow $1/16$ in. lip remaining on either side of the $5/8$ in. wide mortise, the jig is pretty much a must. As shown in Fig. 1, the mortises on the posts must also include two deep hollows to accept the two bed rail prongs. The mortises in the rails have two shallower hollows to fit the back of the prongs. Note that on the post mortises for the top fasteners, you'll probably need to clean out the part of the mortise nearest the miter by hand. The miter interferes with indexing the jig to cut the full mortise length.

With the mortises cut, test assemble the top rails by mounting each fastener plate with just a short center screw. That way, if you need to adjust the mortises and move the plate a little higher or lower, you'll still have the top and bottom screws to provide maximum hold. If the center screw hole overlaps the first, the longer screw should still find good hold.

Chippendale Small Chest

O ur small chest makes an elegant chairside or bedside table. The three drawers provide storage, and the bail handles on either side are handy if you need to move it. It's perfect for a small space, measuring only 14³/4 in. deep by 19 in. wide by 24 in. high. We used cherry, an attractive wood that works easily.

The Case

You'll probably need to edge-glue stock for the top (A) and sides (B). Glue up enough wood to provide both the top and sides from a single length. Later, by crosscutting first one side, then the top, and then the opposite side, in that order, you'll achieve a very attractive detail— the continuous matching of grain as it flows from the sides into the top.

While you are waiting for the edge-glued stock to dry, cut the stretcher (C) and drawer frame parts (G, H). Note that a slip joint is cut on the ends of the drawer frame parts so they may be

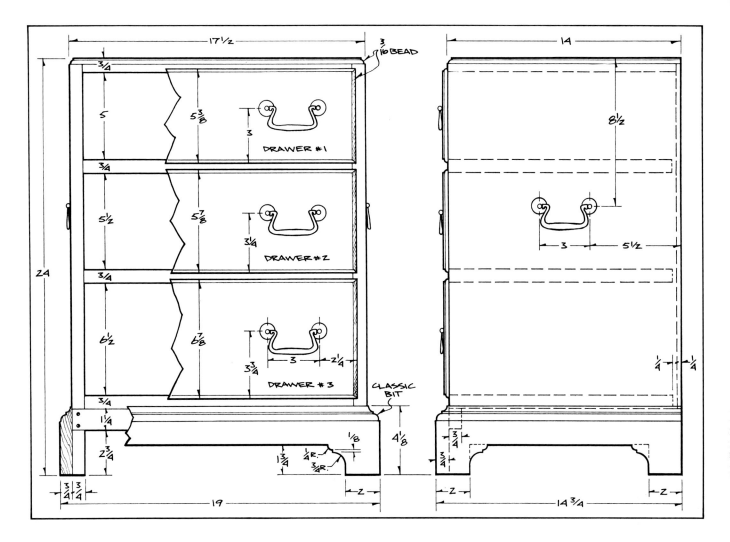

assembled before mounting in the case (see Drawer Frame Detail). Also note the $1/8$ in. by $1/2$ in. notch on the front corners of the drawer frames. This notch enables the drawer frames to fit into the stopped dadoes that are cut into the sides of the case. Drill slotted screw holes in the drawer frame sides, as indicated, to permit wood movement across the width of the case sides. The screw holes near the front are not slotted. This arrangement keeps the drawer frames and sides flush at the front, while directing any movement that might occur toward the back. As you'll note from the Bill of Materials, both the drawer frames and the drawers are sized to stop $1/4$ in. short of the plywood back (D) in order to accommodate this movement.

Once the stock for the top and sides is out of clamps, you can start work on these parts. Crosscut the parts to length in the order noted earlier. The crosscut length of the top will be $17^1/2$ in. The actual final length will be slightly less after the case is assembled and the bead is cut. Now lay out the blind dovetails

that join the top and sides. The dovetail layout is shown in the Top View Detail, and our techniques ''Cutting Full-Blind Dovetails'' techniques article on page 112 provides step-by-step instructions on how to make them. You could substitute other types of joinery to fasten the top to the sides, but the blind dovetails provide maximum strength.

With the dovetails cut, next cut the rabbet in the sides and top to accept the plywood back. Note that the rabbet for the back in the top is $1/4$ in. deep by $1/2$ in. wide, and the rabbets in the sides are $1/4$ in. deep by $3/8$ in. wide. Notch the bottom ends of the sides, as shown, to match the width and height of the base side profile. Notch the front edge of the sides to accept the half-lapped stretcher, and cut the stopped dadoes in the sides to fit the drawer frames. Whether you use the table saw or the router to establish the stopped dadoes, the stopped end of the dadoes must be squared by hand, using a chisel.

Now assemble the top and sides around the three drawer frames. As

explained in the techniques article, you may need to add slips of veneer to fill gaps in the blind dovetails. The drawer frames are glued along the front end of the stopped dado, but not along the back two-thirds. This helps prevent the sides from developing cracks, which could happen if the drawer frames were glued and screwed along their entire length. Remember to keep the frames flush with the case sides at the front. Add the stretcher and the back. The back, if it is cut accurately, serves to help square-up the case. Use glue and screws to secure the back. When dry, use the router and a $3/16$ in. radius ball-bearing guided beading bit to establish the bead on the top front and sides. The depth of cut is set so that there will be a $1/16$ in. shoulder above the bead.

Next, cut the base front and sides (E, F). Start with a length of stock $3/4$ in. thick by $4^1/8$ in. wide by about 50 in. long. Establish the molded edge using the table saw and a molding-head cutter. We used a Sears cutter (their part no. 9BT2352). Then crosscut the base front

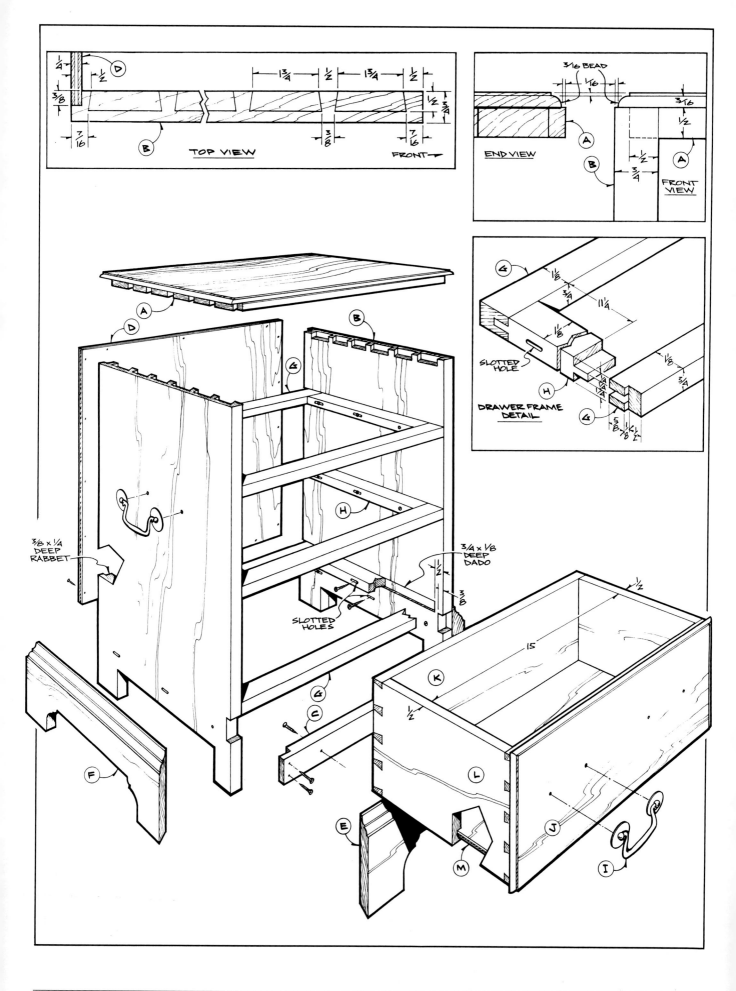

3/16 BEAD

1/16

END VIEW

FRONT VIEW

D

A

B

3/4

1/2

3/8

7/16

1/4

1/2

3/8

13/4

1/2

13/4

1/2

7/16

3/8

G

H

1/8

3/4

11 1/4

1/8

3/4

SLOTTED HOLE

DRAWER FRAME DETAIL

5/8

1/8

1/2

1/4

1/4

A

D

B

G

H

3/8 x 1/4 DEEP RABBET

SLOTTED HOLES

G

C

3/4 x 1/8 DEEP DADO

1/2

3/8

K

1/2

15

1/2

L

J

I

F

E

M

Bill of Materials
(all dimensions actual)

CASE

Part	Description	Size	No. Req'd	Part	Description	Size	No. Req'd
A	Top	3/4 x 14 x 17 1/2 *	1	F	Base Side	3/4 x 4 1/8 x 14 3/4	2
B	Side	3/4 x 14 x 23 3/4	2	G	Drawer Frame Front/Back	3/4 x 1 1/8 x 16 1/4	6
C	Stretcher	3/4 x 1 1/4 x 17 1/2	1	H	Drawer Frame Side	3/4 x 1 1/8 x 12 1/2	6
D	Back	1/4 x 16 3/4 x 19 3/4	1	I	Bail Pull (brass)	3 in. on center **	8
E	Base Front	3/4 x 4 1/8 x 19	1				

DRAWERS

Part	Description	No. Req'd per Drawer	Drawer 1	Drawer 2	Drawer 3
J	Front	1	3/4 x 5 3/8 x 16 3/8	3/4 x 5 7/8 x 16 3/8	3/4 x 6 7/8 x 16 3/8
K	Back	1	1/2 x 5 x 16	1/2 x 5 1/2 x 16	1/2 x 6 1/2 x 16
L	Side	2	1/2 x 5 x 13 1/2	1/2 x 5 1/2 x 13 1/2	1/2 x 6 1/2 x 13 1/2
M	Bottom	1	1/4 x 13 x 15 1/2	1/4 x 13 x 15 1/2	1/4 x 13 x 15 1/2

* Length is before bead is cut.

** Available from Anglo-American Brass Co., P.O. Box 9487, San Jose, CA 95157; tel. (408) 246-0203. Order part no. B-8B.

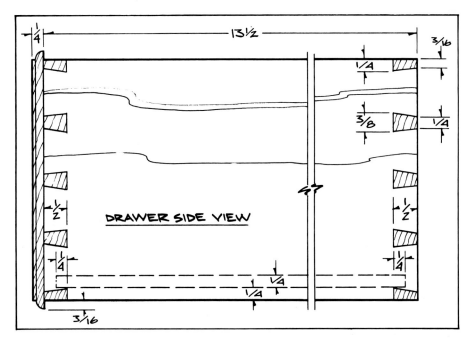

DRAWER SIDE VIEW

and sides to approximate length, cut the profile as shown, and finally miter the ends that meet at the front. Glue and screw the base front and sides to the case. However, on the base sides use glue only toward the front and at the miters. Screws through slotted holes in the case sides allow the sides freedom to move in relation to the base. The slotted holes may seem like a fussy point, but they help to insure that a fine piece like this will stay together for a lifetime and not just a few years.

The Drawers
You can now get to work on the drawers. Start with the drawer fronts (J). Establish the bead around the front, and then cut the 3/16 in. deep by 1/2 in. wide rabbet all around that enables the drawer front to fit into the drawer opening. Don't assume that each drawer opening will be identical to the dimensions we show. Instead, make the drawer fronts to fit the actual drawer openings as measured from your case. Mill stock for the drawer backs (K) and sides (L). We chose a light

colored hardwood, such as maple, for the sides and backs. The lighter sides contrast nicely with the cherry drawer fronts, highlighting the half-blind dovetails. These dovetails are cut using the basic techniques described on page 104. However, the tails on the drawer sides will be easier to cut than the tails on the case top, since they are through and not blind. Use the pin layout illustrated in the Drawer Side View Detail. Each of the drawers features the same number of pins.

Once the dovetails have been cut and test-fitted, you can cut the drawer bottoms (M) to size from 1/4 in. thick plywood (we used birch), and assemble the drawer fronts, backs and sides around them. Make certain that the drawers are square (check with a framing square), and sand the dovetails flush once the drawers are out of clamps.

After final sanding, we finished this piece with several coats of penetrating oil followed by paste wax. We then mounted the Chippendale bail-style brass pulls (see Bill of Materials for ordering information). Note that the brass pulls are slightly off-center in their position relative to the drawer front heights and to the case height. We didn't use levelers on this piece, but you could easily add them if your floors are uneven. ●

Secretary Desk

few small pieces of $1/2$ in. thick stock for the cubbyhole parts. Because you only need a little, it's easiest to plane down some $3/4$ in. stock to get the required $1/2$ in. You'll also need $1^1/2$ in. thick stock for the tapered legs. We used 8/4 stock to achieve the full $1^1/2$ in. width at the top of the legs, but you may be able to get away with 6/4 stock if you don't mind making the legs a little undersized. If you buy the 6/4 stock rough, you'll get usable stock between $1^3/8$ in. and $1^7/16$ in. thick.

You'll also want some poplar or pine for the $3/8$ in. thick inside drawer parts. We used pine because it was available. Of course, you can also use cherry if you happen to have plenty on hand. Finally, you'll need some $1/4$ in. thick plywood for the case and desk backs and drawer bottoms. A cherry veneer plywood is the best choice, but you can substitute pine or mahogany if you want.

Getting Started

The secretary is made in three separate pieces: the base, desk and bookcase. For purposes of discussion we'll treat them separately, but in practice you'll want to mill the stock for all the sections at the same time and also glue up stock for the wider sections at the same time. Make the panels carefully, being sure that all the stock is true and that the edges are jointed perfectly square before glue-up. Depending on the width of your lumber, you may need to glue up stock for the desk top and bottom (A and B), the desk side (C), the desk lid (E), the bookcase top and bottom (Q and S), and the door panels (Z). Since the desk section is the most involved, we started construction there. But it really doesn't matter, so begin with whatever section you're in the mood for.

Desk Section

Start by cutting the stock to the overall dimensions listed in the Bill of Materials and preparing the wider panels as needed. Make sure that the desk lid and the case parts are flat and true after glue-up. A little extra care now will save you a lot of grief trying to fit the lid to a crooked case. If you find that the parts are slightly out of true after they are glued up, use a hand plane to true them.

With the parts cut to size, start on the details and joinery. First, cut the $3/8$ in.

S tately yet delicate, this small secretary will lend an air of elegance to any room of your house. The curly maple details in a cherry case give this traditional design an appeal that's hard to resist.

The door panels, drawer fronts and valance are cut from curly maple. For added interest, we used pieces with dark heartwood as well as the lighter sapwood. The panel we used is $3/4$ in. thick

by $10^5/8$ in. wide, so you'll need to hunt up some wide stock unless you decide to glue up the panels from smaller pieces. Since the visual appeal of the secretary depends so much on the panels, we think it's worthwhile to find some wide stock. If you don't have a local source for hard-to-find woods, refer to the list of mail-order sources on page 131.

Most of the cherry case parts are cut from $3/4$ in. thick stock, but you'll need a wide by $1/4$ in. deep rabbets in the case parts for the back. Then establish the sloping angle on the side sections using a bandsaw.

For the dovetails, first scribe the depth of cut (the thickness of the stock plus $1/32$ in.) onto the ends of the case top and bottom and onto the matching edges of the sides. Then lay out the tails on the sides using the dimensions shown in the side view. (It helps to use a sharp knife for the layout here.) Extend the layout lines across the end grain. Use a dovetail saw to cut out the tail sides and then use a chisel to cut along the depth lines.

Note that before starting the chisel cuts, it's best to use a knife to create a small shoulder to rest the back of the chisel against. Cut down once lightly with the knife at the depth line for each pin, using a straightedge as a guide. Then cut down again with the knife angled toward the waste portion. The two cuts should form a thin cross-grain chip. When you remove the chip, you have a neat shoulder along the bottoms of the tails. If you don't create the shoulder to start with, the chisel tends to creep off the line.

Holding the parts together with a clamp, mark the pins from the completed tails, and extend the lines down from the end grain to the depth lines you established before. Use the dovetail saw and chisel in sequence to cut away the waste. Work carefully and slowly on the

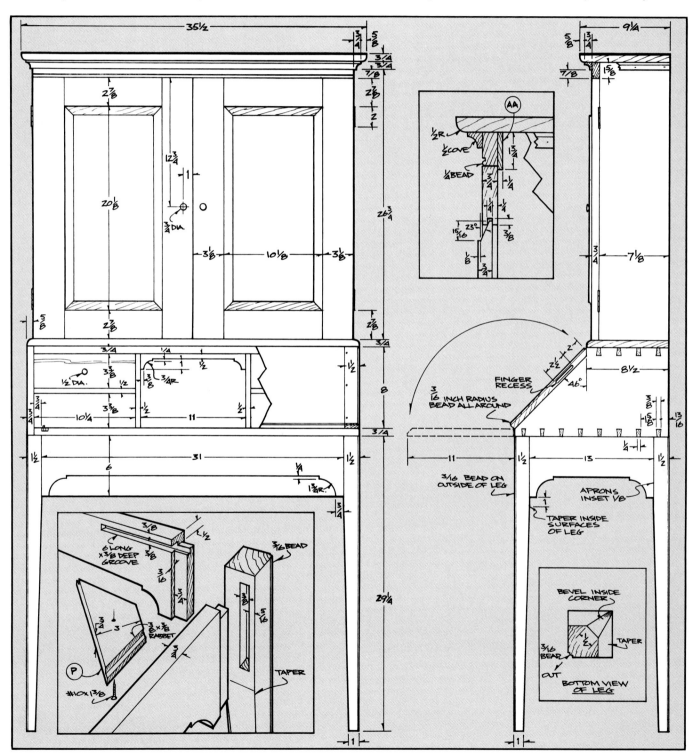

Bill of Materials
(all dimensions actual)

Part	Description	Size	No. Req'd.
Desk Unit			
A	Desk Top	3/4 x 81/2 x 34	1
B	Desk Bottom	3/4 x 16 x 34	1
C	Desk Side	3/4 x 16 x 83/4	2
D	Desk Back	1/4 x 8 x 331/4	1
E	Desk Lid	3/4 x 11 x 33	1
F	Breadboard End	3/4 x 11/2 x 11	2
G	Divider	1/2 x 8 x 73/4	2
H	Shelf	1/2 x 8 x 103/4	2
I	Valance	1/2 x 11/2 x 11	1
J	Drawer Guide	1/4 x 1/2 x 75/8	2
K	Drawer Stop	1/4 x 3/4 x 2	2
Base			
L	Leg	11/2 x 11/2 x 291/4	4
M	Front Apron	3/4 x 6 x 321/2	1
N	Back Apron	3/4 x 6 x 321/2	1
O	Side Apron	3/4 x 6 x 141/2	2
P	Corner Block	3/4 x 3 x 9	4
Bookcase			
Q	Case Top	3/4 x 91/4 x 351/2	1
R	Case Side	3/4 x 71/8 x 281/4	2
S	Case Bottom	3/4 x 81/2 x 34	1
T	Adjustable Shelf	3/4 x 67/8 x 311/4	2
U	Case Back	1/4 x 32 x 281/4	1
V	Rail	3/4 x 15/8 x 323/4	1
W	Cove Molding	3/4 x 3/4 x 521/8	*
X	Door Stile	3/4 x 31/8 x 257/8	4
Y	Rail	3/4 x 27/8 x 121/8	4
Z	Door Panel	3/4 x 105/8 x 205/8	2
AA	Doorstop	1/4 x 13/4 x 311/4	1
Drawers			
BB	Drawer Front	3/4 x 33/8 x 103/16	2
CC	Drawer Side	3/8 x 33/8 x 75/8	4
DD	Drawer Back	3/8 x 27/8 x 95/8	2
EE	Drawer Bottom	1/4 x 75/16 x 95/8	2
Hardware**			
FF	Door Knob	3/4 dia. brass as shown	2
GG	Drawer Knob	1/2 dia. brass as shown	2
HH	Lid Hinge	3/4 x 7 as shown	2
II	Door Hinge	2 x 11/8	4
JJ	Bullet Catch	5/16 dia. as shown	2
KK	Shelf Peg	1/4 dia.	8

* As required.
** Hardware available from Paxton Hardware, 7818 Bradshaw Rd., Upper Falls, MD 21156; tel (410) 592-8505. Door knob (FF) is catalog no. 915; Drawer knob (GG) is no. 913; Lid hinge (HH) is no. 5009; Door hinge (II) is no. 4102; Bullet catch (JJ) is no. 4426; Shelf pegs (KK) are no. 5521.

dovetails so they come out crisp. For more on dovetails, see page 104.

After cutting the dovetails, dry-fit the case and adjust the dovetails to get a snug fit. You shouldn't have to whale on the parts to get them to go together.

With the desk case held together with clamps—but still not glued—make the lid to fit the case. Cut the panel to size and form a 1 in. long tenon as shown on each end. Mortise on the breadboard ends using three pegs. Make slots as shown for the two outboard pegs to allow the panel to move in relation to the ends. Note that the 1 in. tenon is a tad shorter than the length of the groove in the ends. This also allows for expansion.

After gluing on the ends and allowing them to dry, sand the ends flush if needed. Then bevel the top edge and test fit the lid to the case. Shape the 3/16 in. radius bead on the edges of the lid on the router table. Gauge off a fence for the roundover instead of a ball bearing. The bevel cut on the top edge won't allow you a flat for the bearing to ride on.

Then use a 3/8 in. diameter core box cutter to cut a 1/8 in. deep finger recess in the sides of the breadboard ends. Again use the router table and drop the lid onto the core box bit. Use a high fence so it's easy to control the cut. Also mortise in the hinges, and check the fit of the lid to the case. The hinge joint needs to be mortised in so that half the thickness fits within the lid and half within the bottom. If the lid doesn't lie perfectly flat, you can adjust it somewhat by slightly changing the position of the hinges.

Next, remove the lid, take the case apart, and start on the cubbyhole details. The vertical dividers (G) are notched and dadoed into the top and bottom of the case. The horizontal shelves (H) also have blind dadoes where they fit into the dividers and the sides. The decorative valance (I), also made of curly maple, is glued and nailed in place. The drawer guides (J) are screwed in place. Use oversized shank holes to allow the case to move in relation to the guides. The drawer stops (K) are glued in place 3/4 in. back from the edge. Dry-fit the case and all the cubbyhole parts before final assembly and gluing.

When you're sure everything fits, sand all the parts thoroughly, using successively finer grits of 120 to 220 paper. It's a lot easier to sand now than after all the parts are assembled. When you assemble the desk section, use glue sparingly in the dadoes and dovetails. You want enough to hold the parts together but not so much that you have glue squeeze-out all over the desk.

Base

The base is a straightforward tapered leg construction. First, cut the leg blanks (L) to size and chop the mortises. Then cut the tenons on the aprons (M, N and O) to fit the mortises. Note that there's a 3/16 in. shoulder on the tenon sides, and a 1/2 in. shoulder at the top. Establish the profile on the front and side aprons after cutting the tenons.

Next, make the corner blocks (P) and establish the 3/8 in. by 3/8 in. rabbets on the angled ends. Cut the matching 3/8 in. by 3/8 in. grooves in the aprons as shown.

The blocks stiffen the base and also serve as the attachment point of the base to the desk unit.

With the base unit parts roughly shaped, cut the taper on the legs. First, cut the two tapers on the inside of the legs using a tapering jig in the table saw. Then set the legs in V-blocks for support, and plane the secondary tapers by cutting away the inside corner of each leg as shown in the Bottom View of Leg detail. Also cut the 3/16 in. radius beads on the outside corner of each leg.

As with the desk unit, dry-assemble everything before getting out the glue bottle. When you're satisfied with your work, sand up all the parts and clamp and glue the assembly.

Bookcase Section

The bookcase section is comprised of two sides (R) dadoed into the case top (Q) and bottom (S). The back (U) is rabbeted into the case, and the doors are applied to the front. Two adjustable shelves (T) fit inside.

Start by cutting the stock to size and making the 3/8 in. wide by 3/8 in. deep dadoes in the top and bottom. Then cut the corresponding 3/8 in. wide by 3/8 in. deep rabbets on the ends of the sides. Also cut the 3/8 in. wide by 1/4 in. deep rabbets in the edges of the top, bottom and sides to accept the case back.

Next, cut the rail (V) to size and form the bead using a three bead molding cutter (we used Sears cutter number

9BT2352). Also cut the molding (W) from a 3/4 in. thick by 3/4 in. wide strip of cherry using a 1/2 in. radius cove cutter. Round over the edges of the top and bottom with a 1/2 in. radius roundover bit in the router. Then, use the drill press to cut the holes as shown in the sides for the adjustable shelf pegs (KK).

Dry-fit the parts, and if everything fits, sand the parts and assemble the bookcase. The rail, molding and door-stop (AA) go on after the case itself is out of clamps. The rail and doorstop are just glued in place. The side molding is nailed in place with finish nails, with glue only on the first few inches near the corners. The front molding is glued along its entire length.

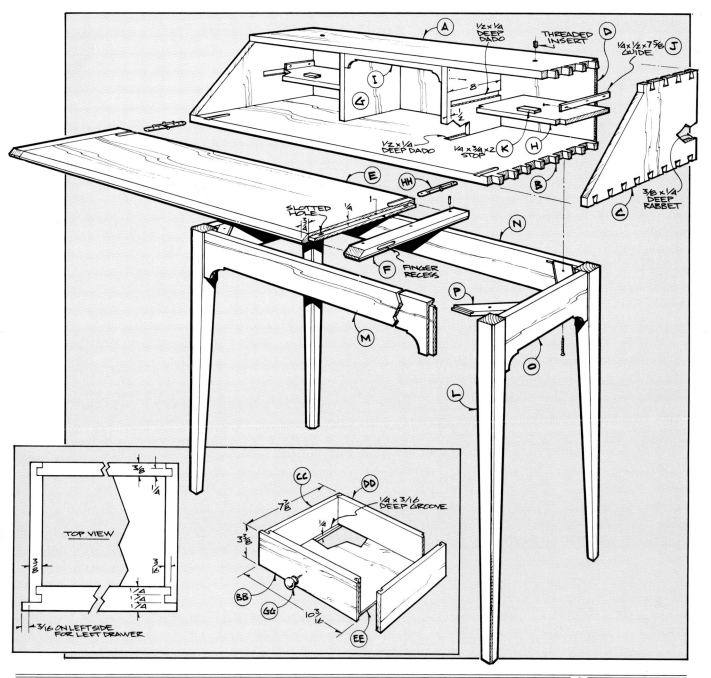

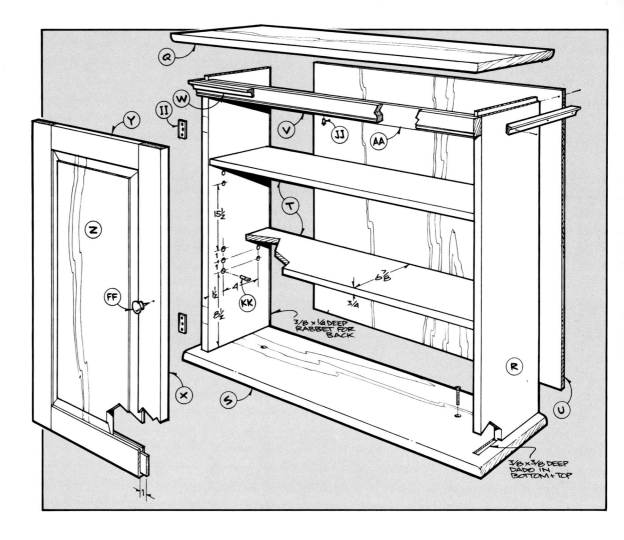

With the case complete, move on to the doors. Mortise the stiles and rails together, leaving a $1/4$ in. shoulder on the tenon sides and a $3/8$ in. shoulder top and bottom. Cut the raised panel using the table saw with the blade set $15/16$ in. high and 23 degrees from vertical. Be sure to use a high auxiliary fence when cutting the raised panel. Note that the grooves in the stiles should allow some room for the panels to expand and contract with seasonal moisture changes. The side-to-side movement is much more pronounced than the top to bottom movement. You don't really need to allow extra room in the rails grooves, but in practice many woodworkers do. It's easier to cut all the grooves at the same depth rather than changing settings.

When you assemble the doors, remember not to glue the panels in place. They float in their grooves.

Drawers

The drawers employ a dado and rabbet to hold the fronts (BB) onto the sides (CC). A $3/16$ in. lip on one side of each drawer helps prevent the drawers from rubbing against the sides of the desk and creating visible wear. The drawer side instead rubs against a $1/4$ in. thick drawer guide, which is hidden by the lip.

Both the dado in the sides and the rabbet in the fronts are made with the $1/4$ in. wide dado head cutter. First set the dado $1/4$ in. from the fence and $3/16$ in. high, then cut the dadoes on the front of all the sides, as well as the rabbets in the backs. You'll need to run the backs through on end, using a tenon jig for support. Adjust the fence to $1/8$ in. from the dado blade and cut dadoes in the back of the sides.

Raise the dado to $3/8$ in., reset the fence to $1/4$ in., and establish the grooves on the insides of the fronts, again running the pieces through on end. Then raise the dado to $9/16$ in. and cut the grooves for the outsides of the fronts. Remove the dado head, replace it with the saw blade and cut the tongues back, as shown, to fit the dadoes. The inside tongues are cut back $3/16$ in. while the outside tongues are cut back $3/8$ in. to allow for the $3/16$ in. overhang.

Use the dado head or router table to cut the $1/4$ in. wide by $3/16$ in. deep grooves in the front and sides for the drawer bottoms (EE). The drawer bottom is slid into place and secured with three small brads driven through the bottom and into the bottom edge of the back.

Finishing Up

Finish sand the three sections and apply three coats of tung oil. Then add the door knobs (FF), drawer knobs (GG), lid hinges (NH), door hinges (II), bullet catches (JJ) and the shelf pegs. Apply the backs to the sections with finishing nails and a small bead of glue. Use threaded inserts to hold the bookcase section onto the desk section. Screws through the corner blocks into the desk bottom secure the desk section. With threaded inserts, the bookcase is easily separated for moving. ●

Techniques

Hand-Cut Dovetails

Everyone appreciates handcut dovetails. Whether on an antique or a contemporary piece of furniture, they're a mark of quality. Still, how many have actually built a project with handcut dovetails?

Are dovetails really that hard? Perhaps you recall the first time you admired their symmetry and marveled at the way the pins and tails interlocked. Maybe you felt *I really like that, but . . .*

Well, get out that bevel square, dovetail saw and marking gauge. Sharpen up the pencil and those chisels, and buy a few new blades for the coping saw. Dovetails—arguably the strongest handcut joint you can make—needn't be so great a challenge. If you need any further encouragement, consider this: When then-novice woodworker Dennis Preston set to work on his handsome Connecticut River Valley Highboy (page 38), it was only the second time he had ever tried cutting dovetails. As Dennis aptly notes, "By the time I had

that chest finished, I had the technique down pat."

Dovetails, Anyone?
Just listing all the types of dovetail joints would take a page. Describing how the different versions are used, and how they're made, could easily fill a book. For the dovetail aficionado, there's a smorgasbord of possibilities. But, from secret-miter dovetails to sliding dovetails and compound angle dovetails, all share one common principle—that of an angled pin or tenon fitting within a like-shaped housing to create a strong mechanical connection.

Here we'll concentrate on the basic through-dovetail used in case and drawer construction. It's the type of dovetail joint you'll encounter most frequently. It consists of a series of angled tenons called *pins* cut on the end of one board, fitting neatly into what's essentially a negative image cut on the end of another board. After the mortises

for the pins have been cut into the mating board, the remaining dovetail-shaped pieces between the pin mortises are appropriately referred to as the *tails*.

Methodology
We'd be remiss in telling you that there's only one approved method for handcutting through-dovetails. Almost every book on woodworking touts a slightly different method for cutting dovetails, and many employ modern power tools for much of the work. Some use the band saw or table saw to establish the sides of pins or tails, others use the router for most of the cleanout work, and still others show the age-old method of dovetail saw and chisel.

While there's no right or wrong way, we think our step-by-step method allows the beginner the best chance for success. Key to it is the use of a coping or bow saw to remove most of the waste from between the pins and tails. The chisel is the more traditional tool for this task, but unless you're experienced with chisel work, it's difficult to get a smooth cut. Beginners often end up with chipping and tear-out as they cut across grain.

The coping saw, or a bow saw with a fine blade, produces a clean cut that requires little paring or filing. Overall, this results in a better glue surface and therefore a stronger joint.

There are two divisions of labor with dovetail work. The first part is largely cerebral. Its focus is layout, pin size, angle and spacing. This is the part that's important if the dovetails are to fit properly, have maximum strength, and show that handsome hand-done look. The second part is the sweat and glory of actually cutting all those dovetails. It may seem like a monumental chore now, but once you've got your confidence up, the work really does go quickly.

Layout
Many find that the biggest challenge in dovetails isn't in cutting the joint, but in doing the layout. The usual questions are "How big should the pins and tails be?" and "What spacing should I use?" and "How do I get the layout right?"

Ideally, both for strength and aesthetics, through-dovetails are laid out evenly and balanced. But don't try to make the widths of the pins and tails exactly equal or get the spacing between every pin identical. If you did that, the dovetails would take on a machine-made look. The most pleasing effect is usually achieved when the pins are narrow, allowing the tails to be broader.

Let's consider pin size and shape first. On $^3/_4$ in. thick stock, an attractive pin size is $^3/_8$ in. on the broad end tapering to $^1/_8$ in. at the narrow end (Fig. 1). But there's nothing wrong with using larger pins. On $^3/_4$ in. thick stock, a pin can be as large as $^3/_4$ in. on the wide end tapering to $^1/_2$ in. on the narrow end. Deciding what size pin to use often depends on the application. For example, you might opt for the larger pins on a blanket chest or a large case, and use the narrower pins on drawers and small boxes. But whatever the application, it's usually a good idea to first draw the dovetails out full-size to make sure the proportions are pleasing.

The angle of the dovetail sides is key to both how the dovetail looks and how strong the joint will be. There are several ways to express this angle, such as a taper, a slope ratio, or a bevel angle. If expressed as a slope, the slope should not exceed about 1 in 8 (which translates to a bevel angle of about 7 degrees), or be less than 1 in 4 (which translates to a bevel angle of about 14 degrees). As

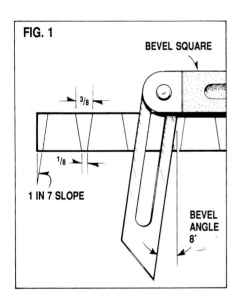

FIG. 1

BEVEL SQUARE

$^3/_8$

$^1/_8$

1 IN 7 SLOPE

BEVEL ANGLE 8°

referred to here, slope is expressed in parts, meaning that for a slope of 1 in 7 there is 1 part of run for every 7 parts of rise. Although dovetail router bits come with sides angled anywhere from about 7 to 14 degrees, a good safe range for handcut dovetails is 8 to 12 degrees of taper, slope or bevel. More taper than

that and you'll risk breaking off short grain on the tails (Fig. 2); any less and there won't be enough angle to keep the joint from slipping apart. As a rule, steeper angles are for hardwoods, the lesser angles for softwoods.

But, to lay out dovetails in the simplest way possible, it helps to just

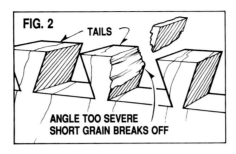

FIG. 2 TAILS

ANGLE TOO SEVERE
SHORT GRAIN BREAKS OFF

have a specific size and work with that. Using our example of dovetails cut on $^3/_4$ in. thick stock, a pin that's $^3/_8$ in. wide at the broad end tapering to $^1/_8$ in. at the narrow end will have sides that are angled at about 9–10 degrees, well within our suggested parameters.

Next up is spacing. On stock that's $^3/_4$ in. thick, a good rule of thumb when using narrow pins is to space the pins somewhere between 1 and 1$^1/_2$ in. apart on-center. Spacing between pins should never exceed about 2$^1/_2$ in. on stock that's less than 1 in. thick. The advantage of using fewer pins is that the amount of work required is reduced, and that's one of the big reasons you'll see narrow pins and wide spacing on so many antiques. Increasing the spacing to more than 2$^1/_2$ in. doesn't provide the joint with enough strength.

Using our suggested 1$^1/_2$ in. pin spacing often works out nicely where stock widths are multiples of 1$^1/_2$ in.— such as a 6 in. wide board. But what about those instances where the numbers don't work out perfectly? You could get that calculator out and transfer the decimals into fractions of an inch, but a much faster and easier method is to just use the technique shown in Fig. 3. Here, by angling a steel ruler across the board, you can get an evenly spaced layout no matter what the actual board width. Just decide how many pins you want, and at what spacing, then angle the ruler to get the pin center points.

Here's an example to show how this works. Let's say your board width is 6$^7/_8$ in. instead of 6 in. If the board were 6 in. wide, you'd use five pins (three full pins

with half-pins on each edge) with a 1$^1/_2$ in. spacing. But with the 6$^7/_8$ in. wide board, five pins would leave a little too much space between. Using six pins (four full pins with half-pins on the edges) would make the pin spacing a hair over 1$^1/_8$ in. on-center, a more attractive layout. Just use the next multiple of 1$^1/_2$ in., which in our example would be 7$^1/_2$ in. Angle the ruler across the board so that the end of the ruler is on the corner and the 7$^1/_2$ in. mark is even with the far side. Then tick off a mark at every 1$^1/_2$ in. Transfer those marks to the end of the board and you've got your pin centers!

Those of you who are calculus majors will probably recognize that depending on the size of the half-pin at the edges, the actual spacing between pins on a board with more than three pins may not be exactly equal. You're correct, although the naked eye will never notice! To explain, the term half-pin does not refer to a pin that's been neatly halved. Rather it refers to the fact that the pin is angled on one side only. To halve a pin that's only $^1/_8$ in. wide at its narrow end would produce a half pin that's too narrow. More properly, half-pins are sized so their width at the narrow end is the same or a little more than the full

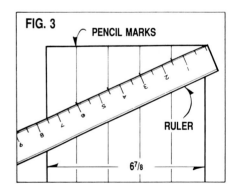

FIG. 3 PENCIL MARKS

RULER

6$^7/_8$

pins. Anything less than that and you risk splitting the stock. With case and drawer construction, always try to use a dovetail layout that has half-pins at either edge. This is important for the integrity of the joint, since locating a tail at the edge provides little if any strength.

Take a deep breath. All the above instruction notwithstanding, dovetail layout can be as simple as gauging the center point across the width of the board by eye, making a pencil mark there, and then eyeing and marking the center point of each half. Even the angles can be gauged by eye, or simply cut with the saw, no bevel square or dovetail template required. If you doubt this, just take a board, judge and then mark what you think is the center point, and check your mark with a ruler. Surprised at how close you were? Now take the dovetail saw and freehand the sides of a few test pins. Surprised at how good the cuts look?

We've really only hit the basics here on dovetail layout. You can purchase dovetail templates, make your own, and for repetitive work such as drawers, even make full templates. This latter option is a huge timesaver if you've got several drawers that are the same size, but can also be a timesaver on carcase work where you've got dovetails on all four corners. Just remember, with dovetails you'll usually be laying out and cutting the pins first and then the tails.

Once you've got your basic dovetail size and spacing decided, do your actual

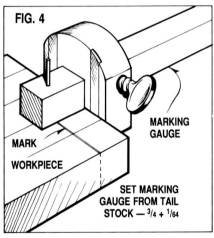

FIG. 4
MARKING GAUGE
MARK WORKPIECE
SET MARKING GAUGE FROM TAIL STOCK — 3/4 + 1/64

layout on the end of the board. First scribe a depth line with your marking gauge. Set the marking gauge from the board that will be your tail stock, and add about $1/64$ in. Scribe the depth line on both faces (Fig. 4). Using the center lines you marked earlier, lay out the pins on the end. You can use either a dovetail template or a bevel square set to the appropriate angle. Then use a square to carry the lines down the faces, both front and back, to meet your depth line (Fig. 5). Now you're ready to start cutting.

Cutting Dovetails
The biggest mistake we can make in cutting dovetails is to confuse the pins and tails. Here's the real beauty of a layout that uses narrow pins with a wide space between. There's no confusing

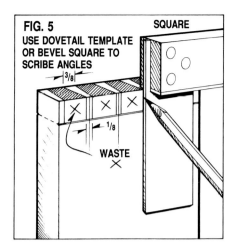

FIG. 5
USE DOVETAIL TEMPLATE OR BEVEL SQUARE TO SCRIBE ANGLES
3/8
1/8
SQUARE
WASTE
X

what parts are the pins, and exactly what's the waste between the pins. Now try looking at the end of a board where the pins and tails are roughly the same width. It's hard to judge just what's what without marking the waste area. To be safe, though, and until you are familiar and confident with cutting dovetails, mark out the waste area by making an "X" or cross-hatching with a pencil.

Now clamp the board vertically in your bench vise and cut the sides of the pins. The important thing here is to get a clean start for each cut and make sure each cut is right on the waste side of the pencil line, straight up and down. The choice of tool makes all the difference. A sharp dovetail saw, either Western or Japanese style, is the best tool for the job. The finer and sharper the teeth, the better and neater the cut. Don't bother with guideblocks. By the time you've properly positioned and clamped the block in place for just the first pin, you could have all the pins cut.

Practice on some scrap first. Start your cut on the corner (Fig. 6) and use firm even strokes to cut to your depth line. The first few times you'll probably want to stop and check your progress regularly to see if there's been any deviation from the guide lines. But once

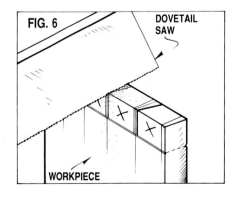

FIG. 6
DOVETAIL SAW
WORKPIECE

you've got a smooth stroke down pat, you'll find that it only takes a few good strokes to reach the depth line. Concentrate on holding the saw so that the blade is vertical, especially as you start the cut, and position your body so that it's in line with the cut being made. In other words, if you are facing the narrow end of the pins as in Fig. 6, for all the right side cuts you should be facing slightly to the right. Then switch your position to the left and make all the left side cuts.

The next step is to clean the waste from between the pins. With a fine blade in the coping saw you should be able to get a cut that needs little if any cleanup. But first you'll want to provide a guide cut so the coping saw blade doesn't wander. Following the depth line you scribed earlier with the marking gauge, use a sharp knife and a straight edge to cut about $1/16$ in. deep between the pins (Fig. 7). Then make a second cut with the knife to establish a "V".

Now use the coping saw to clean the

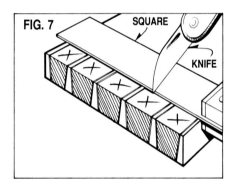

FIG. 7
SQUARE
KNIFE

waste. Make an initial cut down through the waste, then angle the cut as you near the bottom, and cut to the pin while staying even along the bottom. A second cut cleans the remaining waste (Fig. 8). Then use a chisel or a file to smooth the bottom of the waste cut. After a few test pieces, you'll find that your coping saw cuts are so accurate that only touch-up work with the file is needed. As a tip, with delicate dovetails on thin stock, you may want to substitute a deep-throat fretsaw for the coping saw.

Now transfer the profile of the pins to the tail stock. First, though, you'll need to scribe a depth line. Use the same sequence you followed earlier, setting the marking gauge from the pin board and once again adding an extra $1/64$ in. Connect the depth lines across each edge. Now position the pin board on this depth line, and using a sharp pencil,

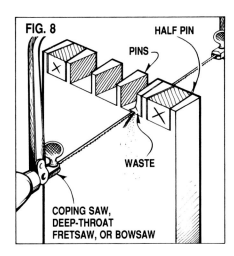

FIG. 8

PINS

HALF PIN

X

WASTE

X

COPING SAW,
DEEP-THROAT
FRETSAW, OR BOWSAW

trace around the pins (Fig. 9). Use a square to carry the lines for the tails across the end grain. With the pins clearly marked, use an "X" or cross-hatching to indicate the waste.

Establishing the sides of the tails isn't much different from making the pin cuts. Clamp the workpiece in the bench vise, but angle it so that your saw cuts will be vertical. Using the dovetail saw and keeping your cuts just on the waste side of the pencil line, make all the tail cuts on one side first, then reposition the board so it tilts to the other side, and make the cuts on the opposite side of the tails (Fig. 10).

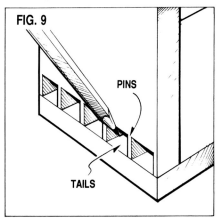

FIG. 9

PINS

TAILS

Use the knife to deepen the scribed depth line from the marking gauge on the waste between the tails, then use the coping saw to cut away this waste (Fig. 11). For the waste at the edges of the board, reposition the piece in the bench vise and cut along the scribe line with your dovetail saw (Fig. 12).

All that remains is to test-fit the dovetails. On your first try you've probably stayed well on the waste side of the lines, which typically produces a tight-fitting joint. But as you gain experience you'll learn to pretty much halve

the pencil line with your dovetail saw cuts, a technique that should produce a smooth-fitting joint with little adjustment required. Where all the pins seem to be a little too tight, use a triangular file or a sharp chisel to pare the bottom of the waste cuts between the tails. If only

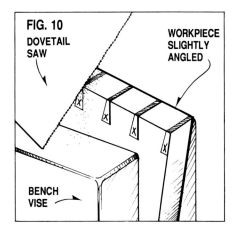

FIG. 10
DOVETAIL
SAW

WORKPIECE
SLIGHTLY
ANGLED

BENCH
VISE

one or two pins are binding, you can try paring just the sides of the pins or tails that are binding.

For easy assembly, dovetails shouldn't be too tight. The joints should slide easily together in a test assembly. Once glue has been added, the wood will swell slightly and make assembly more difficult. Don't worry if there are a few small gaps in your dovetails. Using a

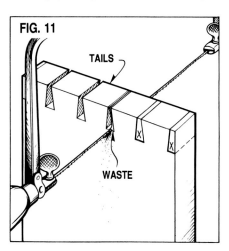

FIG. 11

TAILS

X

WASTE

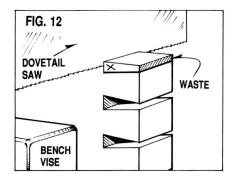

FIG. 12

DOVETAIL
SAW

X

WASTE

BENCH
VISE

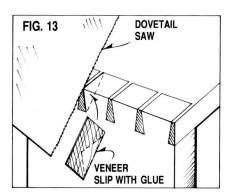

FIG. 13

DOVETAIL
SAW

VENEER
SLIP WITH GLUE

gap-filling glue will fill most minor gaps. Where a gap is too large to fill with glue, after assembly use the dovetail saw to cut down on the corner right along the joint line. Fill the saw-blade-wide gap with a sliver of a similar wood or veneer dipped in glue (Fig. 13). Once the excess veneer has been trimmed, your repair will pass even the most rigid inspection.

When assembling most dovetailed constructions, you'll be dealing with dovetails at all four corners. Use blocks to tap the corners together, rather than using a mallet or hammer directly on the boards. If you need to apply pressure right at the corner, use a dadoed finger block (Fig. 14). With most dovetailed boxes and cases, the primary need for clamps is not to hold the pieces together, but to insure that they're square. With tight-fitting dovetails, the pieces should automatically square themselves up, but if the dovetails are a little loose, you'll need to rely on adjusting the clamp

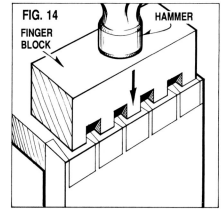

FIG. 14
FINGER
BLOCK

HAMMER

pressure to get a square construction. One way to square a box is to add a clamp diagonally from corner to corner. Check the corners with a framing square, adjust as needed, and let dry. The protruding ends of the dovetails can be pared flush with a chisel or block plane (work in from the edges) or flushed up on the belt or disk sander.

Compound Angle Dovetails

The difference is that instead of the dovetails being cut on the ends of boards that are oriented on perpendicular vertical planes, the dovetails are cut on the ends of boards that are both tilted at an angle.

There are several ways to lay out and cut compound angle dovetails. Our method simplifies the technique by keeping the layout basic, without any advanced mathematics. In addition to a table saw, you'll need a dovetail saw, fretsaw, bevel square, some needle files, a sharp knife and a $1/8$ in. chisel. If you are careful, you can go to work on your actual project stock, but a better choice would be to first cut a sample joint on some scrap that's the same thickness and width as the project stock.

Before cutting the dovetails you'll need to determine the tilt of the sides, and cut the ends and edges of the sides to establish that angle of tilt. The Compound Angle Chart lists the blade tilt and miter gauge angles required to produce constructions with sides that tilt from 5 degrees to 45 degrees. The chart doesn't include any steeper tilt angles because it isn't practical to cut a dovetail joint on sides that exceed 45 degrees. Our illustrations show the sides of the Cutlery Tray project, which are tilted at 25 degrees, but the basic steps are the same whether the sides of the project you are working on tilt 5 or 45 degrees.

Step-by-Step

Step 1: Take the settings from the Compound Angle Chart, and make your cuts on the ends of the boards. Since the Cutlery Tray has sides tilted at 25

P art of the excitement of woodworking is seeing an attractive joint in use. When we discovered the lovely Cutlery Tray on page 26 at a local antique shop, we couldn't help but marvel at how well crafted the compound angle dovetails were. Although it was built some 200 years ago, the tray is still in excellent condition—a testament to the strength of its dovetailed construction.

Compound angle dovetails are not a common joint, but they have several applications. The most common uses are for cutlery trays, knife boxes, and canisters, but also for larger work, such as

dough boxes, cradles and case construction. It's possible to cut a compound angle dovetail by machine with modern fixtures and jigs, but machine-cut compound angle dovetails aren't cut so the dovetails parallel the edges, which results in end grain and therefore a weaker joint. This is one technique where the hand tool method is definitely superior.

It's not mandatory that you have experience with 90-degree dovetails before trying the compound angle version, but it helps to have an understanding of how dovetails fit together before you start. Compound angle dovetails fit together exactly as regular dovetails.

Compound Angle Chart		
(Table Saw Settings*)		
Tilt of Sides (from Vertical)	**Table Saw Blade Tilt** (from Vertical)	**Miter Gauge Angle** (from Saw Blade)
5	$1/2$	85
10	$1^1/2$	$80^1/4$
15	$3^3/4$	$75^1/2$
20	$6^1/4$	$71^1/4$
25	10	67
30	$14^1/2$	$63^1/2$
35	$19^1/2$	$60^1/4$
40	$24^1/2$	$57^1/4$
45	30	$54^3/4$
* All figures are in degrees		

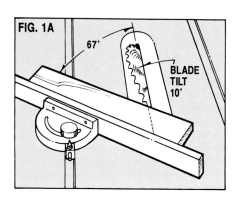

FIG. 1A

67°

BLADE TILT 10°

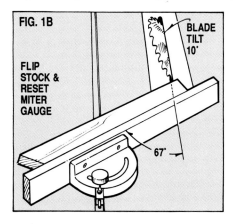

FIG. 1B

FLIP STOCK & RESET MITER GAUGE

BLADE TILT 10°

67°

degrees from the vertical, the table saw blade should be tilted 10 degrees from vertical, and the miter gauge should be angled 67 degrees from the saw blade. Cut one end of each of the four sides (Fig. 1A), then reverse the miter gauge angle setting and cut the opposite ends

of the sides (Fig. 1B). Be sure to first make some test cuts on scrap after you reverse the miter gauge angle setting, or you may find that the butt miters don't meet quite right.

Step 2: Angle the table saw blade equal to the desired tilt of the sides (25 degrees for the Cutlery Tray) and make a ripping cut on the top and bottom edges. The second ripping cut (Fig. 2) establishes the overall width ($4^5/8$ in. for the Cutlery Tray). As shown, you'll need to include a spacer board under the project stock for this second ripping cut. This will prevent the sharp edge created by the first ripping cut from accidently wedging under the rip fence.

Step 3: Lay out the pin spacing. Since the Cutlery Tray dovetails have narrow pins and wider tails, we found that it was easiest to lay out and cut the pins first and then mark the tails from the pins. It's not practical to cut the tails first because you can't fit a pencil between them to then mark for the pins. The layout in Fig. 3A shows the actual pin and tail spacing

as laid out on the ends of the sides. The total adds up to more than the width of the sides because the measurements are being taken along the angle. Start the layout at the top edge and work down. If

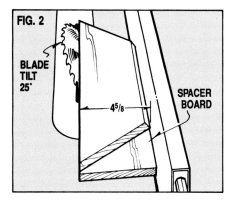

FIG. 2

BLADE TILT 25°

$4^5/8$

SPACER BOARD

you've been accurate in cutting the side width and in cutting the compound angle, you'll find that the layout leaves a little extra on the bottom pin. After assembly, this extra allows you to make adjustments along the bottom edge to get a good flush fit where the sides and ends meet the tray bottom, without the danger of ending up with a pin that's fragile.

We scribed the pin depth mark to allow for the thickness of the sides as measured at the compound angle cut,

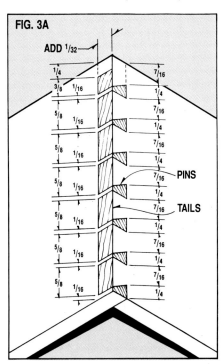

FIG. 3A

ADD $^1/32$

$^1/4$ $^7/16$
$^3/8$ $^1/16$ $^1/4$
$^5/8$ $^1/16$ $^7/16$
         $^1/4$
$^5/8$ $^1/16$ $^7/16$
         $^1/4$
$^5/8$ $^1/16$ PINS
         $^7/16$
         $^1/4$
$^5/8$ $^1/16$ $^7/16$ TAILS
         $^1/4$
$^5/8$ $^1/16$ $^7/16$
         $^1/4$
$^5/8$ $^1/16$ $^7/16$
         $^1/4$
$^5/8$ $^1/16$ $^7/16$
         $^1/4$

and then added an extra $^1/32$ in. The extra results in the pins showing a little proud after assembly and thus allows for final sanding. The pins widen from $^1/16$ in. on the outside face to $^1/4$ in. on the inside

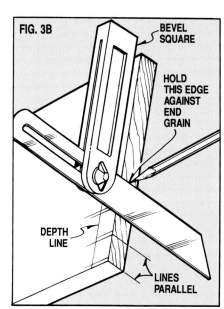

FIG. 3B

BEVEL SQUARE

HOLD THIS EDGE AGAINST END GRAIN

DEPTH LINE

LINES PARALLEL

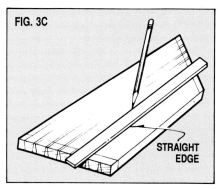

FIG. 3C

STRAIGHT EDGE

face. To carry the bottom lines of the pins from the outside face across the end grain, set your bevel square from the actual board (it should be 67 degrees), and then just move it up and mark each bottom line (Fig. 3B). *Don't make the mistake of holding the bevel square flat to the face of the board.* As shown, to scribe lines that are parallel to the top and bottom edges, you'll need to hold the bevel square so the blade is flat on the board end. If you have a craftsman's protractor with a movable arm, it's a little handier for this sort of work than the bevel square.

To scribe the top lines of the pins, just turn the sides over and tick off the measurements on the inside face so the pin width is $^1/4$ in. and the distance between the pins is $^7/16$ in. Then extend the lines across the end grain to connect the scribed lines on the inside and outside faces. Don't forget to also mark your depth line on the inside faces of the boards. The best way to accurately transfer the depth line from the outside face is to carry the depth line on the front across at the top and bottom edges, and then scribe a line connecting the points on the inside face.

Note how the pins are parallel to the edges. More than anything else, it's important to make certain the pins are parallel if the dovetails are to fit together easily. To get it right: Tick off the pencil points for the pin spacing on both ends of each board, then use a straightedge to mark the cut lines on both ends at once (Fig. 3C). After you have carried the lines for the pins across the ends to the inside face and made your pencil marks for the 1/4 in. pin width there, just repeat the straightedge technique to mark the pins on the inside faces of the boards. Once the pins are all marked, identify

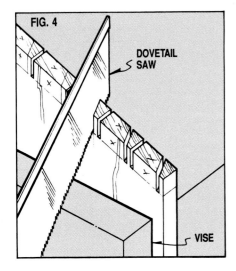

the waste between with an ''X'' so you won't make a mistake during cutting.

Step 4: Use a fine-tooth dovetail saw to establish the pins. The easiest way to get a true cut is to position the board straight up in the vise so your saw cuts are vertical. We used a Japanese dozuki dovetail saw. The advantages of the Japanese saw are its exceedingly thin blade and razor teeth that start the cut with no slipping or wandering, even when working on a slope as we are here. Make your cuts on the waste side of the pins so the saw kerf just grazes the pencil layout lines. Check both faces of the board as your cut nears the depth line. You don't want to cut past the line. Instead of trying to cut both sides of each pin before moving on to the next pin, make all the bottom line cuts first. Then reposition yourself so your body is in line with the top line of the pins and make the top cuts (Fig. 4). After your first few cuts, you'll have the rhythm down and the work will go quickly.

Step 5: The best way to clean the

waste from between the pins is with a fretsaw. But first use a sharp knife to make a starting V-cut along the depth line between the pins on both faces. The V-cut will help guide the fretsaw cut (Fig. 5). If you are careful, there should

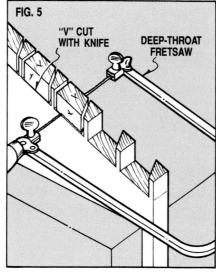

be only minimal work with a triangular needle file and the 1/8 in. chisel to clean out the corners and level the bottom of the waste area between the pins. With a sharp chisel you should be able to just pare the fuzz from the fretsaw cut to get a smooth bottom.

Step 6: Use the pins as a template to mark for the tail cuts. First mark your depth lines on the remaining sides, adding a little extra as before so the dovetails will stand proud when assembled. Then hold the sides with pins on

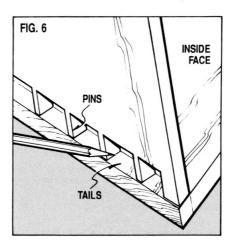

end and flush to the depth line, and mark the tails on the inside face (Fig. 6). A sharp pencil or scribe is important here for accuracy. Use the bevel square to carry the lines across the end grain, making certain the end grain lines are all

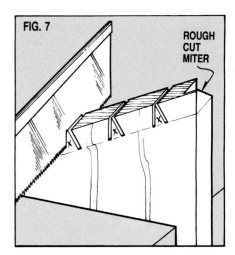

parallel to the top and bottom edges. Finally, mark out the tails on the outside face and identify the waste area between the tails with an ''X''.

Step 7: The top cut on the tails is made with the sides held vertically in the vise. This way your saw will also be straight up and down. For the bottom cuts, reposition the workpiece in the vise so it's angled slightly but so the saw can again be held vertically (Fig. 7). As before, locate the cut on the waste side of the pencil or scribe line. The fretsaw and the 1/8 in. chisel or a triangular needle file are used to clean up the waste between the tails. Be careful not to accidently cut away the stock at the top edge, though. The topmost pin and the corresponding part of the topmost tail are cut on a miter. The miter is cut a little long now and then is trimmed back for a flush fit at the same time that the dovetails are final fitted.

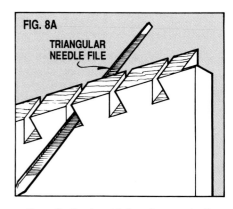

Step 8: It shouldn't take much fine tuning to fit the dovetails and get the miter to close up tight. Clamp the tail side in the vise and try to fit the side with pins. If your saw cuts have been accurate, you can usually make the pins fit by just deepening the cut at the depth line between the tails. The 1/8 in. chisel or a

triangular needle file is perfect for this (Fig. 8A). Try to avoid paring the pins or tails away. It's easy to mess up an otherwise carefully cut dovetail at this stage. If as you slide the dovetails together you identify an area that's

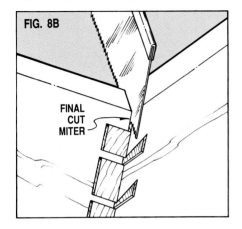

FIG. 8B

FINAL CUT MITER

binding, file or pare only a little bit away at a time. One way to find those pins that are binding is to rub some pencil lead on the sides of the tails. If a pin is binding, you'll see a lead smudge transferred to the part of the pin that needs adjusting.

In fine tuning the dovetails don't make the mistake of having them fit too snugly. The dovetails should slide together smoothly and not require force to assemble. If the fit is too tight, you'll invite a serious assembly problem come glue-up. Since the wood swells a little after the glue is applied, too tight a fit may result in the dovetails failing to fit or seat properly. It's best to use white instead of yellow glue for an assembly like this, since white glue allows a little extra assembly time. There's no sacrifice of strength with the choice of white glue.

As the dovetails are final fitted you'll also trim back the miters at the top edge. One way to get a perfect miter joint here is to make a final miter cut with the dovetail saw positioned right on the corner, but with the dovetails not quite fully seated (Fig. 8B). When you slide the dovetails home, the miter will close up neatly, leaving no unsightly gaps. Don't worry about trying to allow just enough stock for one final miter cut. Leave a generous amount of extra length (about $1/16$ in.) on each mitered end, and then just make as many cuts as are needed to fully seat the dovetails.

Assembly Notes: On the Cutlery Tray project, the V-cuts for the center divider and the scalloping on the top edges of the sides are cut after the dovetails have been final fitted, but before glue-up. ●

Cutting Full-Blind Dovetails

The question could reasonably be asked: Why use dovetails as a case joinery method if they will not be visible? In the Chippendale Small Chest, on page 94, we used full-blind dovetails to join the top and sides. Other methods of joinery, such as a rabbet or spline, are easier than full-blind dovetails, but none is as strong. Also, given the unusual arrangement of a non-overhang top with an applied bead, there are few options for joinery to accommodate the bead detail.

We call these dovetails full-blind because they are totally concealed. Half-blind dovetails are those used to join a drawer front to the sides, where the dovetails are not visible from the front, but show from the sides. Full-blind dovetails are similar to half-blind dovetails, with the exception that both the pins and the tails are stopped partway through the thickness of the board. This means that considerable chisel work is required to cut them. While it's a good idea to have cut at least a few dovetails before you try the full-blind variety, it's by no means a prerequisite. If your dovetails aren't perfect, you can just shim the gaps with slips of veneer before the joint is assembled.

The chest sides and top are made from $^3/_4$ in. thick stock. Note, as shown in the exploded view, that the tails are cut in the top and the pins are cut in the sides. The tails and pins measure $^1/_2$ in. deep and $^1/_2$ in. long.

Start by marking for and then cutting the pins. But, before putting the pencil to the wood, it's a good idea to first set the marking gauge to the thickness of the sides, and scribe a line on the inside surface of the top (see Fig. 1), delineating the depth of the cut that you'll make later between the tails for the pins. With the marking gauge set to scribe a line $^1/_2$ in. from the edge, mark the depth lines on the end grain of the sides, and on the inside face (Fig. 1).

Next, find and mark the center points of the pins. Now make up a hardboard (Masonite) template of a pin. Although you could use a sliding bevel to mark the angled sides of the pins, a template makes the job a little quicker and the pin layout a little more consistent. Line up the center line on the pin template with the center lines that you've marked on the sides for the pins and, using a pencil

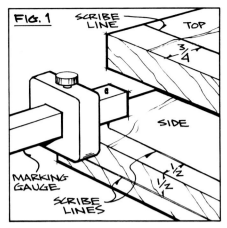

FIG. 1
SCRIBE LINE
TOP
3/4
SIDE
MARKING GAUGE
SCRIBE LINES
1/2
1/2

or scratch-awl, mark the profile of the pins (Fig. 2). Using a square, continue the lines from the pins down the inside face of the sides to meet with the depth line you scribed earlier with the marking gauge (Fig. 3). Use a pencil to cross-hatch the waste area between the pins. This helps eliminate any confusion when you start to cut.

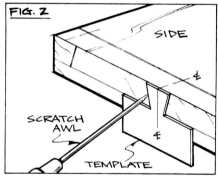

FIG. 2
SIDE
SCRATCH AWL
TEMPLATE

Now use a dovetail saw to make a cut across the corner, establishing the pins (Fig. 4). As shown, the saw must be angled slightly to follow the bevel of the pin. The cut will stop at the depth lines you scribed earlier. Try to keep the saw on line with the pencil lines both on the end grain and on the inside face. If you haven't cut dovetails before, it's a good idea to practice on some scrap first to get the technique down pat.

The saw cut establishes exactly one-

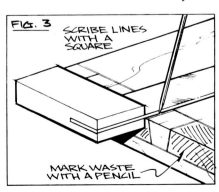

FIG. 3
SCRIBE LINES WITH A SQUARE
MARK WASTE WITH A PENCIL

half the sides of the pins. It doesn't reach the inside half. Some woodworkers continue the saw cut past the scribe line on the inside face, until the cut achieves close to full depth. Others recommend using an old scraper blade, inserted into the saw kerf, to finish the cut into the corner. The scraper is the better method, since it doesn't leave an unsightly assortment of saw cuts that would be visible on the inside of the case once it is assembled. Insert the scraper into the saw kerf, and hit it with the hammer as needed to finish the cut. A sharp tap on

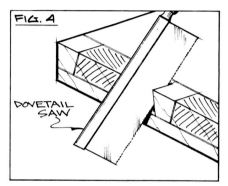

FIG. 4
DOVETAIL SAW

the opposite edge of the scraper is needed to knock it back out. If you don't have an old scraper blade, you could substitute an old saw blade or steel rule. Your only other option is to use the chisel and cut out the corner as you remove the rest of the waste.

The next step in cutting the pins is to establish a starting point for your chisel work. Removing the waste between the pins is a two-step process of repeatedly severing the wood fibers across the grain, and then cleaning out the chip by using the chisel with the grain. The starting point for the chisel is made by scoring with a utility knife (Fig. 5A). Clamp a framing square in place as a straightedge, and make a $1/16$ in. deep score line, as shown, between the pins. Then, with the knife held at an angle, remove the chip (Fig. 5B). This step gives the back of the chisel a flat to bear against for the chisel work that follows. Without this small flat, you'll be starting the chisel on the flat plane of the board, a situation that typically results in chisel creep when the tool is first hit with the mallet. The bevel of the chisel tends to force the tool toward the flat back, compressing the wood fibers on that side. Also, on widely spaced dovetails, without a starting groove for the chisel, you end up with a somewhat ragged

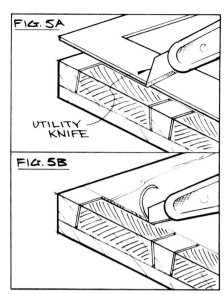

FIG. 5A
UTILITY KNIFE

FIG. 5B

edge, since it's hard to line each cut up perfectly with the previous one.

With your starting point established, now use the chisel and a mallet to sever the fibers down through the grain, as shown in Fig. 6. Don't attempt to cut deep. It's better to make a series of small cuts, rather than trying to clean out the waste in one large chip. After each cut down (remember to keep the flat of the

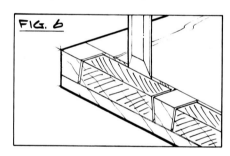

FIG. 6

chisel against the back), use the chisel in from the end of the board, with the bevel facing up, to pop out the waste (Fig. 7). You'll need several repetitions of Figs. 6 and 7 to clean out between each of the pins. Use the chisel to pare the sides of the pins, and the bottom and back of the cutouts between them, to clean up any raggedness. Remember that it's best to slightly undercut the bottom of the waste area between the pins, since this will help insure that the tails seat fully.

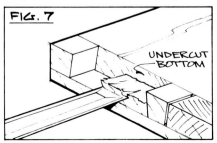

FIG. 7
UNDERCUT BOTTOM

You now have the pins cut on the ends of the sides. Next, you'll cut the tails on the chest top. As noted earlier, you should have a scribe line on the top establishing the depth of cut. The first step in cutting the tails is to use the table saw with the dado head to establish a $1/4$

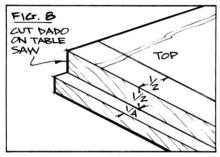

in. wide by $1/2$ in. deep rabbet on the ends of the top (Fig. 8). With the rabbet cut, you can mark out the tails, using the pins as a template. Hold the side in position as shown in Fig. 9, and scribe the lines with a sharp awl. Note that we used a guide board and stopblock to align the edges of both pieces, and the end of the top with the outside face of the side. Then carry the lines across the end grain. Remember, with the tails you'll be removing the areas into which the pins will fit. As before, cross-hatch the waste to avoid any confusion.

The tails are cut using the same basic technique that you used for the pins (Fig. 10). But be sure to keep the saw kerf on the waste side of the line. If the dovetails are a little tight, it's always easier to pare them back a tad, rather than filling the gaps with slips of veneer. Start with the saw, cutting across the corner, then use the scraper blade to finish the inside corner of the cut. When using the saw, note that you'll be able to achieve even less of the cut than with the pins, because of the lip remaining from the

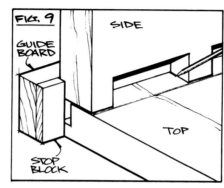

rabbet. Be careful not to cut deeply into this lip. However, if you miss a little and touch it there won't be a problem, because about $1/16$ in. of the lip is cut away when the bead detail is applied after the sides and top are assembled.

Use the straightedge and a utility knife to establish the start line for the chisel as before, and the chisel to sever the fibers and clean out the waste, as with Figs. 6 and 7.

Now dry assemble the sides and top. The dovetails should be a little tight at

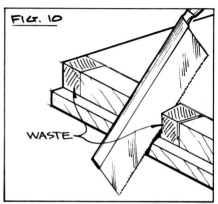

first. Inspect the joint as you start to fit the pieces together, and mark with a pencil the areas that need paring. After paring them back a bit, try the assembly again. Repeat as needed until the fit is just snug. If the dovetails show any significant gaps, fill them by gluing slips of veneer to the insides of the pins or tails. A few gaps won't affect the strength of the joint as long as most of the pins and tails fit snugly. ●

The cabriole leg, as we know it today, is actually a refinement of animal-shaped legs used on furniture in ancient Egypt. Although we might not think of it at first, it's not hard to see the connection as the leg evolved from its initial animal shape to the stylized Queen Anne version popularized in the 18th century. Even the terminology that we use to describe the various parts of the cabriole leg, such as the knee, ankle and foot, reflects this origin.

Our step-by-step illustrations show the Queen Anne style leg used on the Connecticut River Valley Highboy on page 38, but the basic steps involved in making most cabriole legs are similar. Some may have a carved ball-and-claw foot, a lion's foot, a club foot, pad foot, trifid or even a webbed foot. And depending on the piece on which the cabriole leg is used—be it a chair, stool, table, or chest—the proportions and length will vary. Consistent throughout, though, are the common steps that are used to achieve the easily identified cyma-curved shape of the cabriole leg.

Differences are mainly in the carving and detailing that's done after the leg has been shaped.

Start with the pattern. Because you'll usually be making four legs, it makes sense to use a full-size template to trace the shape directly to your leg stock. To make the template, lay out a 1 in. square grid pattern on stiff cardboard or some thin plywood, transfer the profile using the grid pattern provided along with the Highboy project, and then cut and smooth the template edges (Fig. 1).

Based on the pattern, you'll need to rough-size the blanks for the legs. As shown in Fig. 2, you can either use a single block for each leg, or to save stock just laminate additional blocks as needed to achieve the necessary thickness at the knee and foot. Unless you've got a near perfect grain match, though, the single block is the preferred method for the leg. The ears (Fig. 3) are added and shaped after the case is assembled, and are not a part of the leg at this stage. Adding and shaping the ears is described in the highboy project.

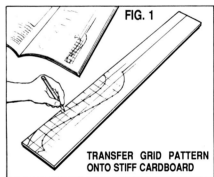

FIG. 1

TRANSFER GRID PATTERN
ONTO STIFF CARDBOARD

As shown in Fig. 3, the length of the leg includes the four corners of the base section of the highboy, so the overall length is 35^1/4 in. You'll need 12/4 stock for the 3 in. square leg blanks for the highboy if you are to avoid any laminations and glue lines. Make sure the leg blank is square, and that the two inside faces have been jointed smooth and square. This is especially important if you are to achieve a good fit when the case parts are joined to the legs.

With your leg blanks sized, now use your full-size template to trace the leg profile to the stock. As shown in Fig. 4, you'll be tracing the pattern onto two adjacent faces of each leg blank. Use tape to hold the template in position. Be sure to locate the template so the long flat edge is flush with what will be the

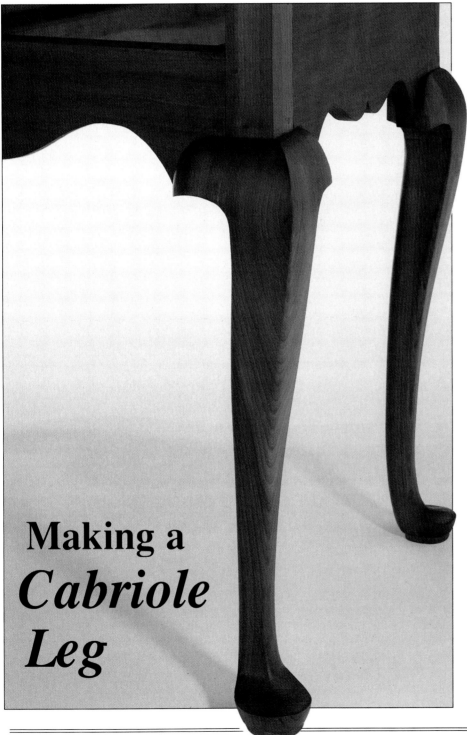

Making a
Cabriole
Leg

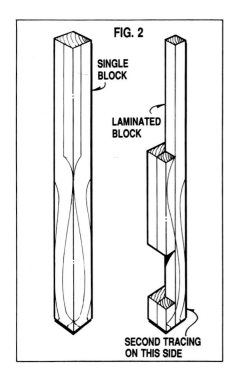

FIG. 2

SINGLE BLOCK

LAMINATED BLOCK

SECOND TRACING ON THIS SIDE

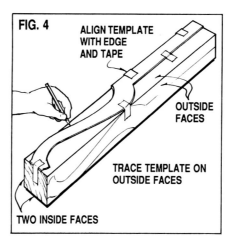

FIG. 4

ALIGN TEMPLATE WITH EDGE AND TAPE

OUTSIDE FACES

TRACE TEMPLATE ON OUTSIDE FACES

TWO INSIDE FACES

The foot is still square at this stage, so you'll need to pencil in the foot profile. As shown in Fig. 7, the pad foot shown has a 2 in. radius at the narrowest point (the base of the pad), and a $2^3/4$ in. diameter across the width of the flare. But a cross-section of the foot at the flare is not a pure radius. Instead, it has more

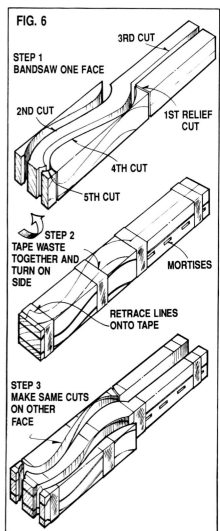

FIG. 6

STEP 1 BANDSAW ONE FACE

3RD CUT

2ND CUT

1ST RELIEF CUT

4TH CUT

5TH CUT

STEP 2 TAPE WASTE TOGETHER AND TURN ON SIDE

MORTISES

RETRACE LINES ONTO TAPE

STEP 3 MAKE SAME CUTS ON OTHER FACE

inside face of the leg, where the case parts will be joined. Repeat this procedure when tracing the profile on the adjacent face.

Next, lay out for the mortises that will accept the tenons on the sides, frame stretchers and apron (Fig. 5). Since your leg blank is still just a block, it's important that you locate the mortises properly. Mark what will be the waste area of the blank to eliminate any confusion. Then use a drill press to rough out the mortises, and a chisel to dress the mortise sides.

As shown in Fig. 6, cutting the legs to

shape is actually a 3-step process. We used the band saw, but a bow saw would have been the traditional tool of choice. With the leg blank laying on its side, make your initial cuts. Note the use of a relief cut at the knee, which eliminates having to back the blade out through a rather long cut. Once the relief cut is made, the cut sequence isn't all that important. Save the short cut at the foot for last, again to avoid having to back the blade out.

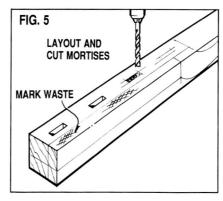

FIG. 5

LAYOUT AND CUT MORTISES

MARK WASTE

After the initial cuts are made, take some masking tape and tape the waste pieces back in place. Flip the block over so the adjacent face is now facing up and use your full-size template to retrace the pattern lines over the masking tape. Then follow the same basic cut sequence as before, making the relief cut at the knee as before to avoid having to back the blade out.

With the cabriole leg on our highboy, very little shaping remains to be done. A traditional cabinetmaker might have reached for the spokeshave here, but that's a tool that takes some skill to wield, especially when faced with the reversing grain direction of a cyma curve. Instead, we recommend that you use just a gouge, if you have one, and some files and scrapers.

of an elliptical or spoon shape, with the $2^3/4$ in. dimension being the measurement across the width of the spoon. The length of the spoon shape at the flare is about $3^1/4$ in. A compass can be used to scribe the 2 in. radius on the bottom of the leg, but for the shape at the flare you'll need to hold the leg upright and draw the profile in freehand.

Use the gouge to rough-shape the pad foot. You'll need to hold the leg securely for shaping. The best advice is to anchor it firmly between the bench vise and a stopblock or bench dog, if your bench is so equipped. Work from the flare down to the 2 in. radius to take advantage of the grain direction (Fig. 8). Then work

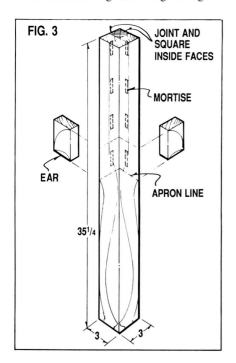

FIG. 3

JOINT AND SQUARE INSIDE FACES

MORTISE

EAR

APRON LINE

$35^1/4$

3

3

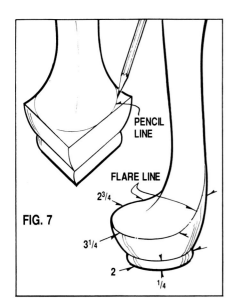

FIG. 7

PENCIL LINE

FLARE LINE

2³/₄

3¹/₄

2

1

¹/₄

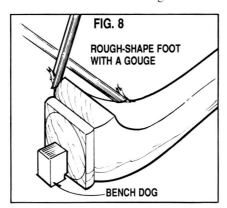

FIG. 8

ROUGH-SHAPE FOOT WITH A GOUGE

BENCH DOG

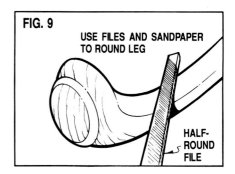

FIG. 9

USE FILES AND SANDPAPER TO ROUND LEG

HALF-ROUND FILE

leg through the ankle shows not a pure radius, but rather the remnant of the four-cornered shape, though the corners are softened and the sides rounded.

All that remains of the leg is to final

on the opposite side of the flare to shape the top of the pad and remove the square corners at the front and sides. Work slowly. Remember, don't remove too much stock here. A cross-section of the

shape with files, scrapers and sandpaper (Fig. 9). But take care not to accidentally round over the corners where the ears will be added later. It's best to just leave the shape rough and then final smooth

the knee after the ears are added. That way you'll not risk removing too much stock before the ears are in place.

Your eye is the best judge of when you have gone far enough with the shaping. For the highboy leg, keep in mind that while a delicate leg may look sophisticated, on a large chest like this the leg needs to retain some heft or it will look out of proportion. And, of course, with all that weight to support, spindly legs are hardly an advantage. ●

Two Traditional Inlay Methods: The Line & Berry and Banding

The line-and-berry and banding inlays shown here appeared on the Small Chest on page 66. Paula Garbarino tells us she learned these techniques at the North Bennet Street School, in Boston, Massachusetts.

The Line-and-Berry

Line-and-berry inlays were traditionally laid out with a compass. Feel free to use the compass to come up with your own line-and-berry design, or you can use our full-size pattern and some carbon paper (Fig. 1) to trace the pattern shown to your stock. In either case, note that the inlay work is completed before the dovetail work on the box begins.

The lines in the line-and-berry inlay are formed by scratching out the various curved channels, and then inlaying these channels with strips of veneer placed on edge. Tools needed for making the lines are a good quality compass (approximately 6–8 in. long) and a $1/4$ in. or $5/16$ in. (whichever best fits in your compass) drill bit. You'll need the type of compass shown, which is sized to accept a pencil.

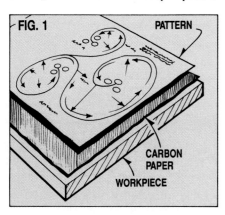

Most stationery stores carry this type of compass. Grind the tip of the drill bit flat and square to a length of $3/32$ in., as shown (Fig. 2). The thickness of the protruding square section should be equal to the thickness of the inlay veneer plus a hair to account for expansion when glue is added. Use anything from a

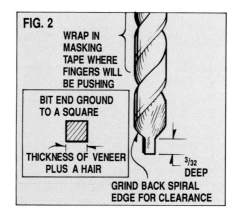

$1/28$ in. to a $1/16$ in. thick maple or holly veneer. To make sure that your scratch cutter is properly sized, make a test channel in some scrap to fit a test piece of the veneer. You should start with the scratch cutter a little larger than necessary, and then grind it back until it's just a little wider than the veneer is thick.

The veneer is now cut into $3/32$ in. wide strips (Fig. 3). Be sure to select veneer that has a consistent straight grain, or it will have trouble making the tighter curves without splitting out. Make a fresh table saw insert, raise the blade up through the insert, and clamp an auxiliary wood fence tight to the saw table. A wooden guideblock screwed to the fence directly above the blade holds

the veneer down and prevents its shattering. The use of a fresh insert insures that the narrow strips don't get caught in the gap between the blade and your regular insert, and the auxiliary fence prevents the veneer from accidentally sliding under the regular fence. A fine-tooth blade is best for cutting the veneer to the $3/32$ in. width, since it's less likely to catch and perhaps shatter the delicate veneer. You can also resaw your own inlay veneer from some holly or maple stock. Just make sure that the strips you cut are flat-sawn so, when on edge, the veneer is best able to make the various curves without splitting.

Now get to work scratching out the inlay channels. As shown (Fig. 4), you'll need to locate stopblocks at the end of

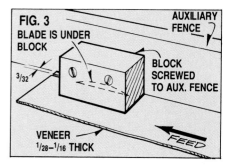

each channel as you work. The blocks—located at the termination point of each arc—prevent you from overswinging your mark and gouging the surface where you don't want a channel. When

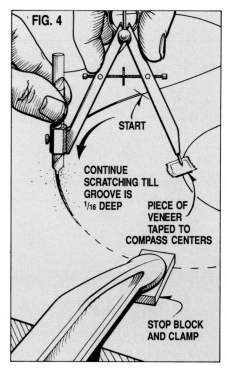

moving from one arc to another, start the scratch cutter in the end of the channel that you just cut. This insures a smooth transition from one arc to the next. Don't try to get two arcs to meet coming from opposite directions; most likely one of the arcs will be a little off and you'll get a step instead of the smooth transition. The arrows on the full-size pattern indicate the direction of the scratch motion. Note the starting point for the scratch work is the spot where the S-curve reverses.

For best results, position the compass so the drill bit is held perpendicular to the work surface. When changing from one radius arc to another, you may need to readjust the length of the bit in the compass to maintain this perpendicular-

ity. As you cut into the wood, make the channel by repeatedly scratching over the same arc line. As shown in the full-size pattern, each inlay is just a combination of several different radius arcs. You'll be scratching out one arc at a time. Set the compass directly from the pattern on your stock, then keep scratching until you've achieved the desired $1/16$ in. channel depth. The $1/16$ in. channel depth will leave the inlay veneer standing just a little proud of the surface, so it can later be sanded flush. Note that for best results you should scratch in one direction only, rather than going back and forth. If you attempt to scratch in the opposite direction, the scratch cutter will be prone to jumping out of the channel. Scratching across end grain is more

difficult, so go slowly in these sections.

The center point of the compass leaves a small hole. These holes can be found on some of the original pieces with compass inlay, but by steaming with an iron the holes can be made to almost disappear. If you'd rather not have any holes, just tape a small scrap of veneer over the compass center points to serve as protection.

Don't be concerned with the end point of your lines, since the berry that the lines terminate in will cover any small error. Once your scratch work is complete, cut the veneer strips that you made earlier to length and dry-fit them. Start with the long strip (A), cut it a little longer than the $28^{1}/2$ in. indicated, dry fit it, final trim the length, and then glue it

FULL-SIZE PATTERN

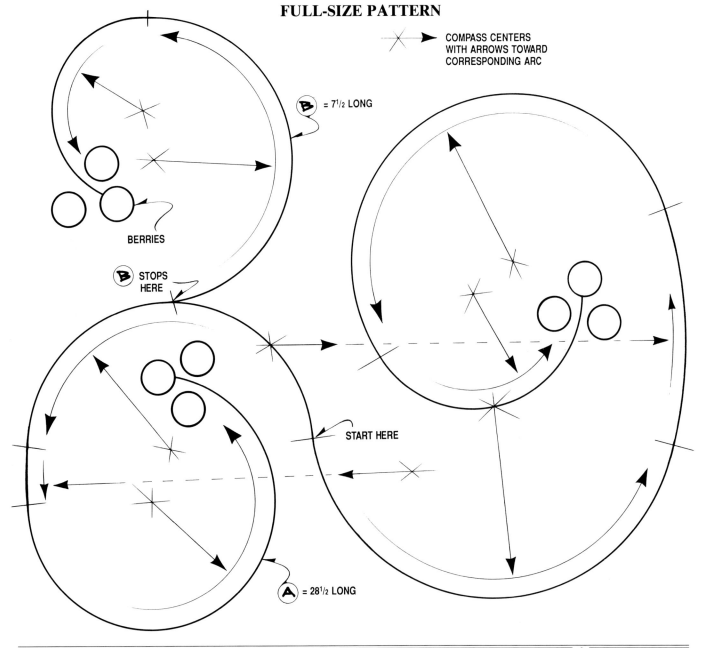

COMPASS CENTERS WITH ARROWS TOWARD CORRESPONDING ARC

B = $7^{1}/2$ LONG

BERRIES

B STOPS HERE

START HERE

A = $28^{1}/2$ LONG

in place. Cut and fit the short strip (B), again starting with the veneer a little longer than the 7½ in. length shown.

The gluing procedure is to first use a syringe glue applicator with a needle tip

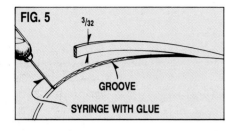

FIG. 5

3/32

GROOVE
SYRINGE WITH GLUE

to squeeze a line of glue into the channel, and then press the veneer into place (Fig. 5). Don't be afraid of excess glue squeezing out; that will be cleaned

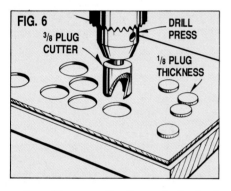

FIG. 6

3/8 PLUG CUTTER

DRILL PRESS

1/8 PLUG THICKNESS

up later. Use a small roller or the back of a spoon to apply a gentle, even pressure to firmly seat the veneer. Remember, too much pressure risks crushing the inlay. Once seated, wipe away excess glue, let

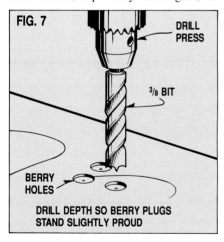

FIG. 7

DRILL PRESS

3/8 BIT

BERRY HOLES

DRILL DEPTH SO BERRY PLUGS STAND SLIGHTLY PROUD

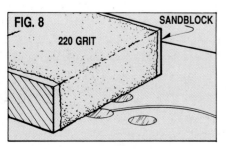

FIG. 8

SANDBLOCK

220 GRIT

dry, then carefully plane, scrape or sand the veneer flush.

The berries are made with a ³/₈ in. diameter plug cutter (Fig. 6), and should fit neatly into a hole drilled with a ³/₈ in. diameter brad-point drill bit (Fig. 7). But it's a good idea to first confirm that this is the case, since occasionally there's a frustratingly poor match between a particular bit and plug cutter. I used maple for the berries, but another nice choice would be a mixture of contrasting colors such as maple, cherry, cedar and mahogany. The berries need not be any thicker than about ⅛ in., but there's nothing wrong with cutting them from heavier stock—up to about ³/₈ in. Whatever the thickness of the berries, set the depth stop on your drill press to drill a hole that will leave the berries, like the veneer inlay, standing a little proud of the surface. Glue the berries in place, let dry, then sand flush (Fig. 8).

The Banding
Each side of the chest has an outline of banding that's made from several contrasting woods. The woods I used here are elm and purpleheart with a maple outline, but combinations of ash and padauk or white oak and mahogany would also work nicely, either with the maple or perhaps a holly outline instead. Similar bandings can also be purchased.

This banding uses the traditional technique of stacking, cutting, restacking and cutting to create usable lengths of finished banding. Start with ¼ in. thick by 2 in. wide by 12 in. lengths of stock. You'll need two pieces each of the light and dark woods. Glue them face to face, alternating the light and dark woods and staggering the ends at a 45-degree angle as shown (Fig. 1) to create a 1 in. thick lamination.

When the four-piece lamination is dry, use the table saw with the miter gauge, angle the blade 45 degrees, and cut the lamination into three 4 in. lengths (Fig. 2). Be sure to use a good quality hollow-ground combination blade, since it's important that your cuts produce a smooth, clean surface.

Now glue and stack the three lengths one atop the other to create a 3 in. thick lamination (Fig. 3). The important thing with this glue-up is to keep the three 45-degree edges perfectly flush to maintain a true 45-degree angle. As shown,

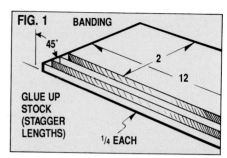

FIG. 1

BANDING

45°

2

12

GLUE UP STOCK (STAGGER LENGTHS)

1/4 EACH

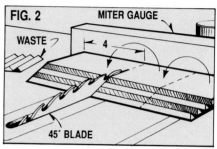

FIG. 2

MITER GAUGE

WASTE

4

45° BLADE

clamping against a block with wax paper will help accomplish this. You'll also need two 45-degree angle clamp blocks (one on each end) to hold the lamination together.

When this lamination is dry, clean any glue squeeze-out off the 45-degree surface that faced the wax paper, and from

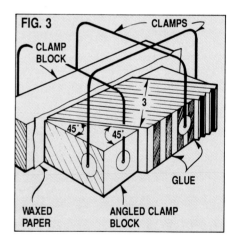

FIG. 3

CLAMPS

CLAMP BLOCK

3

45° 45°

GLUE

WAXED PAPER

ANGLED CLAMP BLOCK

the two sides, and use the table saw to slice off a series of ¼ in. thick strips (Fig. 4). Make a notched pushstick, and glue some fine sandpaper in the notch to help the pushstick control the ¼ in. thick sections after they've been severed. The pushstick is needed to push the sections clear of the blade. Use either the hollow-ground combination blade or a good thin-kerf blade to yield a smooth surface.

Next, glue and stack four of the sections that you just cut end-to-end to yield a total length of about 12 in. The easiest way to make this assembly is to lay some wax paper on a piece of ³/₄ in.

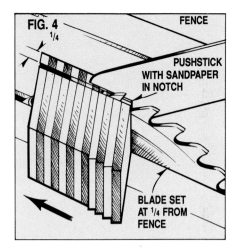

FIG. 4

FENCE

1/4

PUSHSTICK WITH SANDPAPER IN NOTCH

BLADE SET AT 1/4 FROM FENCE

thick plywood that's at least 12 in. long and then assemble the four sections end-to-end on the wax paper (Fig. 5). A 1/4 in. thick waxed block on one edge will serve to help line the four sections up evenly, and you'll need an angled clamp block on each end to provide end-to-end pressure with a pipe or bar clamp. Finally, add some more wax paper topped by another piece of plywood—or a waxed clamp block instead—over the glued-up sections. Several C-clamps will provide top-to-

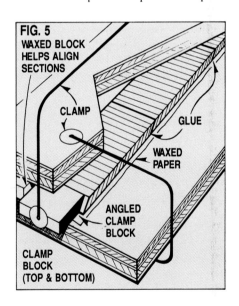

FIG. 5
WAXED BLOCK HELPS ALIGN SECTIONS

CLAMP

GLUE

WAXED PAPER

ANGLED CLAMP BLOCK

CLAMP BLOCK (TOP & BOTTOM)

bottom pressure on the assembly until the glue dries.

With the assembly out of the clamp blocks, clean any glue squeeze-out from the top and bottom faces, and add a layer of maple or holly veneer both top and bottom (Fig. 6). Use the same clamping system of wax paper and plywood, but there's no need for the alignment or end blocks. Once that assembly is dry and out of clamps, trim the excess veneer both top and bottom.

Now move once more to the table saw, and again using a thin-kerf or a hollow-ground combination blade, rip the 1/16 in. thick banding strips (Fig. 7). Use either a new insert or clamp a section of plywood to the saw table and raise the blade up through the plywood. In either case, the idea is to end up with

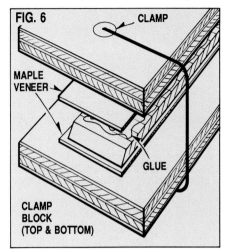

FIG. 6

CLAMP

MAPLE VENEER

GLUE

CLAMP BLOCK (TOP & BOTTOM)

a blade without any gaps on either side into which the thin strips of banding could slip. Cut enough banding to satisfy your needs for the chest. The lamination shown should yield sufficient banding for our chest.

The banding recesses are cut using the table saw dado head. Set the dado head width to equal the width of the banding

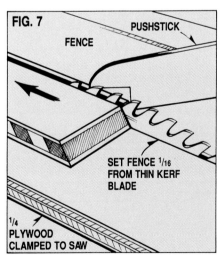

FIG. 7

FENCE

PUSHSTICK

SET FENCE 1/16 FROM THIN KERF BLADE

1/4 PLYWOOD CLAMPED TO SAW

that you just cut. The dimension should be about 5/16 in., but will vary depending on the thickness of the holly or maple veneer that you sandwiched the banding between. To insure that the dado head is set properly, cut a recess in a scrap board and test-fit a piece of banding. If the fit is proper, move on to the chest parts. The height of the dado head should be a little

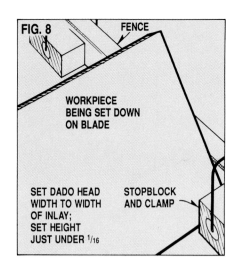

FIG. 8

FENCE

WORKPIECE BEING SET DOWN ON BLADE

SET DADO HEAD WIDTH TO WIDTH OF INLAY; SET HEIGHT JUST UNDER 1/16

STOPBLOCK AND CLAMP

less than 1/16 in., which should produce a recess that will leave the banding just slightly proud of the surrounding surface. The fence will be located 3/4 in. from the dado head for the horizontal bandings, and 1 1/2 in. from the dado head for the vertical bandings. Set up stopblocks to limit the length of cut, and lower the stock down over the cutter (Fig. 8). You'll need two different stopblock setups, one for the horizontal banding recesses, and another for the vertical cuts. Use a chisel to square the corners of the banding recesses.

Once all the recesses have been cut, all that remains is to cut and fit the banding (Fig. 9). You can arrange the banding as I did or try your own design. The banding is cut to length using a sharp chisel, a mallet and a combination square. Glue and clamp the banding, using clamping blocks to seat the banding in the recesses. Then immediately remove the clamping blocks, wipe away any excess glue, and re-clamp. Wax paper between the clamping blocks and the banding prevents the blocks from being glued to the work. When dry, scrape or sand the banding flush. ●

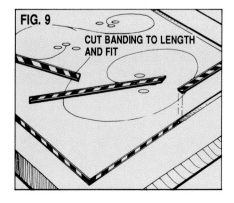

FIG. 9

CUT BANDING TO LENGTH AND FIT

Making the Continuous Bracket Foot

The traditional shaped and molded bracket foot had its origins in Renaissance Europe, and reached a culmination of refinement and design with Chippendale in the 1700's. Understandably, it is widely recognized as one of the loveliest details of classic furniture design.

The molded continuous bracket foot that we employ in the curio cabinet (page 29) is derived from the traditional foot, but features a more contemporary flavor. In building the curio cabinet, we discovered that a unique step-by-step procedure, involving first cutting the bracket profile, and then making a frame and molding the cove shape, vastly simplified the construction process. Taking this new procedure one step further, we found that, with a few modifications, the same concept could be applied to making the traditional shaped and molded individual bracket foot.

Steps 1 and 2: The continuous bracket foot base assembly is simply made to the size needed. The frame size will depend on the project and the size foot required, but for clarity, our illustrations use dimensions and settings as they apply to the curio cabinet.

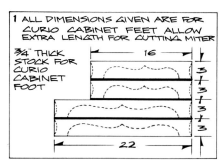

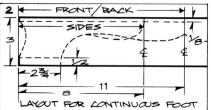

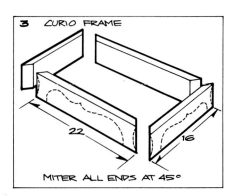

Step 3: Miter the ends of the frame stock at 45 degrees.

Step 4: Lay out the bracket foot profile, and band saw the inner profile. There is no need to either lay out or band saw a profile on the back frame piece,

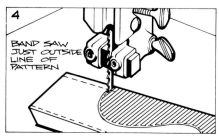

since this side will not be visible. However, the cove must be cut across the back, or the mitered corners will show end grain where the cove is supposed to be.

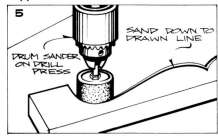

Step 5: Now use various size drum sanders in the drill press to smooth the profiles you have just cut.

Step 6: Glue up the four pieces into a frame. Corner blocks and a band clamp should insure a square frame, as long as the miters were cut accurately.

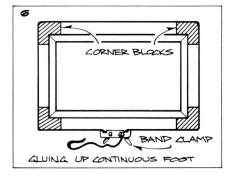

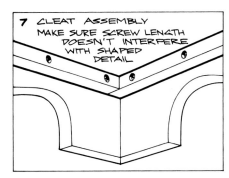

7 CLEAT ASSEMBLY
MAKE SURE SCREW LENGTH
DOESN'T INTERFERE
WITH SHAPED
DETAIL

Step 7: Now add cleats as shown, gluing and screwing them in place. The cleats are simply held flush with the top edge of the frame.

Step 8: Add corner blocks, which are tucked in flush under the cleats.

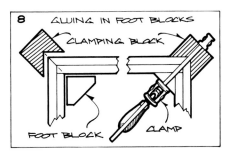

8 GLUING IN FOOT BLOCKS
CLAMPING BLOCK
FOOT BLOCK
CLAMP

Step 9: Now move to the table saw to cut the bracket foot cove. The profile of the cove will depend on four factors: the saw blade height (depth of cut), the fence angle, whether the blade is at 90 degrees or inclined at an angle, and the degree of blade inclination. Fig. 2 shows the shapes that can be achieved with different fence settings when the blade is at 90 degrees. As shown in Fig. 2A, if the stock is passed directly across the blade at 90 degrees, the resulting cove would be a perfect radius equal to the radius of the saw blade. However, as the angle decreases from 90 degrees, the cove cut becomes an increasingly narrow parabolic shape, as illustrated by Figs. 2B and 2D. The blade height will control the depth of cut.

If we now introduce some degree of inclination (tilt) to the saw blade, and set

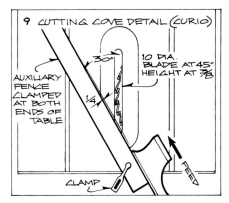

9 CUTTING COVE DETAIL (CURIO)
AUXILIARY FENCE CLAMPED AT BOTH ENDS OF TABLE
30°
10 DIA. BLADE AT 45° HEIGHT AT ⅞
¼
FEED
CLAMP

the fence at any angle except 90 degrees, we will produce a curve with one end deeper than the other, similar to one-half of a teardrop. The side that the blade is tilted toward will always be the deeper end of the teardrop. It is important that you use *only a carbide rip blade* and no other type of blade for this operation. Figs. 1A–D show the various profiles, ranging from the flattened parabola to the exaggerated teardrop, that can be achieved when the blade is tilted.

For any of these cove-cutting table saw operations, we discovered that an 18-tooth carbide tipped ripping blade is most effective for quick removal of a

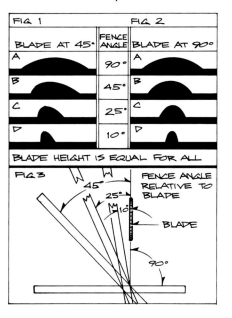

FIG 1		FIG 2
BLADE AT 45°	FENCE ANGLE	BLADE AT 90°
A	90°	A
B	45°	B
C	25°	C
D	10°	D
BLADE HEIGHT IS EQUAL FOR ALL		

FIG 3
45°
25°
10°
FENCE ANGLE RELATIVE TO BLADE
BLADE
90°

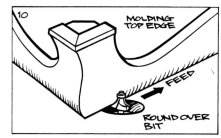

10 MOLDING TOP EDGE
FEED
ROUND OVER BIT

maximum amount of stock. The number of passes needed will depend on the fence setting and the desired cove depth. It is always safer to remove a little stock (¹/₁₆ in.) with each pass and then increase the blade height, rather than attempt to hog all the stock out in a single pass. A final light pass will clean up the cut nicely prior to sanding. We suggest that you use scrap stock to experiment when making the bracket foot to insure that the profile is as desired.

Step 10: (Not required with Curio Cabinet foot). Most bracket feet have a rounded "return" at the top of the cove profile, but we chose not to incorporate

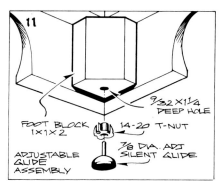

11
9/32 X 1¼ DEEP HOLE
FOOT BLOCK 1 X 1 X 2
¼-20 T-NUT
ADJUSTABLE GLIDE ASSEMBLY
⅞ DIA. ADJ SILENT GLIDE

this detail on the Curio Cabinet. If, with some other continuous bracket foot design, a roundover is required, use a ball bearing guided bit of an appropriate radius in the router table, as shown, to round the top edge of all four sides of the base.

Step 11: Drill for and add adjustable glides, as shown. T-nuts and glides are found at most hardware stores. ●

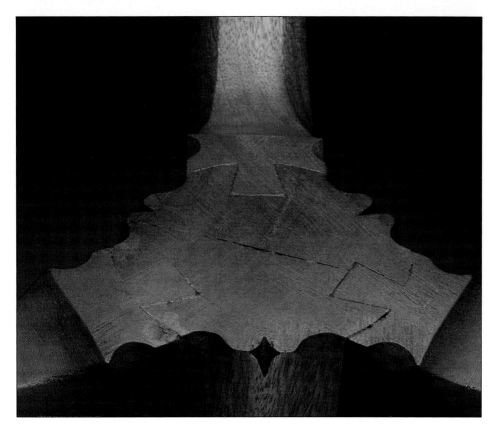

Making Tripod Legs

One of the more fascinating elements of traditional furniture design is the use of dovetails to join shaped table legs to a turned central pedestal. When carefully cut and fit, the result is an exceptionally strong joint.

Paula Garbarino, who built the 18th-Century Philadelphia Tilt-Top Table, tells us that when breakage does occur, it is typically a splitting of the bottom end of the pedestal and not a failure of the dovetail joint. For this reason it is important to make the pedestal as wide in diameter as design limits permit. On large tables, you should also increase the depth and width of the dovetails.

This technique applies specifically to the tilt-top table on page 16, as do the dimensions and angles shown in the following steps. However, the basic technique can be used anywhere you need to join legs to a central pedestal. Except for the use of the band saw and table saw, which speed the work and provide better accuracy, little in the technique has changed from the time when the original version of this tilt-top table was built, about 200 years ago.

To begin, rough cut the three 2 in. thick by 6 in. wide by 16 in. long blanks for the legs. If you have never tried this technique before, we recommend making a practice leg first to test all the setups. Now lay out the side profile of the leg on each of the three blanks. Use a full-size cardboard or plywood template to lay out the profiles so all three legs are consistent. Also note the grain orientation, which is important for maxi-

mum strength. Use the band saw to cut the corners at the sole of the foot and dovetail joint close to—but not touching—the line. Next, as shown in Step 1, clamp the three legs together in the bench vise, and hand plane to the line. The joint and sole surfaces that you are planing must be perpendicular to each other. The template should have provided an accurate pattern, but check with a framing square to be sure.

Next, remove the leg blanks from the vise, and cut the side profiles on the band saw, keeping outside of the pencil line (Step 2). Then re-clamp the legs in the vise, and use the rasp to fair all three legs to the same profile (Step 3). This will help to insure that the legs turn out looking the same.

Using a small block drilled to accept a pencil so the point of the pencil is 1 in. up from your bench surface, mark the center line all the way around each leg (Step 4). As shown, the pencil block is clamped to the bench, and the leg is rotated past the pencil point. This line is needed for alignment of the leg with the pedestal, and also serves as a guide when shaping the leg.

Now make a cardboard or plywood circle template the diameter of the leg end of the pedestal. Lay out the dovetail dimensions (see page 16) on the template. Then transfer a centered dovetail

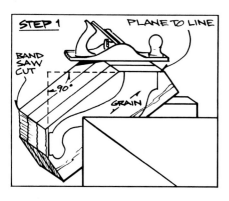

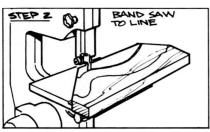

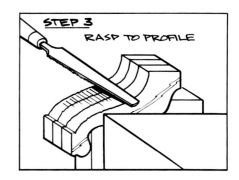

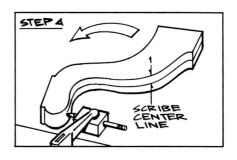

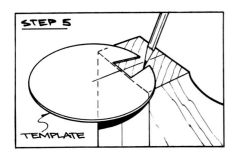

STEP 5

TEMPLATE

to each leg, top and bottom, and draw the curve of the cylinder at the base of the dovetail using the circle template (Step 5). With the foot in the air, first cut the sides of the dovetail on the table saw (Step 6). As the illustration shows, the table saw blade will be tilted to an 80-degree angle. Set the fence so the cut will leave the pencil line. Clamp a hand screw to the leg and riding the top of the fence for extra support and security. Next, with the leg flat on its side, cut the

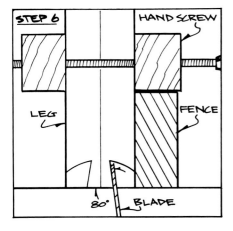

STEP 6   HAND SCREW

LEG

FENCE

80°   BLADE

shoulders (Step 7). Tilt the blade to 70 degrees and cut as close as possible to the curve drawn from the template, but leave the line. Have scrap wood behind this second cut to push out the waste and avoid kickback of the cut-off.

In Step 8 you'll clamp each leg in the bench vise, notch the top end of the dovetail back ³/₄ in., and then use a flat spoon gouge to cope the shoulders of the dovetail to fit the curve of the pedestal. You may want to undercut a bit to insure a flush fit, but the visible line where the

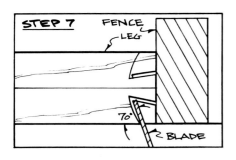

STEP 7   FENCE
             LEG

70°
       BLADE

leg meets the pedestal must remain very straight. This straight edge is required if the leg is to fit properly to the pedestal. The top of the leg where the dovetail was notched back must also be coped to

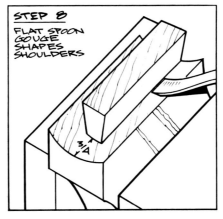

STEP 8
FLAT SPOON
GOUGE
SHAPES
SHOULDERS

³/₄

match the curve of the pedestal.

Next, you'll use the band saw to taper the sides of the leg. Make a paper template that is 2 in. at the dovetail, 1¹/₄ in. at the ankle, and quickly returns to 2 in. at the foot as a guide for tracing the top profile on the legs. Then, using an auxiliary plywood table on the band saw, as shown in Step 9, cut to the scribed line. Note that the leg rests on two points for this operation.

Now shape each leg, roughing in with

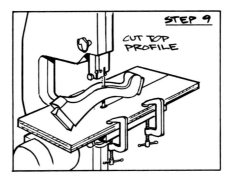

STEP 9
CUT TOP
PROFILE

the mallet and chisel or with the spoke-shave. Cross sections of the leg are shown in the project on page 16. Use a rasp, files, and the cabinet scraper to smooth the legs to final form. The ³/₁₆ in. high pad under the foot is carved with a V-parting tool and small gouges.

Next, you'll cut the dovetail mortises in the pedestal. First, lay out the center points of the three dovetails, 120 degrees apart on the bottom end of the pedestal, and carry the lines to the edge. Then use the dovetail of each foot as the pattern for laying out each of the dovetail mortises, and number the legs and corresponding dovetails so that they

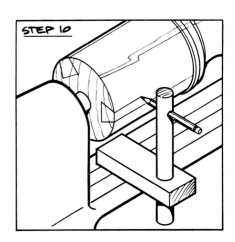

STEP 10

won't be confused later. Returning the pedestal to the lathe, use a pencil holding jig to extend the scribed lines for each dovetail up the pedestal the length of the dovetail. As shown in Step 10, the jig rides off the bed of the lathe.

Now clamp the pedestal in the bench vise, using bandsawn blocks that match

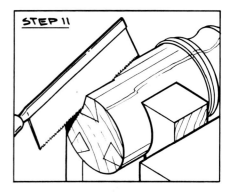

STEP 11

the pedestal curve, and saw up to the pencil lines with a dovetail saw (Step 11). Chisel out the waste, and pare the mortise walls and floor to fit the leg dovetail (Step 12). The fit of the leg should not be forced. If the fit is a little loose, the tail can be shimmed with a piece of veneer. The critical point is that the shoulder edge of the leg be tight against the cylinder. Legs should be glued on only when all other cutting and fitting is completed.   ●

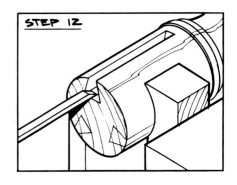

STEP 12

Making the Rule Joint

The rule joint is a traditional fine furniture feature used most commonly with tables having one or more drop leaves. When properly executed the joint makes for an especially attractive detail along the edges where the hinged leaves and fixed table surface meet. The design of the joint serves to effectively conceal the hinge plate whether the leaves are in the open or closed position.

The term "rule joint" is believed to have derived from the brass bound folding boxwood rules that were popular from the 1600's on. The knuckles where these rules folded closely resemble the rule joint. By the time of the William and Mary period the rule joint was quite common, as evidenced by its use on the Gate Leg Table featured on page 54.

Before the era of power tools, the rule joint was fashioned by hand with molding planes and the scratch beader, but the ease of modern methods has made this process impractical. Today's wood-

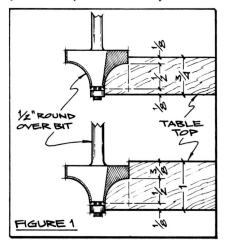

FIGURE 1

½" ROUND OVER BIT

TABLE TOP

worker can accurately reproduce the rule joint using either the router or the table saw equipped with molding head cutters.

When using the router or router table to make the rule joint, you will need matching cove and round-over bits. Bearing guided bits are best since they will not burn the surface along which the bearing rides. The table saw molding head cutter is also an accurate method for making the rule joint. Most standard cutter sets include the ½ in. cove and round-over cutters which we specify here.

No matter which technique is used, the first and most important step is to correctly lay out the position of the joint. There are two key elements to consider: the hinge location and the coordinates of the radius. The thickness of the stock and the size of the bits or cutters can also be factored in, however for practical purposes we have assumed that the stock thickness will be in the area of $^3/_4$ to 1 in., a range which encompasses the thicknesses of most common tabletops. Although theoretically the bit or cutter is determined by the stock thickness, we have found that matching ½ in. cove and roundover bits or cutters can be used to shape a nearly perfect rule joint in stock $^3/_4$ to 1 in. thick. As shown in Fig.

1 the only difference will be a deeper shoulder on the thicker material.

As noted earlier the key elements in making the rule joint work are the hinge location and the position of the radius. If the hinge is to be mortised in place, to accurately lay out its location and the coordinates of the radius, you must first measure the hinge knuckle diameter. By dividing the knuckle diameter in half you can determine the center or pivot

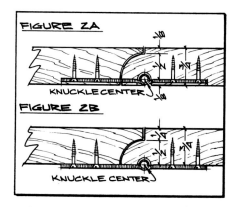

FIGURE 2A

KNUCKLE CENTER

FIGURE 2B

KNUCKLE CENTER

point of the hinge. As shown in Figs. 2A and B the pivot point is important because it dictates exactly where the arc of the joint must begin and end. If the entire hinge is to be mortised (Fig. 2A), then one-half the knuckle diameter is the distance up from the bottom at which the arc begins. If the hinge is to be applied flush (Fig. 2B) with only the knuckle mortised, then the arc simply starts flush at the bottom. Given the same thickness material and the same size bits or cutters, the only variation in the two joints will be the depth of the shoulder.

Fig. 3 shows a basic formula for

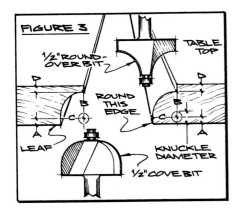

FIGURE 3

locating and cutting a typical rule joint when the hinges are to be mortised in place, as they usually are. Distance A is one-half the knuckle diameter. Distances B and C are the radii of the joint and are equal to the bit or cutter size, which we have set at a constant $1/2$ in. Distance D is the shoulder depth and corresponding lip thickness, which should not be less than $1/8$ in. The critical point to know in all this technical talk is this: For the rule joint to open and close smoothly, the center or pivot point of the hinge knuckle should be located near the intersecting point of radius lines B and C. In actual practice, when mounting the hinge it helps to cheat a little and install the knuckle a hair ($1/32$ in.) toward the leaf side of the joint.

Most experts specify matching bits or cutters for fashioning the rule joint. However the joint works best if the roundover on the tabletop is a tad less than the corresponding cove cut on the leaves. By using the cove bit or cutter to shape a short length of scrapwood and then gluing medium grit sandpaper along the arc, you will have a perfect sanding block with which to reduce the roundover by about $1/32$ in. You may also wish to soften the lower edge of the tabletop (Fig. 3) to avoid tearing along this edge should the joint bind. If, in spite of all these considerations, the joint still binds or catches when mounting the hinges, position the table leaves so that a little space (about $1/64$ in.) remains between the leaves and top along the full length of the joint.

Because the fit of the rule joint can be so critical, and given the fact that a considerable quantity of stock could be wasted should there be a serious problem with the joint, the best way to insure success is to make a sample joint and have a test fitting. With several short lengths of stock the same thickness that you will use for the top and leaves, lay out and cut the rule joint on these test pieces. Mount the hinges exactly as you would on the finished table and check that the joint opens and closes smoothly without catching or binding. If there is a problem, make the necessary adjustments before actually cutting the joint on the finished top and leaves. ●

Making Tambour Doors

The tambour is one of those special elements that make woodworking so fascinating. Rare is the little boy or girl who does not wonder at the way the tambour of Grandpa's rolltop desk works and where it disappears to. Indeed, watching as a well-fitted tambour top or front snakes effortlessly along the hidden grooves can be intriguing, even for adults.

The key words, of course, are "well-fitted." Trying to deal with a tambour that is too tight, too loose, or warped, and that consequently catches, sticks, drags, jams sideways, gets frozen in place, or pops out of its grooves is infinitely frustrating. Although the tambour has been widely used in many different types of furniture ever since its origin in 17th century France, it is every bit as fickle now as it was then. Getting the tambour door right requires careful planning and attention to detail.

Design

There are two specific types of tambour construction: that which is joined by wires, and the fabric backed variety. Although the wired style allows the back of the tambour to be exposed, the fabric backed tambour is better suited to home workshop construction, and we will concentrate on this. The illustrations that accompany this article show the tambour

top of the Rolltop Desk project starting on page 21.

The design of the piece of furniture, the size and shape of the individual tambours, and the size, depth, profile and curve or radius of the tracking groove are all critical elements whose interdependent nature requires that each be precisely worked out and developed with respect to the other.

The Carcase

A strong, stable, well constructed carcase is important since the parts into which the tambour grooves are cut must be absolutely rigid and parallel. Remember that you will probably have to design in a false back (or sides for a vertical tambour) both to isolate the tambour from the contents of the case, and to conceal the fabric side from view when the tambour is open.

The Tracking Grooves

The tracking grooves must be laid out with respect to the radius that the tambour can make without binding. The groove must also be laid out so that the length of the tambour when closed fills the required space, and yet retracts as needed when opened. You will note the tambour groove in the desk is laid out so that, when open, the tambour stops one tambour slat shy of the handle. When

laying out for the groove one must also consider the weight of the tambour. The groove should at least partially balance the tambour weight between opening and closing, so the tambour does not fall back down when fully opened or require too great an effort to control while opening or closing.

As a general rule for size, tracking grooves should fall within a range from $3/16$ in. to $3/8$ in. wide, with the depth dimension usually slightly greater than the width. The groove for the desk is $3/8$ in. deep by $5/16$ wide.

The Tambours

The individual tambours can be made in a variety of shapes, from purely rectangular to half round. The shape of the tambours will be dictated by the general design of the piece, and by factors such as whether or not a reverse curve has been incorporated into the tracking groove. If such is the case, the tambours

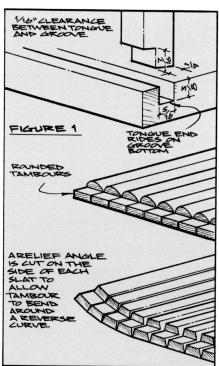

must have a relief cut on either side sufficient to accommodate whatever the reverse curve may be.

Nearly all tambours are made with a shoulder on the exposed side which serves to conceal the tracking groove. The tambour tongue is typically rectangular or slightly wider than it is thick. Fig. 1 shows various tambours and a detail of a tracking groove. The final tambour length is just slightly less than the actual groove-to-groove dimension.

Although on the desk we show a 33¾ in. total tambour length, the actual length will be about ¹/₃₂ in. less to provide clearance. The tambour shoulders are ⁷/₁₆ in. providing ¹/₁₆ in. clearance on either side so the shoulders do not scuff the inside of the case sides. The tambour tongue thickness of ¼ in. allows the tambour to pass freely through the various curves in the ⁵/₁₆ in. wide tracking groove.

Although many simple tambours can be worked out on paper, we strongly recommend making test mock-ups of any unusual or tightly radiused designs. The mock-up need only be of a small

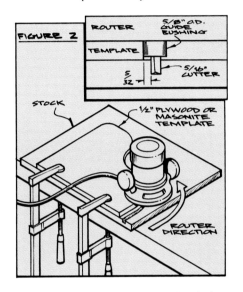

section, but it will insure that the design is feasible. After the carcase has been built, it is too late for a design flaw discovery. We used a mock-up to first test the tambours in the desk.

Routing the Tracking Grooves

After laying out your design, you will need to construct a template as a guide in making the tracking groove. Size the template to accommodate a specific guide bushing and the bit you will use. As shown in Fig. 2, our ½ in. thick plywood template is sized ⁵/₃₂ in. smaller than the inside groove profile and is used with a ⁵/₈ outside diameter guide bushing and the ⁵/₁₆ in. diameter straight cutter. As you will note from the Fig. 2 illustration, the router is moved *counterclockwise* around the perimeter of the template. Naturally, for the opposite or left side groove, the counterclockwise router motion must start at the *back end* of the tracking groove. Also note that we rout the tracking groove *before*

cutting the carcase sides to shape. This way the final profile of the sides can be cut exactly parallel to the tracking grooves. Remember, make your plywood or Masonite template very carefully, since the tracking grooves will ultimately reflect every little hump or inconsistency in the template. The template must be accurately located and clamped to the sides so that both tracking grooves are exact mirror images of each other and precisely parallel to one another. Since it is best that the actual router cuts be as smooth as possible, you do not want to hog out to much stock or labor the router. We used four depth settings to achieve our final ³/₈ in. tracking groove depth.

Once the routing is complete, a dowel wrapped with sandpaper can be used to clean out and smooth the grooves. Pre-finish the inside surfaces, wax the grooves with paraffin, and assemble the case *before* making the individual tambours. Make certain that no glue gets into the grooves, of course.

Making the Tambours

Start with the tambours somewhat longer and wider than the intended final length. We recommend cutting about 30

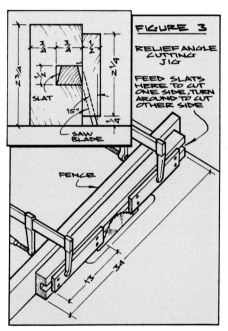

percent more tambours than you actually require, since some will inevitably have to be discarded due to warping.

After flattening and milling stock to achieve final tambour thickness, allow the boards from which you will rip the individual tambours to acclimate. Then

rip the tambours to final width, sticker, and allow to dry for at least 24 hours. Discard any pieces that have warped, twisted, or are otherwise no longer straight.

Since our tracking groove incorporates a reverse curve, the tambours must have a relief angle cut into their sides. Although a router or shaper can be used

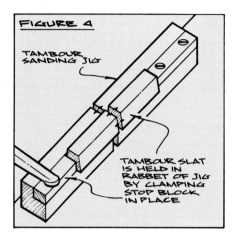

for this, we chose the table saw. Fig. 3 shows a table saw jig for cutting this relief angle. Note that the saw blade must be set at a 15-degree angle, the jig clamped to the saw table, and the blade then raised up slightly into the jig. Slide the tambour through to cut the first side, then reverse it and pass through to cut the opposite side. A second jig (Fig. 4) is made to hold each tambour for final sanding. Sand only the sides; the face will be sanded after tambour glue-up.

Now make a gluing fixture to hold the tambours in place while the fabric or canvas backing is applied to their back side. Our jig (Fig. 5) is made on a particleboard base. The rabbeted side boards must be positioned to hold the tambours tightly. Cut three end pieces the same thickness as the tambours to fit under the rabbet, and also cut a number of wedges, as shown. If your handle is to be glued up on the canvas, make provisions for it. Our handle is applied after, thereby simplifying the glue-up.

Wax the end pieces as indicated, wedge the tambours up tight, and screw the rabbeted side pieces down securely to hold them flush.

Next, apply the fabric back. We used 10 ounce art canvas, sold at most art supply stores. The canvas is sized to come up at least ³/₈ in. short of either carcase side and should overhang several inches on either end. The extra

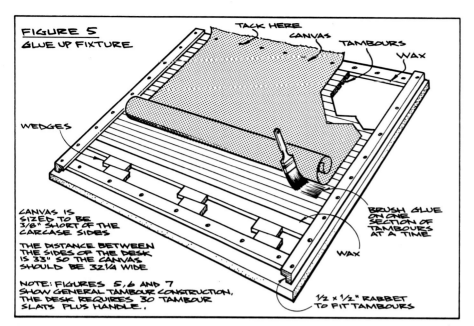

FIGURE 5
GLUE UP FIXTURE

TACK HERE

CANVAS

TAMBOURS

WAX

WEDGES

CANVAS IS SIZED TO BE 3/8" SHORT OF THE CARCASE SIDES

THE DISTANCE BETWEEN THE SIDES OF THE DESK IS 33" SO THE CANVAS SHOULD BE 32¼ WIDE

NOTE: FIGURES 5, 6 AND 7 SHOW GENERAL TAMBOUR CONSTRUCTION, THE DESK REQUIRES 30 TAMBOUR SLATS PLUS HANDLE.

BRUSH GLUE ON ONE SECTION OF TAMBOURS AT A TIME

WAX

½ x ½" RABBET TO FIT TAMBOURS

edge-guide. Use a sanding block to final sand and smooth the tambour tongue.

Test fit and adjust the tambour as necessary. Remember, the tambour shoulder should not rub on the case.

Lastly, make the handle. A variety of handle designs are acceptable. Some are applied while others feature a shaped or extended end tambour serving as a pull. Our handle, which is applied, utilizes a rabbet to conceal the canvas and accept a backing strip. The backing strip actually sandwiches the canvas in the handle rabbet. Location dowels in either end of the handle ride in the tracking grooves to keep it on line. Details of the handle appear in the desk project.

canvas at the front is needed to apply the handle section. We used melt-type hide glue, since it thickens quickly. Start at

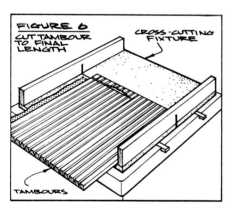

FIGURE 6
CUT TAMBOUR TO FINAL LENGTH

CROSS-CUTTING FIXTURE

TAMBOURS

one end, positioning and lining up the canvas and tacking it to the end piece. Now brush the hot glue over the first section of three or four tambours, making certain coverage is complete. Press the canvas in place, using a block of wood to work out from the center,

smoothing the canvas parallel to the tambours. Peel the canvas back slightly to expose the glue line, then brush glue onto the next three or four tambours, overlapping the glue to insure total coverage. Continue this process until all the tambours are canvassed over. Do not stretch the canvas perpendicular to the tambours. Also, do not brush glue on or work the canvas smooth perpendicular to the tambours, as this will tend to force the glue between the individual tambours. Allow the tambour to dry overnight in the glue-up fixture before removing it.

When completely dry, measure the groove-to-groove distance (narrowest point) and cut the tambour to final length on the table saw using the crosscutting fixture shown in Fig. 6. Next, clamp the tambour end that overhangs the table saw (Fig. 7A), set the blade depth, and establish the tongue shoulders as illustrated in Fig. 7B. Clean out the waste with the router, a straight bit, and the

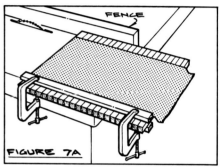

FENCE

FIGURE 7A

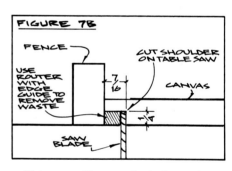

FIGURE 7B

FENCE

USE ROUTER WITH EDGE GUIDE TO REMOVE WASTE

CUT SHOULDER ON TABLE SAW

CANVAS

$\frac{7}{16}$

SAW BLADE

Using paraffin, wax both the tambour tongues and the tracking grooves before final assembly. Final finish must also be applied before the tambour is mounted. It is best to leave the canvas unfinished for maximum life and flexibility. ●

Sources of Supply

The following pages list companies that specialize in mail order sales of woodworking supplies

United States

General Woodworking Suppliers

Constantine's
2050 Eastchester Rd.
Bronx, NY 10461

Craftsman Wood Service
1735 West Cortland Ct.
Addison, IL 60101

Frog Tool Co.
700 W. Jackson Blvd.
Chicago, IL 60606

Garrett Wade
161 Avenue of the Americas
New York, NY 10013

Highland Hardware
1045 N. Highland Ave., N.E.
Atlanta, GA 30306

Seven Corners Ace Hardware
216 West 7th Street
St. Paul, MN 55102

Shopsmith, Inc.
3931 Image Drive
Dayton, OH 45414-2591

Trend-Lines
375 Beacham St.
Chelsea, MA 02150-0999

Woodcraft Supply Corp.
210 Wood County Ind. Park
P.O. Box 1686
Parkersburg, WV 26102

Woodworker's Supply
5604 Alameda, N.E.
Albuquerque, NM 87113

W.S. Jenks and Son
1933 Montana Ave., N.E.
Washington, DC 20002

Hardware Suppliers

Anglo-American Brass Co.
Box 9487
San Jose, CA 95157-0792

Ball and Ball
463 West Lincoln Hwy.
Exton, PA 19341

Horton Brasses
P.O. Box 120
Cromwell, CT 06416

Imported European Hardware
4320 W. Bell Dr.
Las Vegas, NV 89118

Meisel Hardware Specialties
P.O. Box 70
Mound, MN 55364-0070

Paxton Hardware, Ltd.
P.O. Box 256
Upper Falls, MD 21156

Period Furniture Hardware
Box 314, Charles Street Sta.
Boston, MA 02114

Stanley Hardware
195 Lake Street
New Britain, CT 06050

The Wise Co.
6503 St. Claude
Arabi, LA 70032

Hardwood Suppliers

American Woodcrafters
905 S. Roosevelt Ave.
Piqua, OH 45356

Arroyo Hardwoods
2585 Nina Street
Pasadena, CA 91107

Austin Hardwoods
2119 Goodrich
Austin, TX 78704

Berea Hardwoods Co.
125 Jacqueline Dr.
Berea, OH 44017

Bergers Hardwoods
Route 4, Box 195
Bedford, VA 24523

Maurice L. Condon
250 Ferris Ave.
White Plains, NY 10603

Craftwoods
10921-L York Rd.
Hunt Valley, MD 21030

Croffwood Mills
RD #1, Box 14J
Driftwood, PA 15832

Croy-Marietta Hardwoods
121 Pike St., Box 643
Marietta, OH 45750

Dimension Hardwoods, Inc.
113 Canal Street
Shelton, CT 06484

Educational Lumber Co.
P.O. Box 5373
Asheville, NC 28813

Garreson Lumber
RD 3
Bath, NY 14810

General Woodcraft
531 Broad St.
New London, CT 06320

Hardwoods of Memphis
P.O. Box 12449
Memphis, TN 38182-0449

Henegan's Wood Shed
7760 Southern Blvd.
West Palm Beach, FL 33411

Kaymar Wood Products
4603 35th S.W.
Seattle, WA 98126

Kountry Kraft Hardwoods
R.R. No. 1
Lake City, IA 51449

Leonard Lumber Co.
P.O. Box 2396
Branford, CT 06405

McFeely's Hardwoods
& Lumber
P.O. Box 3, 712 12th St.
Lynchburg, VA 24505

Native American Hardwoods
Route 1
West Valley, NY 14171

Niagara Lumber
47 Elm Street
East Aurora, NY 14052

Sterling Hardwoods, Inc.
412 Pine St.
Burlington, VT 05401

Talarico Hardwoods
RD 3, Box 3268
Mohnton, PA 19540-9339

Woodcrafter's Supply
7703 Perry Highway
Pittsburgh, PA 15237

Wood World
1719 Chestnut
Glenview, IL 60025

Woodworker's Dream
P.O. Box 329
Nazareth, PA 18064

Wood Finishing Suppliers

Finishing Products
and Supply Co.
4611 Macklind Ave.
St. Louis, MO 63109

Industrial Finishing
Products
465 Logan St.
Brooklyn, NY 11208

The Wise Co.
6503 St. Claude
Arabie, LA 70032

Wood Finishing
Supply Co.
100 Throop St.
Palmyra, NY 14522

WoodFinishing
Enterprises
1729 N. 68th St.
Wauwatosa, WI 53212

Watco-Dennis Corp.
1433 Santa Monica Blvd.
Santa Monica, CA 90401

Clock Parts Suppliers

The American Clockmaker
P.O. Box 326
Clintonville, WI 54929

Armor Products
P.O. Box 445
East Northport, NY 11731

Klockit, Inc.
P.O. Box 542
Lake Geneva, WI 53147

Kuempel Chime
21195 Minnetonka Blvd.
Excelsior, MN 55331

S. LaRose
234 Commerce Place
Greensboro, NC 27420

Newport Enterprises
2313 West Burbank Blvd.
Burbank, CA 91506

Miscellaneous

Byrom International
(router bits)
P.O. Box 246
Chardon, OH 44024

Brown Wood Products
(balls, knobs, Shaker pegs)
P.O. Box 8246
Northfield, IL 60093

Cherry Tree Toys
(toy parts)
P.O. Box 369
Belmont, OH 43718

Country Accents
(pierced tin)
P.O. Box 437
Montoursville, PA 17754

DML, Inc.
(router bits)
1350 S. 15th St.
Louisville, KY 40210

Floral Glass & Mirror
(beveled glass)
895 Motor Parkway
Hauppauge, NY 11788

Formica Corporation
(plastic laminate)
1 Stanford Rd.
Piscataway, NJ 08854

Freud
(saw blades)
218 Feld Ave.
High Point, NC 27264

Midwest Dowel Works
(dowels, plugs, pegs)
4631 Hutchinson Road
Cincinnati, OH 45248

Homecraft Veneer
(veneer)
901 West Way
Latrobe, PA 15650

MLCS
(router bits)
P.O. Box 4053
Rydal, PA 19046

The Old Fashioned
Milk Paint Co.
(milk paint)
P.O. Box 222
Groton, MA 01450

Sears, Roebuck and Co.
*(miscellaneous tools
and supplies)*
925 S. Homan Ave.
Chicago, IL 60607

Wilson Art
(plastic laminate)
600 General Bruce Drive
Temple, TX 76501

Canada

General Woodworking Suppliers

Ashman Technical
351 Nash Road North
Hamilton, ON L8H 7P4

Canadian Woodworker Ltd.
1391 St. James St. Unit 4
Winnipeg, MB R3H 0Z1

House of Tools Ltd.
131-12th Ave. S.E.
Calgary, AB T2G 0Z9

J. Philip Humfrey Int'l.
3241 Kennedy Rd., Unit 7
Scarborough, ON M1V 2J9

Lee Valley Tools
1080 Morrison Dr.
Ottawa, ON K2H 8K7

Nautilus Arts & Crafts
6075 Kingston Road
West Hill, ON M1C 1K5

Sterling Tools
5043 Still Creek Ave.
Burnaby, BC

Stockade Woodworker's
Supply
291 Woodlawn Rd. West
Unit 3C
Guelph, ON N1H 7L6

Tool Trend Ltd.
420 Millway Ave.
Concord, ON L4K 2V8

Treen Heritage Ltd.
P.O. Box 280
Merrickville, ON K0G 1N0

W. C. Robinson
Woodworking Supplies
1615 Scugog Line, R.R. #1
Port Perry, ON L9L 1B2

Hardware Suppliers

Home Workshop Supplies
RR 2
Arthur, ON N0G 1A0

Lee Valley Tools
1080 Morrison Dr.
Ottawa, ON K2H 8K7

Pacific Brass Hardware
1414 Monterey Ave.
Victoria, BC V8S 4W1

Steve's Shop
Woodworking & Supplies
RR 3
Woodstock, ON M9V 5C3

Hardwood Suppliers

A & C Hutt Enterprises Ltd.
15861 32nd Ave.
Surrey, BC V4B 4Z5

Farrell Lumber Co.
1229 Advance Rd., Unit 3B
Burlington, ON L7M 1G7

Hurst Associates, Ltd.
74 Dynamic Drive, Unit 11
Scarborough, ON M1V 3X6

Longstock Lumber & Veneer
440 Phillip St., Unit 21
Waterloo, ON N2L 5R9

MacVeigh Hardwoods
339 Olivewood Rd.
Toronto, ON M8Z 2Z6

Unicorn Univ. Woods Ltd.
4190 Steeles Ave. W., Unit 4
Woodbridge, ON L4L 3S8

Woodcraft Forest Products
1625 Sismet Road, Unit 25
Mississauga, ON L4W 1V6

Clock Parts Suppliers

Hurst Associates
105 Brisbane Road, Units 7–9
Downsview, ON M3J 2K6

Kidder Klock
39 Glen Cameron Rd., Unit 3
Thornhill, ON L3T 1P1

Murray Clock Craft Ltd.
510 McNicoll Ave.
Willowdale, ON M2H 2E1

Miscellaneous

Arbor Tools, Ltd.
(tool sharpening)
165 Limestone Crescent
Downsview, ON M3J 2R1

Bear Woods Supply Co.
*(pegs, dowel pins, plugs,
toy wheels)*
Box 40
Bear River, NS B0S 1B0

Black & Decker
(power tools)
P.O. Box 9756
St. John, NB E21 4M9

Robert Bosch, Inc.
(power tools)
6811 Century Ave.
Mississauga, ON L5N 1R1

Freud
(saw blades)
100 Westmore Dr., Unit 10
Rexdale, ON M9V 5C3

Laurier Wood Craft
(carving supplies)
P.O. Box 428
South River, ON P0A 1X0

Nautilus Arts & Crafts
(carving supplies)
6075 Kingston Road
West Hill, ON M1C 1K5

R & D Bandsaws
*(custom-made band
saw blades)*
42 Regan Road, Unit 17
Brampton, ON L7A 1B4

Great Britain

General Woodworking Suppliers

Craft Supplies Ltd.
131 The Mills
Millers Dale,
   Buxton SK17 8SN

General Woodwork Supplies
80 Stoke Newington High St.
London N.16

Fine Wood and Tool Store
Riverside Sawmills
Boroughbridge
North Yorks

Hand Tools

Parry's Tools
Old Street
London E2

Sargents Tools
62/64 Fleet Street
Swindon, Wilts.

Alec Tiranti Ltd.
27 Warren Street
London W1

Cecil Tyzack Ltd.
79/81 Kingsland Road
London E2 8AG

Hardwoods

Blumsom Timber Centre
36-38 River Road
Barking
Essex IG11 0DN

Kiln Wood
Unit 18, Gaza Trading Estate
Scabharbour Road
Hildenborough, Tonbridge
Kent TN11 8P1

North Heigham Sawmills
Paddock Street
Norwich
Norfolk NR2 4TW

Tiverton Sawmills
Blundells Road
Tiverton
Devon EX16 4DE

Wessex Timber
Longney
Gloucester GL2 6SJ

Hardware

Classic Brass
1 West Road
Westcliffe
Essex

Woodfit, Ltd.
115 Whittle Low Mill
Chorley
Lancs. PR6 7HB

Miscellaneous

The Cane Store
(cane, bamboo, rush)
207 Blackstock Road
Highbury Vale
London N5 2LL

Griffiths
(router bits)
8 Brynhyfryd Road
Newport
Gwent. NP9 4FX

"K" Toys
(toy wheels)
Brookfield Road
Cotham
Bristol BS6 5PW

M & M Tools
(router bits)
P.O. Box 128
Bexhill-on-Sea
Sussex TN40 2QT

Imperial to Metric Conversion Table

Fractional Equivalents

in.–cms.		in.–cms.	
1/16 = 0.15875		1/8 = 0.31700	
3/16 = 0.47625		1/4 = 0.63500	
5/16 = 0.79375		3/8 = 0.95250	
7/16 = 1.11125		1/2 = 1.27040	
9/16 = 1.42875		5/8 = 1.58730	
11/16 = 1.74625		3/4 = 1.90500	
13/16 = 2.06375		7/8 = 2.22250	
15/16 = 2.38125		1 = 2.54000	

Feet	Inches / Centi-metres	1	2	3	4	5	6	7	8	9	10	11
		2.54	5.08	7.62	10.16	12.70	15.24	17.78	20.32	22.86	25.40	27.94
1	30.48	33.02	35.56	38.10	40.64	43.18	45.72	48.26	50.80	53.34	55.88	58.42
2	60.96	63.50	66.04	68.58	71.12	73.66	76.20	78.74	81.28	83.82	86.36	88.90
3	91.44	93.98	96.52	99.06	101.60	104.14	106.68	109.22	111.76	114.30	116.84	119.38
4	121.92	124.46	127.00	129.54	132.08	134.62	137.16	139.70	142.24	144.78	147.32	149.86
5	152.40	154.94	157.48	160.02	162.56	165.10	167.64	170.18	172.72	175.26	177.80	180.34
6	182.88	185.42	187.96	190.50	193.04	195.58	198.12	200.66	203.20	205.74	208.28	210.82
7	213.36	215.90	218.44	220.98	223.52	226.06	228.60	231.14	233.68	236.22	238.76	241.30
8	243.84	246.38	248.92	251.46	254.00	256.54	259.08	261.62	264.16	266.70	269.24	271.78
9	274.32	276.86	279.40	281.94	284.48	287.02	289.56	292.10	294.64	297.18	299.72	302.26
10	304.80	307.34	309.88	312.42	314.96	317.50	320.04	322.58	325.12	327.66	330.20	332.74
11	335.28	337.82	340.36	342.90	345.44	347.98	350.52	353.06	355.60	358.14	360.68	363.22
12	365.76	368.30	370.84	373.38	375.92	378.46	381.00	383.54	386.08	388.62	391.16	393.70
13	396.24	398.78	401.32	403.86	406.40	408.94	411.48	414.02	416.56	419.10	421.64	424.18
14	426.72	429.26	431.80	434.34	436.88	439.42	441.96	444.50	447.04	449.58	452.12	454.66
15	457.20	459.74	462.28	464.82	467.36	469.90	472.44	474.98	477.52	480.06	482.60	485.14
16	487.68	490.22	492.76	495.30	497.84	500.38	502.92	505.46	508.00	510.54	513.08	515.62
17	518.16	520.70	523.24	525.78	528.32	530.86	533.40	535.94	538.48	541.02	543.56	546.10
18	548.64	551.18	553.72	556.26	558.80	561.34	563.88	566.42	568.96	571.50	574.04	576.58
19	579.12	581.66	584.20	586.74	589.28	591.82	594.36	596.90	599.44	601.98	604.52	607.06
20	609.60	612.14	614.68	617.22	619.76	622.30	624.84	627.38	629.92	632.46	635.00	637.54

Measures of Length—Basic S.I. Unit—
Metre = 100 Centimetres = 39.37 Inches

Example:

(1) To convert 13 feet 6 inches to centimetres, read along line 13 under feet and under column 6 inches read 411.48 cms. To reduce to metres move decimal point two spaces to left; thus, 4.1148 metres is the answer.

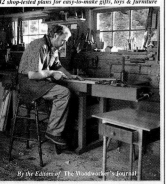

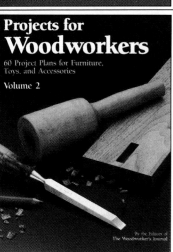
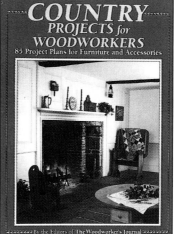

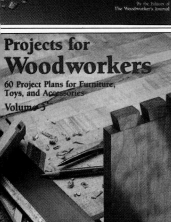

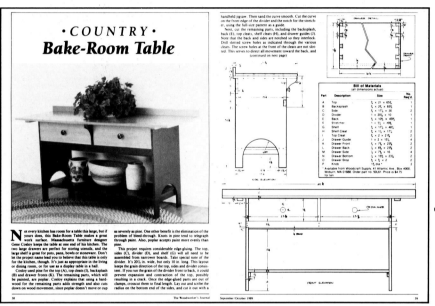